January 25, 2011
Austin, Texas, USA

Association for
Computing Machinery

Advancing Computing as a Science & Profession

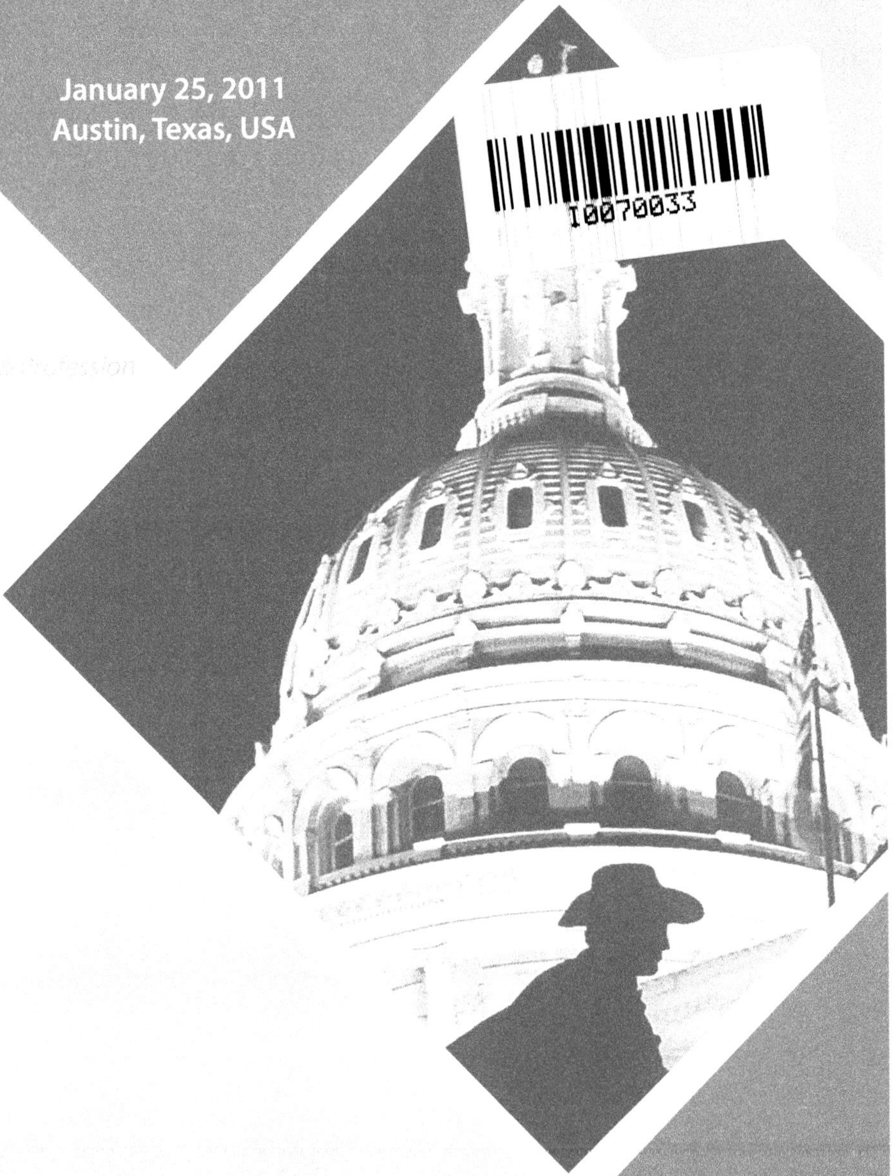

TLDI'11

Proceedings of the 7th ACM SIGPLAN Workshop on

Types in Language Design and Implementation

Sponsored by:

ACM SIGPLAN

In cooperation with:

ACM SIGACT

Supported by:

Google, IBM Research, Intel, Microsoft Research, Mozilla, NEC, NSF, & Computer Science Dept., University of Texas at Austin

Association for Computing Machinery

Advancing Computing as a Science & Profession

The Association for Computing Machinery
2 Penn Plaza, Suite 701
New York, New York 10121-0701

ISBN: 978-1-4503-0484-9

Additional copies may be ordered prepaid from:

ACM Order Department
PO Box 11405
New York, NY 10286-1405

Phone: 1-800-342-6626 (USA and Canada)
+1-212-626-0500 (all other countries)
Fax: +1-212-944-1318
E-mail: acmhelp@acm.org

Printed in the USA

Foreword

It is our great pleasure to welcome you to the *7th ACM SIGPLAN Workshop on Types in Language Design and Implementation – TLDI'11.* The TLDI workshops are a continuation of the *Types in Compilation – TIC* workshops, the first of which was held in 1997. Initially biennial, TLDI is now an annual workshop.

The role of types in all aspects of language design, compiler construction, and software development has expanded greatly in recent years. Type systems, type-based analyses, and type-based reasoning frameworks have led to new concepts in compilation techniques for modern programming languages, verification of safety and security properties of programs, program transformation and optimization, and many other areas. The mission of the TLDI series of workshops is to bring together researchers in all these areas to share novel ideas and stimulate interaction and discussion on the ever-expanding use of types.

The call for papers this year attracted 14 submissions from Asia, Australia, Europe, and the United States. All submissions received at least 3 reviews, with most receiving between 4 and 6 reviews. In addition, every submission received at least one expert review or, failing that, multiple high-confidence reviews. After a weeklong electronic meeting conducted via the Easychair conference management system, the program committee decided to accept 6 papers for presentation at the workshop. The accepted papers concern the application of types to a range of problems, including information-flow security and access control, deadlock avoidance, and the taming of mutable state.

We are grateful to Georges Gonthier (of Microsoft Research, Cambridge), and Chris Hawblitzel (of Microsoft Research, Redmond), for agreeing to give invited talks at the workshop. Our gratitude also goes out to the program committee and external reviewers, who worked diligently in reviewing papers and providing constructive suggestions for their improvement. Finally, we would like to thank our sponsor, ACM SIGPLAN, for their continued support of these successful meetings.

We hope that you will find this program interesting and thought-provoking, and that the symposium will provide you with a valuable opportunity to share ideas with other researchers and practitioners of types from institutions around the world.

Stephanie Weirich
TLDI'11 General Chair
University of Pennsylvania

Derek Dreyer
TLDI'11 Program Chair
MPI-SWS, Germany

Table of Contents

TLDI 2011 Workshop Organization

General Chair: Stephanie Weirich *(University of Pennsylvania)*

Program Chair: Derek Dreyer *(MPI-SWS, Germany)*

Program Committee:
Thorsten Altenkirch *(University of Nottingham)*
Fritz Henglein *(University of Copenhagen)*
Michael Hicks *(University of Maryland, College Park)*
Limin Jia *(Carnegie Mellon University)*
Mark Jones *(Portland State University)*
Neel Krishnaswami *(Microsoft Research, Cambridge)*
Paul-André Melliès *(CNRS & Université Paris Diderot)*
Aleks Nanevski *(IMDEA Software, Madrid)*
Benjamin Pierce *(University of Pennsylvania)*
Tachio Terauchi *(Tohoku University)*
Sam Tobin-Hochstadt *(Northeastern University)*

Steering Committee Chair: Robert Harper *(Carnegie Mellon University)*

Steering Committee:
Amal Ahmed *(Indiana University)*
Nick Benton *(Microsoft Research, Cambridge)*
Derek Dreyer *(MPI-SWS, Germany)*
Andrew Kennedy *(Microsoft Research, Cambridge)*
François Pottier *(INRIA Paris-Rocquencourt)*
Zhong Shao *(Yale University)*
Stephanie Weirich *(University of Pennsylvania)*

Additional reviewers:
Patrick Bahr
Nils Anders Danielsson
Anders Starcke Henriksen
Tom Hvitved
Andrew Kennedy
Oleg Kiselyov
Daniel Licata
Chung-chieh Shan
Kristian Støvring

Sponsor: acm SIGPLAN

Type Design Patterns for Computer Mathematics

Georges Gonthier

Microsoft Research Cambridge
7 JJ Thomson Avenue
Cambridge, United Kingdom CB3 0FB
gonthier@microsoft.com

Abstract

Proof assistants such as the Coq system have traditionally been a laboratory for exotic type features such as dependent and computable types, and first-class type classes. Although these features have been introduced independently, it turns out they can be combined in novel and nontrivial ways to solve some of the more challenging problems posed by the formalization of advanced mathematics. Many of these patterns could also be useful for general programming.

Categories and Subject Descriptors D.3.3 [**Programming Languages**]: Language Constructs and Features – data types and structures, modules, patterns, polymorphism.

General Terms Design, Languages.

Keywords design patterns; type inference; type classes; reflection; user notation; theorem proving.

1. The Challenge of Computer Mathematics

The formalization of advanced mathematics is quite a challenge for the computer language designer. Honed over centuries, mathematical notation depends heavily on contextual information to maximize information content, displaying only the minimal relevant information, e.g., a group quotient expression G / H does not explicitly state which group operation is being used.

Moreover, practicing mathematicians routinely expect to "abuse notation" and use the results and notation of a variety of theories for syntactically incongruent instances, e.g., mixing set and group theory, or applying group theory results to matrix sums. They do not expect to be bothered with checking the myriad of side conditions that justify this usage.

Any significant mathematical formalization project must address these issues, which are basically programming language issues. While solving these seem to call for a host of new exotic features, but luckily it turns out that the handful of general-purpose features that existing proof systems support can be *combined* to achieve a workable approximation of the ideal behavior.

2. The Coq Type Toolbox

Amid the many available proof assistants, the Coq system provides one of the richest type system and typing environment.

TLDI'11 January 25, 2011, Austin, Texas, USA.
ACM 978-1-4503-0484-9/11/01.

While some of the patterns we propose below can be implemented with lesser systems (e.g., Isabelle's or Haskell's type classes), many require the full complement.

Higher-kinded dependent types: types are not segregated from values: type parameters can be data values, and conversely (higher-kinded) data structures can contain types.

Computable types: CiC's conversion rule lets the Coq type checker evaluate type functions; this lets us reprogram (part of) the type system.

Implicit value inference: as types contain values, Coq has an extended "type" inference that can also fill in omitted values in expressions. Crucially, both the type inference and the higher order unification procedure proceed in a predictable order; this lets us reprogram type inference.

Canonical structures: these are basically first-class type classes, and one of the more powerful features of the Coq type system. These are simply hints allowing the unification procedure to solve equations of the form $?r.(\mathsf{p}) = v$, where p is a record projector and $?r$ an indeterminate record, for specific values of v. Specialized to `Structure` records that pack a type with a dictionary of operations this is equivalent to type classes, but the mechanism is much more general; the hints can be computed dynamically by ordinary record-producing functions. Note that Coq also offers a variant of second-class type classes, to which we prefer this more general version.

Coercions: these are simply functions that can be automatically inserted in user code to "fix" type errors. They are not displayed, which makes them quite handy for encoding "abusive" math notation. Coercions were mainly introduced to capture inheritance between `Structure`s, but we propose a more general and better-behaved pattern (packed classes, see below).

User-defined notation: while Coq's facilities in this area are somewhat rudimentary and quirky, they are critical to providing the user with a readable display, hiding ugly implementation details such as the use of a specific argument sequence to control type inference.

Modules: Coq modules package both logical (definitions and theorems) and non-logical (hints and notation) declaration; this lets us hide the exact combination of features needed to capture a particular theory. Modules also provide separate namespaces which let us use uniform names to implement complex patterns.

3. An array of patterns

Almost all of the features described above were introduced independently, with a specific purpose in mind: dependent types and conversion to simplify the logical framework, type inference to compensate for the explicit polymorphism, coercions for structure inheritance, canonical structures to supplement coercions. But, thanks to the foresight of their designers, all turn out to be extremely useful for other purposes, in combination. Here are some of the more interesting ones we have come up with.

3.1 Packed classes

We declare most of our structures using the following pattern:

```
Record mixin_of T := Mixin {op : T -> T; …}.
Record class_of T := Class {
  base :> Base.class_of T; mixin :> mixin_of T}.
Structure type := Pack {
  sort :> Type; class : class_of sort}.
Canonical Structure baseType t :=
  Base.Pack (class t).
```

Thus, each structure gets a specific projector to `Type`, while the dictionary is packaged into a specific record, which is itself composed of a base class dictionary and a mixin record that comprises the extensions introduced for the composite structure. This pattern is meant to be used inside a submodule; here `Base` would be another submodule defining the base structure.

The "`:>`" symbol makes the projector into a coercion, which gets automatically inserted when needed. Thus any `t : type` can also be used as a `Type`, and `x : t` will be read as `x : sort t`. The baseType declaration implements inheritance, as it allows `sort t` to unify with `Base.sort (baseType t)`. This patterns also supports construction from mxins (inferring the base class) and multiple inheritance.

3.2 Phantom types

Structures are meant to be inferred by the type system, so it is preferable to let the user supply the projection rather than the structure, as in:

```
Inductive phantom (T : Type) := Phantom.
Record finset (T : finType)  (phT : phantom T) :=
  Finset { bitset : #|T|.-tuple bool }.
Notation "{ 'set' T }" := (finset (Phantom T)).
Variable A : {set bool}.
```

The `phantom` type uses a dummy dependency to make the (data) argument of its constructor accessible to type inference; thanks to dependent types, this does not require painful data-as-types encodings as in Haskell. The `finset` declaration, which encodes sets over a finite type T and needs a property of this structure (its cardinal `#|T|`), is given a dummy `phantom` argument, which is then hidden by a user notation. In the last line, type inference unifies `phantom bool` with `phantom (Finite.sort` *?T*`)`, using a `Canonical Structure bool_finType` hint.

3.3 Value classes

Unlike its programming language cousin, the canonical structure mechanism does not have to be keyed on types: it is perfectly acceptable to have `Structure`s keyed on data objects such as functions or sets, to capture important mathematical notions such as morphisms, groups, and group actions.

For instance we used this facility in our `bigop` library of generic iterated operators (the kind one gets by typing "`\big`" in LaTeX) to specify arbitrary operators with monoidal properties. This lets us formulate and use directly for all kinds of iterated operators generic lemmas such as

```
Lemma big_split: forall R (idx : R),
  forall op : Monoid.com_law idx,
  forall I r (P : pred I) F1 F2,
    \big[op/idx]_(i <- r | P i) op (F1 i) (F2 i) =
       op (\big[op/idx]_(i <- r | P i) F1 i)
          (\big[op/idx]_(i <- r | P i) F2 i).
```

3.4 Deep reflection

By combining the fact that notation interpretation in Coq is context sensitive with computable types we can "hijack" normal term interpretation and layer new meaning on casual user input. We use this in the interpretation of free group expressions, as in

```
Lemma Grp_dihedral :
  'D_m \isog
     Grp (x : y : (x ^+ q, y ^+ 2, x ^ y = x^-1)).
```

This asserts that the dihedral group of order $m = 2q$ is isomorphic to the group freely generated by x and y, subject to 3 relations. The classical interpretation of the right-hand side is not possible in a constructive setting, and the naïve interpretation would not have the correct parametricity properties. To solve these issues we interpret the entire argument of `Grp` as a formal expression (in higher-order syntax style), and the meaning of the whole statement is defined by running a generic interpreter on that formal expression.

3.5 Shallow reflection

An inconvenience of shallow reflection is that only literal input can be given layered meaning. However it is possible to combine phantom types, value classes and deep reflection to achieve shallow reflection, where arbitrary data expressions are reified (i.e., quoted) and then given additional meaning. For instance we use this to capture the concept of "direct linear sum" in

```
Let sumV := (\sum_(i < h) 'V_i)%MS.
Lemma mxdirect_sum_eigenspace_cycle :
   (sumV :=: 1%:M)%MS /\ mxdirect sumV.
```

Here the `mxdirect` notation hides a phantom which causes type inference to analyse the contents of the constant `sumV` and determine that it is a formal sum of vector spaces (the `\sum` notation uses the `bigop` library); this analysis is then used to define the meaning of "the sum `sumV` is direct".

Indeed this mechanism can in principle be used to perform any kind of quotation, including allocating fresh constants for unknown terms, though we have yet to find a practical mathematical application for such generality.

4. Conclusions and acknowledgements

The patterns described here were developed as part of an effort to formalize the celebrated Feit-Thompson theorem, which asserts that all odd order groups are solvable and was the starting point of the Finite Simple Group Classification proof. They have proved invaluable in the progress of this effort, and we believe they probably are generally useful as well. We acknowledge the help of the many people involved in the Mathematical Components project at the Odd Order effort, as well as the foresight and the work of the designers and developers of the Coq system, which make all of this possible.

Singleton

A General-Purpose Dependently-Typed Assembly Language

Simon Winwood
NICTA and UNSW
sjw@cse.unsw.edu.au

Manuel Chakravarty
UNSW
chak@cse.unsw.edu.au

Abstract

In this paper we present Singleton, a dependently typed assembly language. Based upon the calculus of inductive constructions, Singleton's type system allows procedures abstracting over terms, types, propositions, and proof terms.

Furthermore, Singleton includes generalised singleton types. In addition to the primitive singleton types of other languages, these generalised singleton types allow the values from arbitrary inductive types to be associated with the contents of registers and memory locations. Along with Singleton's facility for term and proof abstraction, generalised singleton types allow strong statements to be made about the functional behaviour of Singleton programs.

We have formalised basic properties of Singleton's type system, namely type safety and a type erasure property, using the Coq proof assistant.

Categories and Subject Descriptors D.3.3 [*Programming Languages*]: Language Constructs and Features; F.3.1 [*Logics and Meanings of Programs*]: Specifying and Verifying and Reasoning about Programs—Logics of programs

General Terms Theory

1. Introduction

The Singleton language attempts to address a gap in the available languages for certificate-bearing code. Morrisett *et al.* [9] gives an elegant translation from a high level language — System F — into a TAL, thus showing that typed assembly languages are natural certification logics for programs compiled from high-level languages. Furthermore, the guarantees provided by the type system of a TAL typically correspond with the low-level safety properties desired of the system: well typed programs cannot 'go wrong'.

However, traditional TALs are restricted to those properties entailed by type safety. While this includes essential properties such as memory safety, these properties are not always sufficient. For instance, while traditional TALs may be able to encode that a particular address contains the root of a tree, they cannot state that the tree is balanced.

Based on the *calculus of inductive constructions* (CiC), Singleton's assertion logic allows programs to abstract over terms in this logic, including types, terms, propositions, and proofs. Singleton also includes a rich type language including *generalised singleton types*; these types carry terms in the assertion logic corresponding to the run-time behaviour of the classified object.

Example 1.1 As an illustrative example of the power of Singleton's type system, consider the higher-order function *map* with type

$$map \; : \; \forall a\, b.\, (a \rightarrow b) \rightarrow list\ a \rightarrow list\ b$$

A traditional TAL may admit an implementation of such a function, but Singleton allows a program to prove that the output is actually the result of applying a given function to every element of the input list; the Singleton type

$$\begin{aligned} \texttt{map} :: \forall (a : Set)(b : Set)(f : a \rightarrow b)(xs : list\ a).& \\ \{\texttt{a}_1 : \forall (v : a).\{\texttt{a}_1 : sgl(v : a),& \\ \texttt{ra} : \{\texttt{t}_1 : sgl(f\ v : b)\}\},& \\ \texttt{a}_2 : sgl(xs : list\ a),& \\ \texttt{ra} : \{\texttt{t}_1 : sgl(map\ f\ xs : list\ b)\}\}& \end{aligned}$$

states that the `map` program takes for arguments the logical types a and b, a function f from a to b, and a list with element type a. The program also takes as run-time arguments a function pointer in $\texttt{a}_1$ which computes $f v$ for any v, a generalised singleton object in $\texttt{a}_2$ representing the input list, and a return address in `ra` expecting as argument $map\ f\ xs$: if the program returns through this address, it must provide a generalised singleton object representing $map\ f\ xs$, that is, the contents of $\texttt{t}_1$ will correspond to the result of mapping f over the elements in xs.

Our original motivation in developing Singleton was in the context of run-time verification: we wished to establish high-level properties of the program which are not implied by type safety alone. In fact, the requirements of run-time verification are more comparable to those of a traditional verification environment such as a Hoare-style logic [8].

Such languages, however, typically assume a much looser view of type safety than run-time verification requires; for example, a reference monitor is usually type safe, and will not need to modify arbitrary memory locations.

Singleton is then a compromise between the simplicity of a typed assembly language and the expressive power of a Hoare logic. The use of generalised singleton types, types which carry detailed information about their run-time contents, allows fine-grained assertions on heap structures; the addition of existential types allows control over the mutability of objects in the heap. Other languages, the DTAL of Xi and Harper [15] for example, typically provide singletons on primitive types, such as the value of words or the length of arrays; Singleton allows user-defined singleton types over inductive data types.

In summary, the main contributions of this paper are the following

TLDI'11, January 25, 2011, Austin, Texas, USA.

$$
\begin{aligned}
&\texttt{head} :: \forall(a : Set)(xs : list\ a).\\
&\qquad \{\texttt{a}_1 : sgl(xs : list\ a),\\
&\qquad\ \ \texttt{ra} : \forall(x : list\ a)(xs' : list\ a)\\
&\qquad\qquad (pf : xs = cons\ x\ xs').\{\texttt{t}_1 : sgl(x : a)\}\}
\end{aligned}
$$

head :

$$
\begin{aligned}
&\texttt{case}\ \texttt{t}_1,\ \texttt{a}_1,\ [\texttt{hNil}\ @\ (a, xs),]\\
&\qquad\qquad \texttt{hCons}\ @\ (a, xs)
\end{aligned}
$$

$$
\begin{aligned}
&\texttt{hNil} :: \forall(a : Set)(xs : list\ a)(pf : xs = nil).\\
&\qquad \{\texttt{t}_1 : \langle word(0)\rangle,\\
&\qquad\ \ \texttt{ra} : \forall(x : list\ a)(xs' : list\ a)\\
&\qquad\qquad (pf : xs = cons\ x\ xs').\{\texttt{t}_1 : sgl(x : a)\}\}
\end{aligned}
$$

hNil :

(handle error for empty list)

$$
\begin{aligned}
&\texttt{hCons} :: \forall(a : Set)(xs : list\ a)(x : a)(xs' : list\ a)\\
&\qquad (pf : xs = cons\ x\ xs').\\
&\qquad \{\texttt{t}_1 : \langle word(1), sgl(x : a), sgl(xs' : list\ a)\rangle,\\
&\qquad\ \ \texttt{ra} : \forall(x : list\ a)(xs' : list\ a)\\
&\qquad\qquad (pf : xs = cons\ x\ xs').\{\texttt{t}_1 : sgl(x : a)\}\}
\end{aligned}
$$

hCons :

```
load t1, t1(1)
apply ra, ra, (x, xs', pf)
jump ra
```

Figure 1. A Singleton implentation of the *head* function. The argument register $\texttt{a}_1$ contains the input list.

- We introduce the idea of *generalised singleton types*, that enable user-defined singleton types corresponding to arbitrary inductive data types (Section 2).
- We present Singleton, a dependently-typed assembly language, that includes an assertion logic based on the calculus of inductive constructions (Sections 3 and 4)
- We give an operational and a static semantics for Singleton (Sections 5 and 6).
- We establish fundamental properties of Singleton's type system; refer for proofs to [14] (Section 7)

We will discuss related work in more detail in Section 8.

2. Singleton by Example

We give two short examples to introduce Singleton and also to serve as a running example through the remainder of this paper.

2.1 Taking the head of a list

Consider the list data type

$$
\begin{aligned}
&\textbf{Inductive}\ list\ (t : Set) : Set :=\\
&\quad |\ nil : list\ t\\
&\quad |\ cons : t \to list\ t \to list\ t
\end{aligned}
$$

and the *head* function

$$
\begin{aligned}
&head \quad :: \forall a.\ list\ a \to a\\
&head\ xs = \textbf{match}\ xs\ \textbf{with}\\
&\qquad\qquad nil \to error\\
&\qquad\qquad cons\ x\ xs' \to x\\
&\qquad\quad \textbf{end}
\end{aligned}
$$

where *error* indicates a runtime error when the list is empty. We can, of course, make this function total by requiring a proof that xs isn't *nil*; see Sect. 2.1.4. Fig. 1 gives the Singleton implementation of this function.

2.1.1 The two types

We claim that the Singleton implementation is somehow related to *head*. To see why we can make this claim, consider the type of *head*

$$head :: \forall a.\ list\ a \to a$$

and that for **head**

$$
\begin{aligned}
&\forall(a : Set)(xs : list\ a).\\
&\ \{\texttt{a}_1 : sgl(xs : list\ a),\\
&\ \ \texttt{ra} : \forall(x : list\ a)(xs' : list\ a)\\
&\qquad (pf : xs = cons\ x\ xs').\{\texttt{t}_1 : sgl(x : a)\}\}
\end{aligned}
$$

We can read this type as a code block which takes the *logical* arguments a and xs, and two *run-time* arguments in the registers $\texttt{a}_1$ and ra. The register ra contains a reference to a code block with logical arguments x, xs', and pf, and a single register argument, $\texttt{t}_1$.

Both the type of *head* and **head** are polymorphic in the contents of the list; this is the logical parameter a in the Singleton version. Similarly, both accept the input list, although in the Singleton version this occurs both as the logical parameter xs and as the register argument in $\texttt{a}_1$: the type

$$sgl(xs : list\ a)$$

connects the logical variable xs to the machine register $\texttt{a}_1$; we discuss what this means in the next section.

Finally, both return a value of type a. In the Singleton case, this can be seen by examining the type of the return address: if **head** returns through this address, it will provide the logical parameters x and xs' representing the head and tail of the list respectively, and a *proof* that xs is, in fact, composed of these two values. As with the argument to **head**, the head of the list, x, appears as the register argument $\texttt{t}_1$.

Therefore, we claim that if **head** returns through the given return address, then the result in $\texttt{t}_1$ will correspond to the head of the list xs.

2.1.2 Singleton types

In the previous section we noted that the register $\texttt{a}_1$ somehow contains the list xs, and the register $\texttt{t}_1$ should contain the value x when **head** returns. We now examine more closely the types of these two registers to see precisely how the argument and result of *head* correspond to their Singleton counterparts.

Recall the list argument to **head**: the *generalised singleton type* $sgl(xs : list\ a)$ represents the logical value xs with logical type $list\ a$; we say that xs is the (logical) value associated with the singleton type, and similarly for its type, $list\ a$.

Objects with singleton type have an underlying object, the type of which, the *representation type*, is determined by the value associated with the singleton. How this type is determined in general we leave to Sect. 6.3; here we will focus on the details required for *head*.

We start by noting that xs has two possible forms: either it is nil, or it is $cons\ x\ xs'$ for some x and xs'. In the first case, $sgl(nil : list\ a)$ is represented by the tuple

$$\langle word(0)\rangle$$

that is, the tuple containing the singleton word 0 indicating a nil node; in the second case, $sgl(cons\ x\ xs' : list\ a)$ is represented by the tuple

$$\langle word(1),\ sgl(x : a),\ sgl(xs : list\ a)\rangle$$

that is, the word 1 indicating a $cons$ node, followed by an element for x and then an element for xs'.

Thus, depending on the contents of xs, the register a_1 may contain a tuple with a single member, or a tuple with three members. We can then say that the argument in a_1 corresponds to the argument to *head*, xs, in that the first element of xs is the second entry in the tuple in a_1, the second element of xs is second entry of the tuple in third entry of this tuple, and so on.

2.1.3 The implementation of head

We now turn our attention to the actual implementation of head. As noted above, the value associated with a singleton determines the shape of the representation object. Conversely, by examining this object, specifically the first element, we can determine the shape of the associated value: there is a one-to-one correspondence between the first element of a representation object and the associated value.

Thus, by examining the first element of a list singleton we can determine whether it is *nil* or $cons\ x\ xs'$ for some x and xs'. In fact, this is precisely the behaviour of case: the instruction

$$\texttt{case}\ \texttt{t}_1,\ \texttt{a}_1,\ [\texttt{hNil} @ (a,\ xs),\ \texttt{hCons} @ (a,\ xs)]$$

examines the singleton value in a_1 and branches to hNil if the value associated with a_1 is *nil* and to hCons if the value is *cons*. The unpacked singleton value is passed in t_1. In both cases we pass the additional logical arguments a and xs.

In addition to these explicit arguments, the case instruction passes to the target label any constructor arguments, along with a proof. This proof states that these additional arguments, applied to the corresponding constructor, give the associated value.

The logical arguments to hNil are then the two explicit arguments followed by a proof that the list is indeed empty. As this case is undefined, and will result in some implementation-specific error, we shall treat it no further.

The hCons case, however, is more interesting. In addition to the element type and argument list, this code block also accepts the two arguments to the *cons* constructor, x and xs', along with a proof that these do actually form xs, namely

$$pf\ :\ xs = cons\ x\ xs'$$

Furthermore, the type of register t_1 is the representation type for $cons\ x\ xs'$, that is, a tuple containing the tag 1, an element for x, and an element for xs'. We then load the second entry to get x.

Before we can return to the address in ra we need to communicate to this label the new variables and the new proof; this is done via the instruction

$$\texttt{apply ra},\ \texttt{ra},\ (x,\ xs',\ pf)$$

where $(x,\ xs',\ pf)$ is an *argument sequence*, that is, a sequence of logical arguments and a sequence of type arguments, although in this case we have no type arguments. This instruction applies the arguments in this sequence to the code type in ra. After applying the new variables, we jump to the resulting address.

2.1.4 Aside: a total version of *head*

Our version of *head* above raises an error in the case that xs is *nil*. If we know that xs is *not nil*, that is, we have $xs = cons\ x\ xs'$, then we can give a total version of head as follows

```
totalHead :: ∀(a : Set)(xs : list a)(x : list a)(xs' : list a)
                (pf : xs = cons x xs').
                {a₁ : sgl(xs : list a),
                 ra : {t₁ : sgl(x : a)}}
totalHead :
    coerce t₁, a₁ using pf
    project t₁, t₁
    load t₁, t₁(1)
    jump ra
```

We take advantage of two Singleton-specific instructions in this implementation of *head*, coerce and project. Firstly, the instruction

$$\texttt{coerce}\ r_d,\ r_s\ \texttt{using}\ pf$$

rewrites the value associated with the singleton in r_s with the equality in pf, placing the result in r_d. In our example above, we have

$$sgl(xs : list\ a) \xrightarrow{rewrite\ with\ pf} sgl(cons\ x\ xs' : list\ a)$$

Secondly, the instruction

$$\texttt{project}\ r_d,\ r_s$$

extracts the representation of the singleton in r_s into r_d, when the shape of the associated value is known. In the above case, we have

$$sgl(cons\ x\ xs' : list\ a) \xrightarrow{project} \langle word(1),\ sgl(x : a),\ sgl(xs' : list\ a)\rangle$$

noting that the destination register of project will have the same type as if after a case operation. This instruction is thus an optimised version of case: project simply extracts the representation type for a *known* value, while case examines an *unknown value* and branches to the appropriate label.

2.2 Adding an element to a list

We have seen how to destroy a singleton object: use case if the shape of the associated value is unknown, and project if the value is known. In this section we will discuss how to *construct* a singleton.

Continuing with our example of lists, the cons procedure should act like the *cons* constructor, that is, it should add the given element to the start of the given list.

If we wish to create a new singleton object, we use the inject instruction. This operation performs the inverse of project: given an object of the correct type, it creates a singleton such that the object represents the singleton. Recall from Sect. 2.1.2 that a *cons* term is represented by a triple: the tag 1, the head of the list, and the tail of the list.

Given the head of the list in a_1 and the tail in a_2, our implementation needs to allocate a tuple and initialise the first element with the word 1 and the remainder with the contents of a_1 and a_2. The code is then as follows

```
cons :: ∀(a : Set)(x : a)(xs : list a).
           {a₁ : sgl(x : a),
            a₂ : sgl(xs : list a),
            ra : {t₁ : sgl(cons x xs : list a)}}
cons :
    alloc t₁, [word(1), sgl(x : a), sgl(xs : list a)]
    ldi t₂, 1
    store t₂, t₁(0)
    store a₁, t₁(1)
    store a₂, t₁(2)
    inject t₁, t₁ as sgl(cons x xs : list a)
    jump ra
```

The alloc instruction creates a new, uninitialised tuple with the given type in t_1. We then use the ldi instruction to move the constant 1 into t_2 so we can initialise the first element of the new tuple. After storing the two arguments, we create the new singleton using the inject instruction. We then return to the given address.

$$
\begin{array}{lcl}
A,\ B,\ v,\ T & ::= & \mathit{Set} \mid \mathit{Prop} \mid \mathit{Type} \\
 & \mid & x \mid \lambda x : A.\ B \mid A\ B \mid \forall x : A.\ B \\
 & \mid & \mathit{Ind}(X : A)\{\vec{B}\} \\
 & \mid & \mathit{Ctor}(n,\ A) \\
 & \mid & \mathit{Elim}(C,\ A)\{\vec{B}\} \\
\Upsilon & ::= & x_1 : A_1,\ \ldots,\ x_n : A_n
\end{array}
$$

Figure 2. The calculus of inductive constructions, used by Singleton as an assertion logic.

2.3 Discussion

The natural question to ask is: what have we achieved by the extra type machinery involved in a (type-correct) Singleton program.

Firstly, if the return address is invoked, the contents of the register $\mathtt{t}_1$ will have the singleton type $\mathit{sgl}(x : a)$; Singleton provides a logic of *partial* correctness only, and so the `head` function may not return through the given label (calling some other function, for example) or may not return at all.

Secondly, objects with singleton type have a specific layout: given the type, we can make strong statements about the contents of values of this type in the heap.

Finally, any object in the heap retains the type it had before the invocation of `head`. Although this is not the same as saying that the remainder of the heap is unmodified, Singleton's precise types imply that either such modifications are trivial (that is, equivalent to the identity mutation), or the element modified had existential type and therefore any mutation does not violate invariants about the particular value of that cell.

3. The Calculus of Inductive Constructions

In this section we summarise the syntax of CiC and briefly justify its use. Space limitations prevent us from giving a complete treatment of CiC; we direct the reader to Paulin-Mohring [11].

The syntax of CiC is given in Fig. 2. Apart from sorts (*Set*, *Prop*, and *Type*) and the usual lambda terms, application, and (dependent) function spaces, CiC includes inductive datatypes ($\mathit{Ind}(X{:}A)\{\vec{B}\}$), along with their inhabitants ($\mathit{Ctor}(n,\ A)$). Elimination ($\mathit{Elim}(C, A)\{\vec{B}\}$) takes apart inductive terms, generalising recursive functions and structural induction. Following the Coq system [2], we will use a concrete syntax for inductive types, like that above for the definition of list.

The CiC has a number of features which make it a good fit as an assertion logic for Singleton, namely

- dependent types allow a uniform syntax for both terms and proofs, including their abstraction;
- inductive types give structure to singleton values. A primitive notion of an inductive type allows Singleton to give rules for automatically generating this structure;
- separating informative types (that is, those in *Set*) from non-informative types (that is, those in *Prop*) allows the values associated with singleton types to include proof objects without a run-time penalty; and
- the construction of a formal model of Singleton in the Coq system requires no extra machinery for the assertion logic beyond that provided by the system.

We shall revisit these first two points in the remainder of this paper, particularly Sect. 6.3. We direct interested in the final point to the first author's dissertation [14].

The typing judgement $\Upsilon \Vdash A : B$ states that the term A has type B under the context Υ, while the equivalence relation $A \equiv_{\beta\iota} B$ states that the two terms A and B are equivalent under

Initialisation flags

$$
\begin{array}{lcl}
\varphi & ::= & \mathbf{0} \mid \mathbf{1}
\end{array}
$$

Registers

$$
\begin{array}{lcl}
r & ::= & \mathtt{r}_1 \mid \ldots \mid \mathtt{r}_N
\end{array}
$$

Kinds and machine types

$$
\begin{array}{lcl}
\kappa,\ \pi & ::= & \mathfrak{U} \mid \mathfrak{B} \\
\sigma,\ \tau,\ \xi & ::= & \alpha \\
 & \mid & \mathit{word}(n) \\
 & \mid & \mathit{sgl}(v : T) \\
 & \mid & \exists(x : A).\tau \\
 & \mid & \langle \tau_1^{\varphi_1},\ \ldots,\ \tau_n^{\varphi_n} \rangle \\
 & \mid & \forall \Upsilon, [\Delta].\Gamma
\end{array}
$$

Type contexts

$$
\begin{array}{lcl}
\Delta,\ \Omega & ::= & \{\alpha_1 :: \kappa_1,\ \ldots,\ \alpha_n :: \kappa_n\}
\end{array}
$$

Register file types

$$
\begin{array}{lcl}
\Gamma & ::= & \{\mathtt{r}_0 : \tau_1,\ \ldots,\ \mathtt{r}_n : \tau_n\}
\end{array}
$$

Heap types

$$
\begin{array}{lcl}
\Psi & ::= & \{0 : \tau_1,\ \ldots,\ n : \tau_n\}
\end{array}
$$

Figure 3. Syntactic classes for Singleton: types

β- and *iota*-reduction (elimination of inductive terms). Both typing and term equivalence are decidable.

4. Syntax

In this section we present the syntax of Singleton, and discuss some of the syntactic forms; the remainder are discussed in the following sections. The various syntactic forms constituting the Singleton language are shown in Fig. 3 and Fig. 4.

4.1 Types and Values

In this section we discuss the various types supported by Singleton, along with their value forms. Briefly, kinds classify types into *unboxed* and *boxed* types, while types classify both word values and heap values. Heap values are code blocks and tuples of word values, while word values appear in registers and in tuples. In the remainder of this section we will discuss types and their corresponding values.

Type variables. Type variables refer to variables bound by code types. We assume α-equivalence on type variables, renaming where necessary to avoid capture.

Word types. Word types represent the exact run-time value of their members. For example, a register with type $\mathit{word}(3)$ will contain the integer[1] 3.

The values classified by word types are simply the natural numbers, $\mathbb{N}$.

Generalised singletons. Singleton types carry an abstract representation of their run-time value as a logical term; the singleton type $\mathit{sgl}(v : T)$ classifies objects which correspond to the logical value v with (logical) type T.

This correspondence between an object of singleton type and the associated value is through that value's *representation type*, a machine type derived from the constructor and arguments which form the value; this derivation is discussed in Sect. 6.3.

A singleton value has the form $\mathit{sgl}\ (v : T)\ \mathit{in}\ \mathit{wv}$ where v and T are the value and type associated with the singleton. The word value wv is a reference to the *representation object* for the singleton, that is, wv should have the representation type derived from v; we shall discuss the structure of this object in Sect. 6.3 with the representation type.

[1] For simplicity, we assume unbounded machine words

Arguments sequences and extended labels

$$\Sigma \quad ::= \quad (\vec{A};\, \vec{\tau})$$
$$\mathcal{L} \quad ::= \quad \mathbb{N} @ \Sigma$$

Instructions and instruction sequences

$$
\begin{array}{lll}
I & ::= & \texttt{add}\ r_d,\ r_1,\ r_2 \\
 & | & \texttt{ldi}\ r,\ n \\
 & | & \texttt{move}\ r_d,\ r_s \\
 & | & \texttt{beq}\ r_1,\ r_2,\ \mathcal{L}\ \texttt{as}\ x \\
 & | & \texttt{apply}\ r_d,\ r_s,\ \Sigma \\
 & | & \texttt{lda}\ r,\ \mathcal{L} \\
 & | & \texttt{load}\ r_d,\ r_s(n)\ |\ \texttt{store}\ r_d,\ r_s(n) \\
 & | & \texttt{alloc}\ r_d,\ \vec{\tau} \\
 & | & \texttt{pack}\ r_d,\ r_s\ \texttt{as}\ \tau\ \texttt{hiding}\ v \\
 & | & \texttt{unpack}\ r_d,\ r_s\ \texttt{as}\ x \\
 & | & \texttt{inject}\ r_d,\ r_s\ \texttt{as}\ \tau \\
 & | & \texttt{project}\ r_d,\ r_s \\
 & | & \texttt{coerce}\ r_d,\ r_s\ \texttt{using}\ p \\
IS & ::= & I\ ;\ IS \\
 & | & \texttt{case}\ r_d,\ r_s,\ \vec{\mathcal{L}} \\
 & | & \texttt{br}\ \mathcal{L}\ |\ \texttt{jump}\ r\ |\ \texttt{halt}\ [\tau]
\end{array}
$$

Word values

$$wv \quad ::= \quad ?\tau\ |\ \mathbb{N}\ |\ \mathcal{L}\ |\ pack\ v\ in\ wv\ |\ sgl\ (v:\ T)\ in\ wv$$

Heap values

$$hv \quad ::= \quad \langle wv_1, \ldots, wv_n\rangle\ |\ \Lambda\Upsilon, [\Delta].IS$$

Heaps, register files, and programs

$$
\begin{array}{lll}
H & ::= & \{0 \mapsto hv_1,\ \ldots,\ n \mapsto hv_n\} \\
R & ::= & \{\texttt{r}_0 \mapsto wv_1,\ \ldots,\ \texttt{r}_N \mapsto wv_N\} \\
P & ::= & (H,\ R,\ IS)
\end{array}
$$

Figure 4. Syntactic classes for Singleton: instructions and values

Existential types. Singleton and word types are sometimes *too* precise: we may not care about the particular value associated with a type, only its general shape. The existential type $\exists(x : T).\tau$ then hides a logical value inside the type τ. In particular, an existential can hide the value associated with a singleton type.

Example 4.1 We can implement the non-dependent word type by

$$WORD \triangleq \exists(n : nat).word(n).$$

that is, a word type where the associated value is hidden by an existential.

Existential types are not limited to hiding logical values (that is, objects with a type in the sort Set): other logical terms can be hidden, including proof terms[2].

Example 4.2 The type

$$\exists(b\ :\ nat)(p\ :\ if\ b\ >\ 0\ then\ P\ else\ Q).word(b)$$

that is, a word type with a hidden value along with a (hidden) proof, can be used to simulate a boolean type. Depending on the value of b, p is equivalent to a proof of the proposition P or a proof of Q.

Tuple types. Tuple types are sequences of types classifying sequences of corresponding word values in the heap. Tuple types also track the initialisation status of the tuple contents: each type in the sequence has an associated *initialisation flag* which tracks the initialisation status of that entry [9]. For clarity, the initialisation flag may be omitted if it is set.

Values of tuple type occur both as heap values and as word values; in the heap, a tuple type classifies a sequence of word values, while as a word value, a tuple type classifies a label. Such labels then refer to a sequence of values in the heap.

Code types. Program blocks may abstract over both types and logical terms. The code type $\forall\Upsilon, [\Delta].\Gamma$ classifies code blocks abstracting over the logical variables in Υ and the type variables in Δ. The term Γ gives the expected types of each register; not all registers need to have a type.

Example 4.3 The type of a function which doubles the word in $\texttt{t}_1$ and preserves the word in $\texttt{t}_2$, returning to the label in $\texttt{ra}$ is

$$\forall(x : nat), [\alpha :: \mathbb{B}].\{\texttt{t}_1 : word(x), \texttt{t}_2 : \alpha,$$
$$\texttt{ra} : \{\texttt{t}_1 : word(x + x), \texttt{t}_2 : \alpha\}$$

where the logical argument is $(x\ :\ nat)$, the type argument is α, and the register arguments are $\texttt{t}_1$ with word type $word(x)$, $\texttt{t}_2$ with parametric type α, and the return register $\texttt{ra}$ with the code type $\{\texttt{r}_1\ :\ word(x\ +\ x),\ \texttt{r}_2\ :\ \alpha\}$.

Code values reside in the heap and take the form $\Lambda\Upsilon, [\Delta].IS$ where the logical variables in Υ and the type variables in Δ are bound in the instruction sequence IS.

Word values may also have code type: *extended labels* contain a reference to a heap object, along with an *argument sequence* containing a list of logical terms and types which have been applied to the label. We discuss argument sequences and extended labels further in Sect. 5.1.

5. Operational Semantics

In this section we present the operational semantics for Singleton, along with a discussion of the various instructions. We shall focus our discussion on those instructions which are Singleton-specific. The remainder, at least operationally, are typical of TALs in general; see [14] for more details.

Definition 5.1 The small-step operational semantics of Singleton are denoted by the following judgement

$$P \longmapsto P'$$

where P and P' are program states. The semantics are given in Fig. 5

5.1 Argument Sequences and Extended Labels

Singleton programs may abstract over both logical terms and machine type. An *argument sequence*

$$\Sigma = (\vec{A};\, \vec{\tau})$$

is used to instantiate any such terms, and is simply a tuple containing a sequence of logical arguments and a sequence of type arguments. Given two argument sequences Σ and Σ', $\Sigma \frown \Sigma'$ is their pairwise concatenation.

Argument sequences appear in a number of places in Singleton: as an argument to the `apply` operation and as arguments to branching instructions In addition, some instructions, namely `beq` and `case`, generate argument sequences containing proof terms.

An *extended label* is a label along with a (possibly empty) argument sequence. Operationally, extended label values collect the arguments to a function; partially applying code values complicates the proof of type erasure, and so the actual substitution occurs only when the final value is required, that is, when the label is used as a branch target.

[2] Hiding a proof term is essentially hiding the *existence* of a proof, as CiC has the proof-irrelevance property.

$(H, R, IS_0) \longmapsto P'$

if IS_0 is	and P' is
`move` $r_d,\ r_s;\ IS$	$(H,\ R\{r_d \mapsto R\ r_s\},\ IS)$
`add` $r_d,\ r_1,\ r_2;\ IS$	$(H,\ R\{r_d \mapsto R\ r_1 + R\ r_2\},\ IS)$
`ldi` $r_d,\ n;\ IS$	$(H,\ R\{r_d \mapsto n\},\ IS)$
`pack` $r_d,\ r_s$ `as` τ `hiding` $o;\ IS$	$(H,\ R\{r_d \mapsto \mathit{pack}\ o\ \mathit{in}\ R\ r_s\},\ IS)$
`unpack` $r_d,\ r_s$ `as` $x;\ IS$	$(H,\ R\{r_d \mapsto wv\},\ IS[x := v])$ when $R\ r_s = \mathit{pack}\ v\ \mathit{in}\ wv$
`alloc` $r,\ \tilde{\tau};\ IS$	$(H\{l \mapsto \langle ?\tilde{\tau}_0,\ \ldots,\ ?\tilde{\tau}_{\vert\tilde{\tau}\vert}\rangle\}, R\{r \mapsto l\ @\ ()\}, IS)$ when l fresh in H
`load` $r_d,\ r_s(n);\ IS$	$(H,\ R\{r_d \mapsto \tilde{v}_n\},\ IS)$ when $R\ r_s = l\ @\ \Sigma$ and $H\ l = \langle\tilde{v}\rangle$
`store` $r_s,\ r_d(n);\ IS$	$(H\{l \mapsto \langle\tilde{v}\{n \mapsto R\ r_s\}\rangle\}, R, IS)$ when $R\ r_d = l\ @\ \Sigma$ and $H\ l = \langle\tilde{v}\rangle$
`apply` $r_d,\ r_s,\ \Sigma';\ IS$	$(H,\ R\{r_d \mapsto l\ @\ \Sigma \frown \Sigma'\},\ IS)$ when $R\ r_s = l\ @\ \Sigma$
`lda` $r_d,\ \mathcal{L};\ IS$	$(H,\ R\{r_d \mapsto \mathcal{L}\},\ IS)$
`beq` $r_1,\ r_2,\ \mathcal{L}$ `as` $p;\ IS$	$(H,\ R,\ IS_{br})$ when $(pf\ :\ R\ r_1 = R\ r_2)$ and $H \models \mathcal{L}@\ (pf) \rhd IS_{br}$ and $(H,\ R,\ IS[p := pf])$ when $(pf\ :\ R\ r_1 \neq R\ r_2)$
`br` $\mathcal{L}$	$(H,\ R,\ IS)$ when $H \models \mathcal{L} \rhd IS$
`jump` r	$(H,\ R,\ IS)$ when $H \models R\ r \rhd IS$
`coerce` $r_d,\ r_s$ `using` $p;\ IS$	$(H,\ R\{r_d \mapsto R\ r_s\},\ IS)$
`inject` $r_d,\ r_s$ `as` $sgl(v : T);\ IS$	$(H,\ R\{r_d \mapsto \mathit{sgl}\ (v:\ T)\ \mathit{in}\ R\ r_s\},\ IS)$
`project` $r_d,\ r_s;\ IS$	$(H,\ R\{r_d \mapsto wv\},\ IS)$ when $R\ r_s = \mathit{sgl}\ (v:\ T)\ \mathit{in}\ wv$
`case` $r_d,\ r_s,\ \tilde{\mathcal{L}}$	$(H, R\{r_d \mapsto l\ @\ \Sigma\}, IS)$ when $R\ r_s = \mathit{sgl}\ (v:\ T)\ \mathit{in}\ (l\ @\ \Sigma)$ $H\ l = \langle n, \ldots\rangle$ $H \models \mathcal{L}_n@\ (B_1, \ldots, B_m, \mathit{refl\_equal}\ T\ v) \rhd IS$

Figure 5. Operational semantics for Singleton.

Substitution of logical terms and machine types into the various syntactic forms is defined in the usual fashion; we thus omit the definition from this paper. As a shorthand we use

$$v[\tilde{x} := \tilde{A}][\tilde{\alpha} := \tilde{\tau}]$$

for the *sequential* substitution for $\tilde{x}$ and $\tilde{\alpha}$ into v. Furthermore,

$$v[\Upsilon := \tilde{A}][\Delta := \tilde{\tau}] \triangleq v[\tilde{x} := \tilde{A}][\tilde{\alpha} := \tilde{\tau}]$$

where $\Upsilon = (\tilde{x} : \tilde{B})$ and $\Delta = \{\tilde{\alpha} :: \tilde{\kappa}\}$.

Example 5.1 Recall our *head* example from Sect. 2. If we imagine that `head` is applied to the list $[1,\ 2,\ 3]$, that is, the logical argument a will be *nat* while xs will be the above list, then the `case` instruction in `head` is passed two extended labels:

$$\texttt{hNil}\ @\ (\mathit{nat},\ [1,\ 2,\ 3])$$

and

$$\texttt{hCons}\ @\ (\mathit{nat},\ [1,\ 2,\ 3])$$

Execution of the `case` instruction will find that the list is not empty, and hence will invoke `hCons` with the additional arguments 1, $[2,\ 3]$, and the proof

$$\mathit{refl\_equal}\ (\mathit{list\ nat})\ [1,\ 2,\ 3]\ :\ [1,\ 2,\ 3] = [1,\ 2,\ 3]$$

Because `case` will branch to `hCons`, the substitution will be performed, resulting in the instruction sequence

load $\mathtt{t}_1,\ \mathtt{t}_1(1)$
apply ra, ra, $(1,\ [2,\ 3],\ \mathit{refl\_equal}\ (\mathit{list\ nat})\ [1,\ 2,\ 3])$
jump ra

where x, xs', and pf have been substituted accordingly.

Definition 5.2 (Application) The judgement

$$\models v\ @\ \Sigma \rhd IS$$

holds when substituting the arguments in Σ into the code value v results in the instruction sequence IS.

$$\models (\Lambda\Upsilon, [\Delta].IS)@(\vec{A}; \vec{\tau}) \rhd (IS[\Upsilon := \vec{A}][\Delta := \vec{\tau}])$$

We extend this to application at an extended label at a heap: given a heap H, an extended label $\mathcal{L} = l\ @\ \Sigma$, and an argument sequence Σ', we have

$$\frac{Hl = v \qquad \models v@(\Sigma \frown \Sigma') \rhd IS}{H \models \mathcal{L}@\Sigma' \rhd IS}$$

Application is rather straightforward: we simply substitute any arguments for the corresponding variables. Although substitution may result in a malformed instruction sequence, that is, one containing ill-typed CiC terms, the corresponding static judgement (Defn. 6.2) ensures that substitution occurs only when it results in well-formed instruction sequences.

We finish this section by noting that application has *no* run-time penalty for a Singleton program. Although substitution seems to create a copy of an instruction sequence, all types are erased in the translation from Singleton into machine code and hence all copies of an instruction sequence are identical after erasure.

5.2 Singleton operations

The singleton operations are perhaps the most novel part of Singleton; in this section we discuss their semantics. Singleton operations manipulate values of the form $\mathit{sgl}\ (v:\ T)\ \mathit{in}\ wv$, where wv is the object representing the singleton. We note, however, that only the `case` operation examines this value, requiring that it be a label referring to a tuple with at least one member, and this member being a word.

Rewriting the associated value. The `coerce` instruction rewrites the value associated with the singleton type using a proof of equality; operationally it is equivalent to a `move` operation.

Injection and projection. The `inject` operation creates singleton values by injecting objects of the representation type; the `project` operation does the converse, projecting the singleton type into the representation type. Operationally, `inject` and `project` simply create and destroy singleton values, respectively.

Case elimination. The `case` operation eliminates singleton values. This instruction, given a singleton object, branches depending on the value associated with the singleton. In addition, `case` extracts the representation object from the singleton and passes the destination label this object, and any constructor arguments and a proof relating the branch taken with the associated value.

Example 5.2 Recall the `case` instruction from `head`.

$$\texttt{case}\ \texttt{t}_1,\ \texttt{a}_1,\ [\texttt{hNil} \,@\, (a,\ xs),\ \texttt{hCons} \,@\, (a,\ xs)]$$

If the list associated with the type of $\texttt{a}_1$ is *nil*, then `case` will branch to `hNil`, otherwise `case` will branch to `hCons`. In the former case, the only logical argument generated is the proof

$$pf\ :\ xs\ =\ nil$$

while `hCons` gets the arguments from the *cons* constructor, namely x and xs', along with the proof

$$pf\ :\ xs\ =\ cons\ x\ xs'$$

If we are operating over a singleton with associated type T, then each constructor for T has a corresponding label in the arguments to `case`, where the order of the labels corresponds to the order of the constructors. In general, given the singleton value

$$sgl\ (v :\ T)\ in\ wv$$

where

$$v\ \equiv_{\beta\iota}\ Ctor(n,\ A)\ B_1\ \ldots\ B_m$$

then `case` will branch to the n-th label. We note that, at run-time, all values of an inductive type are equivalent to some fully applied constructor.

The n-th label should refer to a code block with arguments $B_1\ \ldots\ B_m$ along with a proof that

$$v\ =\ Ctor(n,\ A)\ B_1\ \ldots\ B_m$$

Dynamically, this proof is simply the reflexivity of equality at the value v, recalling that equivalent terms in CiC are indistinguishable. The main utility of this proof is to exploit *statically*, in the code for this label, that we are in the correct branch, and hence have discovered the shape of v.

Operationally, this branch target is determined by the representation object wv. A singleton value eliminated by the `case` instruction must have

$$wv\ =\ l\ @\ \Sigma$$

for some label l and argument sequence Σ. Furthermore, this label should point to some tuple in the heap with the tag n; the well-formedness conditions on singletons ensure that this is the case, including that this word is equal to the constructor index.

The new instruction sequence IS is obtained by applying the extended label to $B_1\ \ldots\ B_m$, followed by

$$\mathit{refl\_equal}\ T\ v\ :\ v\ =\ v$$

Finally, the value wrapped by the singleton value constructor is extracted and moved into the destination register.

5.2.1 Existential operations

The existential instructions manipulate values of the form $pack\ v\ in\ wv$. The `pack` operation constructs these values, while the `unpack` operation extracts the hidden v, substituting into the remaining instructions.

Example 5.3 We can implement addition on the non-dependent words from Eg. 4.1 (adding $\texttt{t}_1$ and $\texttt{t}_2$ with the result in $\texttt{t}_1$) by

$$\texttt{unpack}\ \texttt{t}_1,\ \texttt{t}_1\ \texttt{as}\ n_1$$
$$\texttt{unpack}\ \texttt{t}_2,\ \texttt{t}_2\ \texttt{as}\ n_2$$
$$\texttt{add}\ \texttt{t}_1,\ \texttt{t}_1,\ \texttt{t}_2$$
$$\texttt{pack}\ \texttt{t}_1,\ \texttt{t}_1\ \texttt{as}\ WORD\ \texttt{hiding}\ n_1\ +\ n_2$$

5.2.2 Code operations

The code operations manipulate code values in the heap, along with labels referring to such values. Only the branching instructions manipulate code variables directly; the instructions `apply` and `lda` manipulate extended labels only. In our semantics application is deferred until the value is actually used, that is, when the label is used as a branch target; thus simplifies the proof of type erasure.

The `apply` operation applies the given logical arguments to the code value in the source register, simply appending the arguments to any existing arguments for that label, while the `lda` operation creates a new value with the given label and arguments.

The branching operations, `beq`, `br`, and `jump`, perform the actual application by substituting the arguments for the corresponding variables. The `beq` instruction also substitues a proof of the equality (or inequality) of the values in the given registers. In all cases, the result of these substitutions forms the new instruction sequence.

6. Static Semantics

The judgements forming Singleton's static semantics are given in Fig. 6. All judgements are modulo CiC equivalence [11]. Again, we shall concentrate primarily on those which are Singleton-specific.

6.1 Well-formed types

A type is well-formed if all logical terms are well-typed and all type variables are accounted for. In addition, we insist that the value associated with a singleton type has sort Set. This allows us to ignore propositions when constructing the representation type.

We classify types into two kinds, *boxed* ($\mathcal{B}$) and *unboxed* ($\mathcal{U}$). This classification is required primarily to ensure Singleton programs can be safely garbage collected, although we will not address garbage collection in this paper.

In essence, a type is boxed if the object it classifies resides on the heap: tuples, singleton types, and code types are boxed, while words are unboxed. Existential types inherit the kind of the type under the existential.

Definition 6.1 (Well-formed types) The judgement

$$\Upsilon; \Delta\ \vdash\ \tau\ ::\ \kappa$$

holds when type τ is well-formed with kind κ under the logical context Υ and type environment Δ.

6.2 Well-formed applications and labels

As noted in Sect. 5.1, at a number of points within a Singleton program we may apply both logical and type arguments to code values. The resulting object is well-formed only when the arguments are well-formed and match those expected by the target.

Definition 6.2 (Well-formed application) The judgement

$$\Upsilon;\ \Delta\ \vdash\ \tau\,@\,\Sigma\ \rhd\ \sigma$$

holds whenever the application of the arguments in Σ to the type τ is valid and results in the type σ, under the logical context Υ and type context Δ.

We extend this to extended labels and heaps.

Constructing representation types

$$\boxed{\Upsilon \vdash \vec{v} \Downarrow \vec{\tau} \qquad \Upsilon \vdash v \downarrow \tau}$$

$$\frac{}{\Upsilon \vdash \epsilon \Downarrow \epsilon} \qquad \frac{\Upsilon \Vdash v : T : \mathit{Set} \qquad \Upsilon \vdash \vec{A} \Downarrow \vec{\tau}}{\Upsilon \vdash v, \vec{A} \Downarrow \mathit{sgl}(v : T), \vec{\tau}} \qquad \frac{\Upsilon \Vdash v : T : s \qquad \Upsilon \vdash \vec{A} \Downarrow \vec{\tau}}{\Upsilon \vdash v, \vec{A} \Downarrow \vec{\tau}}\,(s \equiv_{\beta\iota} \mathit{Prop}, \mathit{Type})$$

$$\frac{\Upsilon \Vdash n : \mathit{nat}}{\Upsilon \vdash n \downarrow \langle \mathit{word}(n) \rangle} \qquad \frac{\Upsilon \Vdash v : T \qquad \Upsilon \vdash \vec{B} \Downarrow \vec{\tau}}{\Upsilon \vdash v \downarrow \langle \mathit{word}([\![n]\!]), \vec{\tau} \rangle}\,(T \not\equiv_{\beta\iota} \mathit{nat}, v \equiv_{\beta\iota} \mathit{Ctor}(n, T) B_1 \ldots B_m)$$

Well-formed types and contexts

$$\boxed{\Upsilon; \Delta \vdash \tau :: \kappa \qquad \Upsilon; \Delta \vdash \Gamma \qquad \Upsilon; \Delta \vdash \Psi}$$

$$\frac{\alpha :: \kappa \in \Delta}{\Upsilon; \Delta \vdash \alpha :: \kappa} \qquad \frac{\Upsilon \Vdash n : \mathit{nat}}{\Upsilon; \Delta \vdash \mathit{word}(n) :: \mathfrak{U}} \qquad \frac{\Upsilon; \Delta \vdash \tau_i :: \kappa_i}{\Upsilon; \Delta \vdash \langle \tau_1^{\phi_1}, \ldots, \tau_n^{\phi_n} \rangle :: \mathcal{B}}\,(i \leq n) \qquad \frac{\Upsilon \Vdash v : T \qquad \Upsilon \Vdash T : \mathit{Set}}{\Upsilon; \Delta \vdash \mathit{sgl}(v : T) :: \mathcal{B}}$$

$$\frac{\Upsilon \Vdash \Phi \qquad \Upsilon, \Phi; \Delta, \Omega \vdash \Gamma}{\Upsilon; \Delta \vdash \forall \Phi, [\Omega].\Gamma :: \mathcal{B}}$$

$$\frac{\Gamma\, r = \tau \qquad \Upsilon; \Delta \vdash \tau :: \kappa}{\Upsilon; \Delta \vdash \Gamma}\,(r \in \mathit{dom}(\Gamma)) \qquad \frac{\Psi\, l = \tau \qquad \Upsilon; \Delta \vdash \tau :: \mathcal{B}}{\Upsilon; \Delta \vdash \Psi}\,(l \in \mathit{dom}(\Psi))$$

Well-formed application

$$\boxed{\Upsilon; \Delta \vdash \tau @ (\vec{A}; \vec{\sigma}) \rhd \xi}$$

$$\frac{}{\Upsilon; \Delta \vdash \tau @ () \rhd \tau} \qquad \frac{\Upsilon; \Delta \vdash \sigma :: \kappa \qquad \Upsilon; \Delta \vdash \forall \Phi, [\Omega].\Gamma[\alpha := \sigma] @ (\vec{\tau}) \rhd \xi}{\Upsilon; \Delta \vdash \forall \Phi, [\alpha :: \kappa, \Omega].\Gamma @ (\sigma, \vec{\tau}) \rhd \xi}$$

$$\frac{\Upsilon \Vdash b : A \qquad \Upsilon; \Delta \vdash (\forall \Phi, [\Omega].\Gamma)[x := b] @ (\vec{B}; \vec{\tau}) \rhd \xi}{\Upsilon; \Delta \vdash \forall (x : A) \Phi, [\Omega].\Gamma @ (b, \vec{B}; \vec{\tau}) \rhd \xi}$$

Initialisation subtype and well-formed values

$$\boxed{\vdash \sigma \leq \tau \qquad \Upsilon; \Delta; \Psi \vdash wv : \tau \qquad \Psi \vdash hv : \tau}$$

$$\frac{}{\vdash \tau \leq \tau} \qquad \frac{\vdash \sigma \leq \omega \qquad \vdash \omega \leq \tau}{\vdash \sigma \leq \tau} \qquad \frac{}{\vdash \langle \ldots, \tau^0, \ldots \rangle \leq \langle \ldots, \tau^1, \ldots \rangle}$$

$$\frac{}{\Upsilon; \Delta; \Psi \vdash n : \mathit{word}([\![n]\!])} \qquad \frac{\Upsilon; \Delta; \Psi \vdash \mathcal{L} \rhd \sigma \qquad \vdash \tau \leq \sigma}{\Upsilon; \Delta; \Psi \vdash \mathcal{L} : \tau} \qquad \frac{\Upsilon \Vdash v : A \qquad \Upsilon; \Delta; \Psi \vdash wv : \tau[x := v]}{\Upsilon; \Delta; \Psi \vdash \mathit{pack}\ v\ \mathit{in}\ wv : \exists (x : A).\tau}$$

$$\frac{\Upsilon \Vdash v : T \qquad \Upsilon \vdash v \downarrow \tau \qquad \Upsilon; \Delta; \Psi \vdash wv : \tau}{\Upsilon; \Delta; \Psi \vdash \mathit{sgl}\ (v : T)\ \mathit{in}\ wv : \mathit{sgl}(v : T)}$$

$$\frac{\epsilon; \epsilon; \Psi \vdash wv_i : \tau_i}{\Psi \vdash \langle \vec{wv} \rangle : \langle \vec{\tau} \rangle}\,(i \leq |\vec{wv}| \text{ and } \tau_i \text{ initialised}) \qquad \frac{\Upsilon; \Delta; \Psi; \Gamma \vdash \mathit{IS}}{\Psi \vdash \Lambda \Upsilon, [\Delta].\mathit{IS} : \forall \Phi, [\Delta].\Gamma}$$

Instruction sequence prefixes and heap membership

$$\boxed{\mathit{IS} \sqsubseteq \mathit{IS}' \qquad \vdash \mathit{IS} \in H}$$

$$\frac{}{\mathit{IS} \sqsubseteq \mathit{IS}} \qquad \frac{\mathit{IS} \sqsubseteq \mathit{IS}'[x := p]}{\mathit{IS} \sqsubseteq \textsf{beq}\ r_1, r_2, \mathcal{L}\ \textsf{as}\ x; \mathit{IS}'} \qquad \frac{\mathit{IS} \sqsubseteq \mathit{IS}'[x := v]}{\mathit{IS} \sqsubseteq \textsf{unpack}\ r_d,\ r_s\ \textsf{as}\ x; \mathit{IS}'} \qquad \frac{\mathit{IS} \sqsubseteq \mathit{IS}'}{\mathit{IS} \sqsubseteq I; \mathit{IS}'}\,(I \text{ not } \textsf{beq}, \textsf{unpack})$$

$$\frac{H l = \Lambda \Upsilon, [\Delta].\mathit{IS}' \qquad \mathit{IS} \sqsubseteq \mathit{IS}'[\Upsilon := \vec{A}][\Delta := \vec{\tau}]}{\vdash \mathit{IS} \in H}$$

Well-formed heaps, register files, and programs

$$\boxed{\vdash H : \Psi \qquad \Upsilon; \Delta; \Psi \vdash R : \Gamma \qquad \vdash P}$$

$$\frac{\Psi\, l = \tau \qquad H\, l = hv \qquad \Psi \vdash hv : \tau}{\vdash H : \Psi}\,(l \in \mathit{dom}(\Psi)) \qquad \frac{\Gamma\, r = \tau \qquad R\, r = wv \qquad \Upsilon; \Delta; \Psi \vdash wv : \tau}{\Upsilon; \Delta; \Psi \vdash R : \Gamma}\,(r \in \mathit{dom}(\Gamma))$$

$$\frac{\vdash H : \Psi \qquad \epsilon; \epsilon; \Psi \vdash R : \Gamma \qquad \epsilon; \epsilon; \Psi; \Gamma \vdash \mathit{IS} \qquad \vdash \mathit{IS} \in H}{\vdash (H, R, \mathit{IS})}$$

Figure 6. Singleton static semantics judgements (not including instruction sequences). We construct CiC natural numbers from meta-logical numbers using $[\![n]\!]$.

$$\frac{\Psi\ l = \tau \qquad \Upsilon;\Delta \vdash \tau@(\Sigma_1 \frown \Sigma_2) \rhd \sigma}{\Upsilon;\Delta;\Psi \vdash (l@\Sigma_1)@\Sigma_2 \rhd \sigma}$$

Applications are only relevant for code types, although we allow the empty argument sequence to be applied to any type. Otherwise, we apply the arguments from left to right, substituting into the code type for the corresponding variable. An application is well-formed only if the logical arguments are of the expected logical type, and the type arguments are of the expected kind.

Example 6.1 Consider again Eg. 5.1, where we apply `head` to the logical arguments nat and $[1,\ 2,\ 3]$. Recall the type of `head`

$$\begin{array}{l}\forall(a\ :\ Set)(xs\ :\ list\ a).\\ \quad \{\mathtt{a}_1\ :\ sgl(xs : list\ a),\\ \quad\ \mathtt{ra}\ :\ \forall(x\ :\ list\ a)(xs'\ :\ list\ a)\\ \qquad\qquad (pf\ :\ xs\ =\ cons\ x\ xs').\{\mathtt{t}_1\ :\ sgl(x : a)\}\}\end{array}$$

We shall call this type $\tau_{\mathtt{head}}$ in the following.
To apply nat, we must show

$$\Upsilon \Vdash nat\ :\ Set$$

noting that the first argument, a, has type Set. This holds, and so we substitute nat for a to get

$$\begin{array}{l}\forall(xs\ :\ list\ nat).\\ \quad \{\mathtt{a}_1\ :\ sgl(xs : list\ nat),\\ \quad\ \mathtt{ra}\ :\ \forall(x\ :\ list\ nat)(xs'\ :\ list\ nat)\\ \qquad\qquad (pf\ :\ xs\ =\ cons\ x\ xs').\{\mathtt{t}_1\ :\ sgl(x : nat)\}\}\end{array}$$

To apply $[1,\ 2,\ 3]$, we must show

$$\Upsilon \Vdash [1,\ 2,\ 3]\ :\ list\ nat$$

as xs has type $list\ nat$. Again this holds, and so, letting $\sigma_{\mathtt{head}}$ be

$$\begin{array}{l}\{\mathtt{a}_1\ :\ sgl([1,\ 2,\ 3] : list\ nat),\\ \ \mathtt{ra}\ :\ \forall(x\ :\ list\ nat)(xs'\ :\ list\ nat)\\ \qquad\quad (pf\ :\ [1,\ 2,\ 3]\ =\ cons\ x\ xs').\{\mathtt{t}_1\ :\ sgl(x : nat)\}\}\end{array}$$

we can derive $\Upsilon;\ \Delta \vdash \tau_{\mathtt{head}} @ (nat,\ [1,\ 2,\ 3]) \rhd \sigma_{\mathtt{head}}$.

6.3 Pseudo-elimination judgements

In this section we define auxiliary judgements used to eliminate singleton values. A *representation type* is the machine type underlying the singleton type, and the *elimination candidate* describes the possible forms the value associated with the singleton can take.

6.3.1 Representation types

We have informally introduced the concept of a representation type; in this section we define it formally.

Definition 6.3 (Representation types) The judgement

$$\Upsilon \vdash v \downarrow \tau$$

holds when the value v is represented by the type τ under the logical context Υ.

In general, the representation type for a given value is a tuple containing the constructor index for that value as a word, followed by singleton types for those constructor arguments with informative types (that is, types in the sort Set). Natural numbers, however, are represented using a word type boxed by a tuple.

Example 6.2 We can construct the representation type for the list of natural numbers $[1,\ 2,\ 3]$, as

$$\begin{array}{l}\Upsilon \vdash [1,\ 2,\ 3] \downarrow \langle word(1),\ sgl(1 : nat),\\ \qquad\qquad\qquad\quad sgl([2,\ 3] : list\ nat)\rangle\end{array}$$

which matches our description from Sect. 2.1.2.

Example 6.3 The type of lists containing elements which satisfy some predicate P is

$$\begin{array}{l}\textbf{Inductive}\ listP\ (T\ :\ Set)(P\ :\ T\ \rightarrow\ Prop)\ :\ Set\ :=\\ \quad |\ nilP\ :\ listP\ T\ P\\ \quad |\ consP\ :\ \forall(v\ :\ T).\ P\ v\ \rightarrow\ listP\ T\ P\ \rightarrow\ listP\ T\ P\end{array}$$

The list corresponding to $[1,\ 2,\ 3]$ then has the representation type

$$\begin{array}{l}\Upsilon \vdash [1,\ 2,\ 3] \downarrow \langle word(1),\ sgl(1 : nat),\\ \qquad\qquad\qquad\quad sgl([2,\ 3] : listP\ nat\ P)\rangle\end{array}$$

The proofs terms, having sort $Prop$, do not appear as elements in the representation type.

6.3.2 Elimination Candidates

Recall from Sect. 2.1.2 that the type of a label argument to `case` depends upon the corresponding constructor; the types of `hNil` and `hCons`, for example, are partially determined by their being the targets for the nil and $cons$ cases, respectively. In this section we define the *elimination candidates* for a given .

Definition 6.4 (Elimination candidates) Given a value, v, of inductive type T, and n, where

$$\begin{array}{l}\textbf{Inductive}\ T\ :\ Set\ :=\\ \quad \vdots\\ \quad |\ C_n\ :\ \forall(x_1\ :\ A_1)\ \ldots\ (x_m\ :\ A_m).\ T\\ \quad \vdots\end{array}$$

the elimination candidate for v, T, and n is

$$\begin{array}{rl}elims\ v\ T\ n\ = & (Ctor(n,\ T)\ x_1\ \ldots\ x_m,\\ & \ (x_1\ :\ A_1)\ \ldots\ (x_m\ :\ A_m)\\ & \ (p\ :\ v\ =\ Ctor(n,\ T)\ x_1\ \ldots\ x_m))\end{array}$$

where the x_i and p are chosen to be fresh.

The elimination candidate represents the possible head-normal forms for the value v, with new variables for the (unknown) constructor arguments. The candidate consists of the head-normal form, which is used to construct the representation type, and a context containing these new variables along with a proof that v equals the head-normal form, used to construct the target label type.

Example 6.4 The elimination candidates for $list\ T$ and some value v are

$$\begin{array}{rl}elims\ v\ (list\ T)\ 0 = & (nil,\ \epsilon)\\ elims\ v\ (list\ T)\ 1 = & (cons\ a\ as, (a\ :\ T)(as\ :\ list\ T)\\ & \qquad\qquad\qquad (p\ :\ v\ =\ cons\ a\ as))\end{array}$$

where a, as, and p are fresh. The context part of each candidate gives the extra arguments for the `hNil` and `hCons` labels.

Example 6.5 The elimination candidates for $listP\ T\ P$ and some value v are

$$\begin{array}{rl}elims\ v\ (listP\ T\ P)\ 0 = & (nilP,\ \epsilon)\\ elims\ v\ (listP\ T\ P)\ 1 = & (consP\ a\ p\ as,\\ & \ (a\ :\ T)(p\ :\ P\ a)\\ & \ (as\ :\ listP\ T\ P)\\ & \ (q\ :\ v\ =\ consP\ a\ p\ as))\end{array}$$

where a, as, p, and q are fresh. Note that, unlike the representation type for $listP$ (see Eg. 6.3), the elimination candidates *are* effected by the extra proof term: the environment portion of $elims\ v\ (listP\ T\ P)\ 1$ includes the proof p.

These operations, and hence singleton types, are defined only for inductive types without arguments[3]: constructing useful elimination candidates for inductive families is rather involved. Supporting them is left as future work.

6.4 Well-formed instruction sequences

The judgement for well-formed instruction sequences forms the heart of the type system for Singleton.

Definition 6.5 (Well-formed instruction sequence) The judgement

$$\Upsilon;\ \Delta;\ \Psi;\ \Gamma\ \vdash\ IS$$

holds when the instruction sequence IS is well-formed under the logical context Υ, type context Δ, heap type Ψ, and register file type Γ. The rules for this judgement are given in Fig. 7.

Arithmetic operations. The typing rules for arithmetic operations are more specific than with a traditional TAL as they must track the operation performed in the type of the target register: in the addition case, for example, we have that the destination register has type $word(n_1 + n_2)$ where n_1 and n_2 are the word values corresponding to the two argument registers. The rule for loading an immediate also produces a word type.

Existential operations. The typing rules for existential types are straightforward: the `pack` instruction hides a logical term value in a type, so we must check that when we substitute the given value back into the type we get that of the source register. Furthermore, we must check that value being hidden is well-formed.

The `unpack` operation performs the opposite operation, obtaining previously hidden values. We abuse α-conversion here so that the names bound by the existential are identical to the those of the target variables. Thus, we simply extend the logical and type contexts and update the target register with the body of the existential.

Singleton operations. The typing rules relating to singleton operations rely on the auxiliary judgements from Sect. 6.3.

The `inject` operation constructs a singleton type, and thus requires that the type of the source register is the representation type for the target singleton type.

Conversely, the `project` operation destroys a singleton with a specific value, and thus simply updates the destination register with the representation type at that value. Note that this operation is well-typed only when the representation type exists; in the case of non-primitive singleton types, this means that the head of the associated value is equivalent to a constructor.

The `coerce` operation rewrites the singleton value using a proof of equality; we must check that the proof is actually an equality, and that the source register is a singleton with a value equivalent to the left hand side of the equality. This operation is also defined for word types; this case is similar to the general singleton case.

The `case` operation eliminates a non-primitive singleton type by case analysis: the elimination candidates for this type give all possibilities for the associated value, introducing new variables for unknown constructor arguments (see Defn. 6.4). For each elimination candidate the corresponding label must refer to a code type which abstracts over the elimination context. Furthermore, the target register file type must be a subset of the current register context after updating the destination register with the representation type for the elimination value.

Code operations. The branching operations require that the target is fully applied: the `br` operation is well formed if the given (extended) label points to a fully-applied code type, the `jump` operation is similar except that the target label is sourced from a register. The `beq` instruction is slightly different in that the target type abstracts over an equality proof for the argument words. As usual, all instructions require the target register file to be a subset of the current register file.

The `apply` operation is well formed if the arguments are applicable at the type of the source register; application gives the new type, which is used to update the destination register.

Similarly, loading a constant label differs from a traditional TAL only in that the immediate is an extended label. The rule for the `lda` operation then updates the target register with the heap type at the given label, taking into account any arguments.

6.5 Well-formed values and programs

The well-formed value judgements are used to show that register files and heaps are well-formed, and hence that programs are well-formed. These judgements are standard, taking into consideration any extended labels.

Following Hamid et al. [6], a well-formed program requires that the instruction sequence resides in the heap. This property, required to show type erasure, is rather more complicated in Singleton than in a traditional TAL.

Definition 6.6 (Heap suffix membership) The judgement

$$\vdash\ IS\ \in\ H$$

holds when IS is a suffix of some object in the heap H.

In essence, this judgement states that IS can be obtained from some code value in the heap H by dropping instructions and instantiating any bound variables.

Definition 6.7 (Well-formed program) The judgement

$$\vdash\ P$$

holds when P is a well-formed program.

This holds when for some heap type Ψ and register file type Γ, the heap, register file, and instruction sequence are all well-formed, and the instruction sequence exists in the heap.

7. Type Safety and Type Erasure

We have developed [14] a machine-checked model of Singleton in the system Coq, showing both type safety and type erasure properties. Space constraints require that we only broadly discuss the proofs of these properties; the Coq scripts for these proofs are available at

`http://www.cse.unsw.edu.au/~sjw/thesis/proofs/`

An important lemma in the type-safety proof is the soundness of the well-formed application judgement; we show the following progress- and preservation-like lemmas for applications.

Lemma 1 If $\Psi \vdash hv : \tau$ and $\Upsilon; \Delta \vdash \tau @ \Sigma \rhd \sigma$ then $\models hv @ \Sigma \rhd hv'$ for some hv'.

We note that all CiC terms in hv' are well-formed under the context Υ.

Lemma 2 If $\Psi \vdash hv : \tau$, and $\Upsilon; \Delta \vdash \tau @ \Sigma \rhd \Gamma$, and $\models hv @ \Sigma \rhd IS$ then $\Psi \vdash IS : \Gamma$.

We show type safety using the usual progress and preservation lemmas.

Lemma 3 (Progress) If $\vdash (H, R, I)$ then $I = \mathtt{halt}\ [\tau]$ or $(H, R, I) \longmapsto P$ for some P.

[3] Parameters, that is, arguments to the type which are constant for a given type are defined; this is the case for T and P for $listP\ T\ P$ above.

$$\boxed{\Upsilon; \Delta; \Psi; \Gamma \vdash \mathit{IS}}$$

$$\frac{\Gamma\ r_1 = \mathit{word}(n_1) \qquad \Gamma\ r_2 = \mathit{word}(n_2) \qquad \Upsilon; \Delta; \Psi; \Gamma\{r_d \mapsto \mathit{word}(n_1 + n_2)\} \vdash \mathit{IS}}{\Upsilon; \Delta; \Psi; \Gamma \vdash \mathtt{add}\ r_d,\ r_1,\ r_2; \mathit{IS}}$$

$$\frac{\Upsilon; \Delta; \Psi; \Gamma\{r_d \mapsto \Gamma\ r_s\} \vdash \mathit{IS}}{\Upsilon; \Delta; \Psi; \Gamma \vdash \mathtt{move}\ r_d,\ r_s; \mathit{IS}}$$

$$\frac{\Upsilon; \Delta; \Psi; \Gamma\{r \mapsto \mathit{word}([\![n]\!])\} \vdash \mathit{IS}}{\Upsilon; \Delta; \Psi; \Gamma \vdash \mathtt{ldi}\ r,\ n; \mathit{IS}}$$

$$\frac{\Gamma\ r_s = \langle \ldots, \tau_n^{1}, \ldots \rangle \qquad \Upsilon; \Delta; \Psi; \Gamma\{r_d \mapsto \tau_n\} \vdash \mathit{IS}}{\Upsilon; \Delta; \Psi; \Gamma \vdash \mathtt{load}\ r_d,\ r_s(n); \mathit{IS}}$$

$$\frac{\Gamma\ r_s = \tau_n \qquad \Gamma\ r_d = \langle \ldots, \tau_n^{\varphi}, \ldots \rangle \qquad \Upsilon; \Delta; \Psi; \Gamma\{r_d \mapsto \langle \ldots, \tau_n^{1}, \ldots \rangle\} \vdash \mathit{IS}}{\Upsilon; \Delta; \Psi; \Gamma \vdash \mathtt{store}\ r_s,\ r_d(n); \mathit{IS}}$$

$$\frac{\Upsilon; \Delta \vdash \tau_i :: \kappa_i \qquad \Upsilon; \Delta; \Psi; \Gamma\{r \mapsto \langle \vec{\tau}^{0} \rangle\} \vdash \mathit{IS}}{\Upsilon; \Delta; \Psi; \Gamma \vdash \mathtt{alloc}\ r,\ \vec{\tau}; \mathit{IS}}\ (i \leq |\vec{\tau}|)$$

$$\frac{\tau = \exists(x : T).\xi \qquad \Upsilon \Vdash v : T \qquad \Upsilon; \Delta \vdash \tau :: \pi \qquad \Gamma\ r_s = \xi[x := v] \qquad \Upsilon; \Delta; \Psi; \Gamma\{r_d \mapsto \tau\} \vdash \mathit{IS}}{\Upsilon; \Delta; \Psi; \Gamma \vdash \mathtt{pack}\ r_d, r_s\ \mathtt{as}\ \tau\ \mathtt{hiding}\ v; \mathit{IS}}$$

$$\frac{\Gamma\ r_s = \exists(x : A).\tau \qquad \Upsilon, x : A; \Delta; \Psi; \Gamma\{r_d \mapsto \tau\} \vdash \mathit{IS}}{\Upsilon; \Delta; \Psi; \Gamma \vdash \mathtt{unpack}\ r_d,\ r_s\ \mathtt{as}\ x; \mathit{IS}}$$

$$\frac{\Gamma\ r_s = \tau \qquad \Upsilon \vdash v \downarrow \tau \qquad \Upsilon; \Delta; \Psi; \Gamma\{r_d \mapsto \mathit{sgl}(v : T)\} \vdash \mathit{IS}}{\Upsilon; \Delta; \Psi; \Gamma \vdash \mathtt{inject}\ r_d,\ r_s\ \mathtt{as}\ \mathit{sgl}(v : T); \mathit{IS}}$$

$$\frac{\Gamma\ r_s = \mathit{sgl}(v : T) \qquad \Upsilon \vdash v \downarrow \tau \qquad \Upsilon; \Delta; \Psi; \Gamma\{r_d \mapsto \tau\} \vdash \mathit{IS}}{\Upsilon; \Delta; \Psi; \Gamma \vdash \mathtt{project}\ r_d,\ r_s; \mathit{IS}}$$

$$\frac{\Gamma\ r_s = \mathit{sgl}(v : T) \qquad \Upsilon \Vdash p : v = u \qquad \Upsilon; \Delta; \Psi; \Gamma\{r_d \mapsto \mathit{sgl}(u : T)\} \vdash \mathit{IS}}{\Upsilon; \Delta; \Psi; \Gamma \vdash \mathtt{coerce}\ r_d,\ r_s\ \mathtt{using}\ p; \mathit{IS}}$$

$$\frac{\Gamma\ r_s = \mathit{word}(n) \qquad \Upsilon \Vdash p : n = m \qquad \Upsilon; \Delta; \Psi; \Gamma\{r_d \mapsto \mathit{word}(m)\} \vdash \mathit{IS}}{\Upsilon; \Delta; \Psi; \Gamma \vdash \mathtt{coerce}\ r_d,\ r_s\ \mathtt{using}\ p; \mathit{IS}}$$

$$\frac{\Gamma\ r_s = \mathit{sgl}(v : T) \qquad \Upsilon; \Delta; \Psi \vdash \mathcal{L}_i \rhd \forall \Phi_i.\Theta_i \qquad \Upsilon \vdash w_i \downarrow \tau_i \qquad \Theta_i \subseteq \Gamma\{r_d \mapsto \tau_i\} \qquad \text{for } i \text{ s.t. } \mathit{elims}\ v\ T\ i = (w_i, \Phi_i)}{\Upsilon; \Delta; \Psi; \Gamma \vdash \mathtt{case}\ r_d,\ r_s,\ \vec{\mathcal{L}}}\ (T \not\equiv_{\beta\iota} \mathit{nat})$$

$$\frac{\Gamma\ r_1 = \mathit{word}(n_1) \qquad \Gamma\ r_2 = \mathit{word}(n_2) \qquad \Upsilon; \Delta; \Psi \vdash \mathcal{L} \rhd \forall(p : n_1 = n_2).\Theta \qquad \Theta \subseteq \Gamma \qquad \Upsilon, p : n_1 \neq n_2; \Delta; \Psi; \Gamma \vdash \mathit{IS}}{\Upsilon; \Delta; \Psi; \Gamma \vdash \mathtt{beq}\ r_1, r_2, \mathcal{L}\ \mathtt{as}\ p; \mathit{IS}}$$

$$\frac{\Upsilon; \Delta; \Psi \vdash \mathcal{L} \rhd \Theta \qquad \Theta \subseteq \Gamma}{\Upsilon; \Delta; \Psi; \Gamma \vdash \mathtt{br}\ \mathcal{L}}$$

$$\frac{\Gamma\ r = \Theta \qquad \Theta \subseteq \Gamma}{\Upsilon; \Delta; \Psi; \Gamma \vdash \mathtt{jump}\ r}$$

$$\frac{\Upsilon; \Delta; \Psi \vdash \mathcal{L} \rhd \tau \qquad \Upsilon; \Delta; \Psi; \Gamma\{r \mapsto \tau\} \vdash \mathit{IS}}{\Upsilon; \Delta; \Psi; \Gamma \vdash \mathtt{lda}\ r,\ \mathcal{L}; \mathit{IS}}$$

$$\frac{\Upsilon; \Delta \vdash (\Gamma\ r_s)@\Sigma \rhd \tau \qquad \Upsilon; \Delta; \Psi; \Gamma\{r_d \mapsto \tau\} \vdash \mathit{IS}}{\Upsilon; \Delta; \Psi; \Gamma \vdash \mathtt{apply}\ r_d,\ r_s,\ \Sigma; \mathit{IS}}$$

$$\frac{\Gamma\ \mathtt{r}_0 = \tau}{\Upsilon; \Delta; \Psi; \Gamma \vdash \mathtt{halt}\ [\tau]}$$

Figure 7. Well-formed instruction sequences. Recall that $[\![n]\!]$ is the the logical value corresponding to the natural number n.

Lemma 4 (Preservation) If $\vdash P$ and $P \longmapsto P'$ then $\vdash P'$.

Singleton is rather type-heavy, so we show that any well-formed program can be erased to a simple machine state, such that evaluation of the program is matched by machine transitions.

Theorem 5 (Erasure) If $\vdash P$, and $P \longmapsto P'$ and P erases to the machine state s, then s steps (in zero or more steps) to some state s' such that P' erases to s'

We note that the erasure proof is similar to the proofs required to construct a syntactic FPCC [6] system. The main difference lies in the multiple machine steps required by the translation of the `case` instruction: the FPCC approach requires that each machine step correspond to some program step.

The `case` instruction is translated into a computed jump into a table of branches, one entry for each label argument to `case`. The exact steps are (ignoring the register move component): (1) load the index of the tuple under consideration into a temporary register; (2) use this address to calculate the address of a branch instruction inside the array of branches; (3) jump to this computed address; and (4) branch to the target label.

While we have presented the simpler `case` instruction, we believe that it is possible to encode each step as a separate instruction, allowing a straightforward FPCC proof.

8. Related Work

The *type language* (TL) of Shao *et al.* [12] is a variant of the calculus of inductive constructions. TL is intended to be a general-purpose type language for certified programs. As a specific instance, the authors present λ_H, a lambda calculus with singleton words and booleans, conditionals, fixpoints, existentials, and tuples. Existentials hide TL terms, and thus both computational types and logical terms and proofs. The terms in the computational language are outside TL.

TL is used as both the assertion logic and as a language for encoding computational types, which are simply terms in some inductive kind. Thus, it is possible to define multiple classes of computational types; the authors use this to encode their types for λ_H and for a CPS-converted language. Furthermore, types built from existing types need no extra machinery.

We cannot use TL directly to implement Singleton: TL does not include a facility to eliminate inductive kinds as required to construct representation types. We can, however, construct a similar system if we make the representation type explicit in the generalised singleton type.

We use something similar in our encoding of Singleton in the Coq system, described in [14]. The implementation using TL is, due to impredicativity, somewhat simpler; in particular, abstracting over types and representation functions is straightforward.

This approach is not without problems: the representation function can be an arbitrary function, thus making type checking incomplete. The representation function does not need to be a single-level elimination, and so our practice of checking `case` instructions by considering all possible constructors will not necessarily yield a concrete computational type.

Finally, we note that the *sgl* constructor is not actually required; we can use $f\ v$ instead of $sgl\ t\ f\ v$, that is, we identify a singleton and its representation type. Unfortunately, these three pieces of information, the type, the function, and the value, are all required by the `case` instruction: we perform case analysis on v, and discovering f and v through unification is, in general, undecidable .

The *logical type theory* (LTT) of Crary and Vanderwaart [4] takes a similar approach to TL, using linear LF [3] as the assertion logic rather than CiC; see [4, Sect. 7] for a comparison. The core computation language of LTT is the higher-order polymorphic lambda calculus extended with computational products and dependent products over proof kinds and families. The language is instantiated by giving a signature defining the syntax of the assertion logic and language primitives.

The considerable difference between CiC and LF makes it hard to compare Singleton in detail to LTT. Assuming a variant of LLT whose computation language is an assembly language, rather than a lambda calculus, the main difference to Singleton types is clearly the lack of inductive types in LTT.

Our treatment of inductive data types is similar to the *guarded recursive datatype constructors* of Xi et al.[16]; in particular, they show how datatype families can be considered as a combination of recursive, sum, and existential types. Although this approach generalises our representation types, it requires the addition of dependent kinds to our type system; whether their approach is feasible in our system we leave to future work.

Our singleton types are similar to refinement types [1, 5, 13]: the type $\{\ x\ :\ T \mid P\ \}$ is a refinement of the type T such that P holds, where x is bound in P. We can simulate such types in Singleton by

$$\textbf{Inductive}\ \mathit{refinement}\ (t\ :\ \mathit{Set})(P\ :\ t \rightarrow \mathit{Prop})\ :\ \mathit{Set}\ := \\ \mid \mathit{refinementI}\ :\ \forall(v\ :\ t),\ P\ v \rightarrow \mathit{refinement}\ t\ P$$

Although refinement types subsume our singleton types, in that the refinement types $\{x\ :\ T \mid x\ =\ v\}$ corresponds to the type $sgl(v : T)$, we cannot simply replace singleton types by refinement types: our use of representation types requires an associated value. Furthermore, Singleton's use of explicit proof terms obviates the need for refinement types as any restrictions can be more conveniently encoded as a proof assumption.

Xi and Harper[15] propose a *dependently typed assembly language* (DTAL) with singleton word types and length indexed array types. The annotations in DTAL are formulas of linear arithmetic; the typing rules accumulate contexts of refinement types relating to the variables in these formulas. In addition, code blocks can quantify over variables with refinement type; these variables may appear in the indicies of word and array types. As with our system, these indicies limit the mutability of constrained types.

A major difference between DTAL and Singleton lies in the treatment of proofs: in DTAL proofs are discovered by the type checker using linear constraint solvers, compared to the explicit proof-terms found in Singleton. While this reduces the size of type annotations, it requires type indices to be decidable. In addition, constraint satisfaction in DTAL is NP-complete, allowing potential denial-of-service attacks on the type checker. Finally, we note that DTAL programs can be converted into Singleton programs, assuming the constraint satisfaction solver is certifying.

Harren and Necula [7] give a dependently typed assembly language used as a target for their CCured tool [10]. The system is parameterised by a type policy, which takes the form of a set of constraints and constants, along with operations for refining sets of these constraints when given new information. The constants are used to construct expressions for register types.

This system, unlike Singleton, allows mutable dependent fields. This comes at a cost, however, as inter-record dependencies are not allowed: constraints can refer only to the current record. It is unclear as to whether, and to what extent, constraints can refer to records contained in the current record. We note that, like DTAL, type checking requires constraint operations to be decidable.

9. Discussion

While we have given Singleton as an idealised TAL, we believe that it can be extended to support the usual features, such as a stack, of an assembly language.

We presented Singleton as a TAL, although we believe the *idea* of Singleton is not restricted to low-level languages. We chose such a language in order to emphasise the difference between the computational language and the assertion language. However, higher-level languages are certainly also possible.

Acknowledgements The authors wish to thank Gerwin Klein and Toby Murray for their valuable feedback.

NICTA is funded by the Australian Government as represented by the Department of Broadband, Communications and the Digital Econ- omy and the Australian Research Council through the ICT Centre of Excellence program.

References

[1] J. Bengtson, K. Bhargavan, C. Fournet, A. D. Gordon, and S. Maffeis. Refinement types for secure implementations. In *Proc. of CSF'08*, pages 17–32. IEEE Computer Society, 2008.

[2] Y. Bertot and P. Castéran. *Interactive Theorem Proving and Program Development. Coq'Art: The Calculus of Inductive Constructions*. Texts in Theoretical Computer Science. Springer Verlag, 2004.

[3] I. Cervesato and F. Pfenning. A linear logical framework. *Information and Computation*, 179(1):19 – 75, November 2002.

[4] K. Crary and J. C. Vanderwaart. An expressive, scalable type theory for certified code. In *Proc. of ICFP'02*. ACM SIGPLAN, Oct. 2002.

[5] T. Freeman and F. Pfenning. Refinement types for ml. In *Proc. of PLDI'91*, pages 268–277. ACM, 1991.

[6] N. Hamid, Z. Shao, V. Trifonov, S. Monnier, and Z. Ni. A syntactic approach to foundational proof-carrying code. *Journal of Automated Reasoning*, 31(3-4):191–229, 2003.

[7] M. Harren and G. C. Necula. Using dependent types to certify the safety of assembly code. In *SAS'05*, pages 155–170, 2005.

[8] C. A. R. Hoare. An axiomatic basis for computer programming. *Commun. ACM*, 12(10):576–580, 1969. ISSN 0001-0782.

[9] G. Morrisett, D. Walker, K. Crary, and N. Glew. From System F to typed assembly language. *TOPLAS*, 21(3):527–568, 1999.

[10] G. C. Necula, S. McPeak, and W. Weimer. CCured: Type-safe retrofitting of legacy code. In *Proc. of POPL'02*, pages 128–139, 2002.

[11] C. Paulin-Mohring. Inductive definitions in the system coq - rules and properties. In *Proc. of TLCA'93*, pages 328–345. Springer-Verlag, 1993.

[12] Z. Shao, V. Trifonov, B. Saha, and N. Papaspyrou. A type system for certified binaries. *ACM Trans. Program. Lang. Syst.*, 27(1):1–45, 2005.

[13] T. Terauchi. Dependent types from counterexamples. In *Proc. of POPL'10*, pages 119–130, 2010.

[14] S. Winwood. *Singleton: A general-purpose dependently-typed assembly language*. PhD thesis, The University of New South Wales, 2010.

[15] H. Xi and R. Harper. A dependently typed assembly language. *ACM SIGPLAN Notices*, 36(10):169–180, Oct. 2001. ISSN 0362-1340.

[16] H. Xi, C. Chen, and G. Chen. Guarded recursive datatype constructors. In *POPL'03*, pages 224–235, 2003.

A Type and Effect System for Deadlock Avoidance in Low-level Languages

Prodromos Gerakios [1] Nikolaos Papaspyrou [1] Konstantinos Sagonas [1,2]

[1] School of Electrical and Computer Engineering, National Technical University of Athens, Greece
[2] Department of Information Technology, Uppsala University, Sweden
{pgerakios,nickie,kostis}@softlab.ntua.gr

Abstract

The possibility to run into a deadlock is an annoying and commonly occurring hazard associated with the concurrent execution of programs. In this paper we present a polymorphic type and effect system that can be used to dynamically avoid deadlocks, guided by information about the order of lock and unlock operations which is computed statically. In contrast to most other type-based approaches to deadlock freedom, our system does not insist that programs adhere to a strict lock acquisition order or use locking primitives in a block-structured way. Lifting these restrictions is primarily motivated by our desire to target low-level languages, such as C with pthreads, but it also allows our system to be directly applicable in optimizing compilers for high-level languages, such as Java.

To show the effectiveness of our approach, we have also developed a tool that uses static analysis to instrument concurrent programs written in C/pthreads and then links these programs with a run-time system that avoids possible deadlocks. Although our tool is still in an early development stage, in the sense that currently its analysis only handles a limited class of programs, our benchmark results are very promising: they show that it is not only possible to avoid all deadlocks with a small run-time overhead, but also often achieve better throughput in highly concurrent programs by naturally reducing lock contention.

Categories and Subject Descriptors D.3.3 [*Programming Languages*]: Language Constructs and Features—Concurrent programming structures; D.3.2 [*Programming Languages*]: Language Classifications—Concurrent, distributed and parallel languages; D.1.3 [*Software*]: Concurrent Programming—Parallel programming

General Terms Design, Languages, Performance, Theory

Keywords Deadlock avoidance, types and effects, C, pthreads

1. Introduction

In shared memory concurrent programming, deadlocks typically occur as a consequence of cyclic lock acquisition between threads. Two or more threads are deadlocked when each of them is waiting for a lock that has been acquired and is held by another thread. As

TLDI'11, January 25, 2011, Austin, Texas, USA.


```
efs_lookup(struct inode *dir, struct dentry *dentry) {
  efs_ino_t inodenum;
  struct inode * inode = NULL;

  lock_kernel();
  inodenum = efs_find_entry(dir, dentry->d_name.name,
                            dentry->d_name.len);
  if (inodenum) {
    if (!(inode = iget(dir->i_sb, inodenum))) {
      unlock_kernel();
      return ERR_PTR(-EACCES);
    }
  }
  unlock_kernel();

  d_add(dentry, inode);
  return NULL;
}
```

Listing 1. Code from Linux's EFS (`linux/fs/efs/namei.c`)

deadlocks are a serious problem, several methods to achieve deadlock freedom have so far been proposed. In particular, type based approaches aim for static deadlock freedom guarantees. Most of the proposed type systems in this category [6, 14, 19, 22] *prevent* deadlocks by imposing a strict (non-cyclic) lock acquisition order that must be respected throughout the entire program. However, insisting on a global lock ordering limits programming language expressiveness as many correct programs are rejected unnecessarily. Furthermore, the approach is intrinsically non-modular.

An alternative to deadlock prevention is to employ an approach that dynamically *avoids* deadlocks by utilizing information regarding future lock usage which is provided statically by program analysis. An interesting recent work in this direction is by Boudol [1] who presented a type and effect system for deadlock avoidance when locking is block-structured (e.g. as in Java's `synchronized` blocks). Unfortunately, in Boudol's system the fact that locking is block-structured is a crucial assumption that prohibits the use of his method in many situations. For example, there is a lot of important existing code where locking is used in an unstructured way; cf. the code in Listing 1, which is a typical example of systems code. Furthermore note that in low-level languages such as C, even if the programmer adheres to block-structured locking, this is nothing more than a convention: at the source level, any tool needs to deal with separate lock and unlock primitives. Finally, in almost all languages, the restriction that locking is block-structured is usually lifted at the low-level language of the compiler for optimization purposes. This is the type of languages that our work targets.

More specifically, in this paper we present a type-based method to dynamically avoid deadlocks guided by information about the order of lock and unlock operations which is computed statically via program analysis. The analysis is based on a type and effect system that is general enough to be applicable regardless of how locking is used. Our work is part of a long term effort to design and implement a language at the C-level of abstraction, which has explicit support for shared memory concurrency and provides static guarantees for various safety properties. Chief among these properties are memory safety, freedom from data races, and freedom from deadlocks. In this paper we focus exclusively on the last of them. While our work is primarily targeting low-level languages with unstructured locking, and is applied to multi-threaded C programs using the pthreads library, the main ideas in the type and effect system that we present are generic and language independent. To ease their exposition and simplify the presentation, the language we use in the main sections of this paper is a lambda calculus with recursion, conditionals, and of course primitives for creating, acquiring and releasing re-entrant locks. However, even in this simplified language, unstructured locking primitives and unrestricted lock aliasing introduce significant complexity to the type system compared with block-structured locking, where lock operations always match up with implicit unlock operations. Our type and effect system guarantees that locks are safely released and acquired in the presence of unrestricted lock aliasing.

It should be mentioned that this is not the first system for deadlock avoidance in the presence of unstructured locking that we have developed. In a recent workshop paper [10] we presented a rich type and effect system that, besides deadlock freedom, also guarantees race freedom and memory safety. Its effects contain elements that are pairs (n_1, n_2) associating memory cells with two capability counts: n_1 is a cell reference count, denoting whether the cell is live, while n_2 is the lock count, denoting how many times the cell has been locked (as locks are re-entrant). In addition, capabilities can be either unique or possibly aliased: the type system requires aliasing information so as to determine whether it is safe to pass lock capabilities to new threads. More importantly, it also requires that all functions are annotated with an explicit effect, which is used to type check their body. As a result, that type system is probably unsuitable for a language like C/pthreads; instead, it is relevant for a language like Cyclone [11] where it is commonplace for functions to have annotations. In contrast, the type and effect system we develop in this paper is much simpler. It focuses on deadlock avoidance only, captures the temporal order of lock and unlock operations, and imposes no restrictions with respect to aliasing. More importantly, its implementation is amenable to effect *inference*, and there is no requirement that functions are annotated with explicit effects. Instead, the type and effect system gathers effects and validates them at the beginning of the lexical scope of each lock. This simpler system is thus directly applicable to C/pthreads programs.

In short, the contributions of this paper are as follows:

- we present a polymorphic type and effect system that can be used to dynamically avoid deadlocks, guided by information about the order of lock and unlock operations which is computed statically, in a core language without references but with recursion, conditionals, and primitives for unstructured locking;
- we provide an operational semantics for deadlock avoidance in this language and state and provide proofs of the core soundness properties modeling and guaranteeing deadlock avoidance;
- we show the effectiveness of our approach by running existing C/pthreads programs in our prototype implementation and offer preliminary evidence that the approach is viable in practice.

To make the paper self-contained, we review existing type-based approaches to deadlock freedom (Sect. 2), including the recent work of Boudol, and explain why his approach cannot guarantee deadlock freedom in the presence of unstructured locking (first half of Sect. 3). Most of this material is taken more or less verbatim from our previous workshop paper [10]. In the main body of the current paper, we first describe informally how our approach manages to avoid deadlocks when unstructured locking is used (second half of Sect. 3), and then present the syntax of our language, its operational semantics, and a type and effect system for this language (Sect. 4) which we prove type safe (Sect. 5). To show the effectiveness of our approach, we briefly describe our current implementation (Sect. 6) and its performance (Sect. 7). The paper ends with a comparison of our approach with other techniques for providing deadlock freedom (Sect. 8), and with some concluding remarks.

2. Deadlock Freedom and Related Work

According to Coffman *et al.* [3], a set of threads reaches a *deadlocked state* when the following conditions hold:

- *Mutual exclusion*: Threads claim exclusive control of the locks that they acquire.
- *Hold and wait*: Threads already holding locks may request (and wait for) new locks.
- *No preemption*: Locks cannot be forcibly removed from threads; they must be released explicitly by the thread that acquired them.
- *Circular wait*: Two or more threads form a circular chain, where each thread waits for a lock held by the next thread in the chain.

Therefore, deadlock freedom can be guaranteed by denying at least one of these conditions *before* or *during* program execution. Thus, the following three strategies guarantee deadlock freedom:

- *Deadlock prevention*: At each point of execution, *ensure* that at least one of the above conditions is not satisfied. Thus, programs that fall into this category are correct by design.
- *Deadlock detection and recovery*: A dedicated observer thread *determines* whether the above conditions are satisfied and preempts some of the deadlocked threads, releasing (some of) their locks, so that the remaining threads can make progress.
- *Deadlock avoidance*: Using static information regarding thread resource allocation, *determine* at run time whether granting a lock will bring the program to an *unsafe* state, i.e., a state which can result in deadlock, and only grant locks that lead to safe states.

The majority of literature for language-based approaches to deadlock freedom falls under the first two strategies. In the deadlock prevention category, one finds type and effect systems [2, 6, 14, 19, 22] that guarantee deadlock freedom by statically enforcing a global lock-acquisition ordering, which must be respected by all threads. In this setting, lock handles are associated with type-level lock names via the use of singleton types. Thus, handle $\mathtt{lk}_\iota$ is of type $\mathtt{Lk}(\iota)$. The same applies to lock handle variables. The effect system tracks the order of lock operations on handles or variables and determines whether all threads acquire locks in the same order.

Using a strict lock acquisition order is a constraint we want to avoid. It is not hard to come up with an example that shows that imposing a partial order on locks is too restrictive. The simplest of such examples can be reduced to program fragments of the form:

$(\mathtt{lock}\ x\ \mathtt{in}\ \ldots\ \mathtt{lock}\ y\ \mathtt{in}\ \ldots) \parallel$
$(\mathtt{lock}\ y\ \mathtt{in}\ \ldots\ \mathtt{lock}\ x\ \mathtt{in}\ \ldots)$

In a few words, there are two parallel threads which acquire two distinct locks, x and y, in reverse order. When trying to find a partial order $\leq$ on locks for this program, the type system or static analysis tool will fail: it will deduce that $x \leq y$ must be true, because of the first thread, and that $y \leq x$ must be true, because of the second. In short, there is no partial order that satisfies these constraints. Thus, programs containing such patterns will be rejected, both in the system of Flanagan and Abadi which requires annotations [6] and in the system of Kobayashi which employs inference [14] as there is no single lock order for *both* threads. Similar considerations apply to the more recent works of Suenaga [19] and Vasconcelos *et al.* [22] dealing with unstructured locking primitives. Finally, such programs cannot be handled even by the type and effect system of Boyapati *et al.* [2], which allows for some controlled changes to the partial order of locks at runtime by permitting conservative updates on directed acyclic lock graphs, because there is no acyclic data structure that captures the cyclic dependencies between locks x and y of this program fragment.

Recently, Boudol developed a type and effect system for deadlock freedom [1], which is based on *deadlock avoidance*. The effect system calculates for each expression the set of acquired locks and annotates lock operations with the "future" lockset. The run-time system utilizes the inserted annotations so that each lock operation can only proceed when its "future" lockset is *available* to the requesting thread. The main advantage of Boudol's type system is that it allows a larger class of programs to type check and thus increases the programming language expressiveness as well as concurrency by allowing arbitrary locking schemes.

The previous example can be rewritten in Boudol's language as follows, assuming that the only lock operations in the two threads are those visible:

$$(\texttt{lock}_{\{y\}}\ x\ \texttt{in}\ \ldots\ \texttt{lock}_{\emptyset}\ y\ \texttt{in}\ \ldots)\ \|$$
$$(\texttt{lock}_{\{x\}}\ y\ \texttt{in}\ \ldots\ \texttt{lock}_{\emptyset}\ x\ \texttt{in}\ \ldots)$$

This program is accepted by Boudol's type system which, in general, allows locks to be acquired in *any* order. At run-time, the first lock operation of the first thread must ensure that y has not been acquired by the second (or any other) thread, before granting x. The second lock operation need not ensure anything, as its future lockset is empty. (The handling is symmetric for the second thread.)

3. Type System Overview

Boudol's work heavily relies on the assumption that locking is block-structured. In fact, the soundness of his system in the presence of lock aliasing is guaranteed by assuming that locks are re-entrant and are released in the reverse order in which they were acquired. In this section, we discuss the main ideas of a novel type system for a simple language with unstructured locking primitives, recursion, and conditionals, which guarantees deadlock freedom and safe use of operations that acquire and release locks in the presence of aliasing. We first show that a naïve extension of Boudol's system is insufficient to guarantee deadlock freedom when locking is unstructured. The example program in Fig. 1(a) illustrates this point: It uses three shared variables, x, y and z, ensuring at each step that no unnecessary locks are held. It is assumed here that the long computations do not acquire or release any locks.[1]

In our naïvely extended (and broken, as we will see) version of Boudol's type and effect system, the program in Fig. 1(a) will type check. The future lockset annotations of the three locking operations in the body of f are $\{y\}$, $\{z\}$ and $\emptyset$, respectively. (This can be easily verified by observing the lock operations between a specific lock and unlock pair.) Now, function f is used by instantiating both x and y with the same variable a, and instantiating z with a distinct variable b. The result of this substitution is shown in Fig. 1(b). The first thing to notice is that, if we want this program to work, locks have to be *re-entrant*. This roughly means that if a thread holds some lock, it can try to acquire the same lock again; this will immediately succeed, but then the thread will have to release the lock *twice*, before it is actually released.

Even with re-entrant locks, however, it is easy to see that the program in Fig. 1(b) does not type check with the present annotations. The first lock operation for a now matches with the *last* (and not the first) unlock operation; this means that a will remain locked during the whole execution of the program. In the meantime b is locked, so the future lockset annotation of the first lock operation should contain b, but it does not. (The annotation of the second lock operation contains b, but blocking there if lock b is not available does not prevent a possible deadlock; lock a has already been acquired.) So, the technical failure of our naïvely extended language is that the preservation lemma breaks. From a more pragmatic point of view, if a thread running in parallel with the thread in Fig. 1(b) already holds b and, before releasing it, is about to acquire a, a deadlock can occur. The naïve extension also fails for another reason: Boudol's system is based on the assumption that calling a function cannot affect the set of locks that are held. This is obviously not true, if non lexically-scoped locking operations are to be supported.

To avoid such problems, our type system precisely tracks effects as a sequence of lock and unlock events. A *continuation effect* of an expression represents the effect of the function code following that expression (i.e., our continuation effects are intra-procedural, in contrast to the work of Hicks *et al.* [12] where the continuation effects are inter-procedural). As shown in the example of Fig. 1, the future lockset for unstructured locking operations cannot be computed statically as a result of lock aliasing. Therefore, the computation of future locksets given the continuation effects is deferred until run-time (i.e., after substitution has taken place), in contrast to Boudol's system.

The program in Fig. 2 is similar to the program in Fig. 1, except that lock operations are now annotated with continuation effects.

(a) before substitution	(b) after substitution
let $f = \lambda x.\lambda y.\lambda z.$	
$\texttt{lock}_{\{y\}}\ x;$	$\texttt{lock}_{\{a\}}\ a;$
some_long_computation x;	*some_long_computation* a;
$\texttt{lock}_{\{z\}}\ y;$	$\texttt{lock}_{\{b\}}\ a;$
another_long_computation $x\ y$;	*another_long_computation* $a\ a$;
unlock x;	unlock a;
$\texttt{lock}_{\emptyset}\ z;$	$\texttt{lock}_{\emptyset}\ b;$
another_long_computation $y\ z$;	*another_long_computation* $a\ b$;
unlock z;	unlock b;
unlock y	unlock a
in $f\ a\ a\ b$	

Figure 1. A program which is typable by a naïve extension of Boudol's system before substitution (a) but not after (b).

(a) before substitution	(b) after substitution
let $f = \lambda x.\lambda y.\lambda z.$	
$\texttt{lock}_{[y+,x-,z+,z-,y-]}\ x;$	$\texttt{lock}_{[a+,a-,b+,b-,a-]}\ a;$
some_long_computation x;	*some_long_computation* a;
$\texttt{lock}_{[x-,z+,z-,y-]}\ y;$	$\texttt{lock}_{[a-,b+,b-,a-]}\ a;$
another_long_computation $x\ y$;	*another_long_computation* $a\ a$;
unlock x;	unlock a;
$\texttt{lock}_{[z-,y-]}\ z;$	$\texttt{lock}_{[b-,a-]}\ b;$
another_long_computation $y\ z$;	*another_long_computation* $a\ b$;
unlock z;	unlock b;
unlock y	unlock a
in $f\ a\ a\ b$	

Figure 2. The program of Fig. 1 with continuation effect annotations; now the program is typable in both cases.

[1] For simplicity, in the examples of this section, we assume that there is one (implicit) lock for every shared program variable, which is used to avoid data races when this shared variable is accessed. Therefore, by x we denote both the shared variable x and its implicit lock. As we will see, in Sect. 4 we will simplify presentation even further by completely omitting shared variables and mutable state in general from the language.

$\texttt{let}\ f = \lambda\_.\ \ g()_{[z+]};$
$\qquad\qquad\ \texttt{lock}_{\emptyset}\ z\ ;$

$\texttt{let}\ g = \lambda\_.\ \ \boxed{\texttt{lock}_{[y+,\,y-]}\ x;}$
$\qquad\qquad\ \texttt{lock}_{[y-]}\ y;$
$\qquad\qquad\ \texttt{unlock}\ y\ ;$

$f()_{[z-,\,x-]};\ \texttt{unlock}\ z;\ \texttt{unlock}\ x$

(a) lock/unlock in different scope

Stack

$z-, x-$
$z+$

Lock/Continuation

$x+ \quad y+, y-$

lockset = $\{y, z\}$

(b) run-time state

Figure 3. An example program where lock and unlock operations are not in the same scope (a) and the run-time state of this program when the boxed term is executed (b).

For example, the annotation $[y+,\ x-,\ z+,\ z-,\ y-]$ at the first lock operation means that in the future (i.e., after this lock operation) y will be acquired, then x will be released, and so on. If x and y are instantiated with distinct values, the run-time system will compute the future lockset $\{y\}$ from the continuation effect. In terms of the continuation effect, $y+$ precedes $x-$ (i.e., the matching unlock operation).

On the other hand, if x and y are instantiated with the same lock handle a and z with b, the continuation effect of the first lock operation becomes $[a+,\ a-,\ b+,\ b-,\ a-]$ and the future lockset is now correctly calculated as $\{a, b\}$: $a+$ and $b+$ precede the matching unlock operation, which is the last $a-$. More generally, the future lockset computation algorithm takes as input a lock x, a continuation effect γ, assumes an empty future lockset and adds all $y+$ events of γ to the future lockset until the matching unlock operation for x is found.

Our continuation effects are intra-procedural, as mentioned earlier. Therefore, the matching unlock operation for y may not be located in γ. We resolve this issue by annotating application terms with their continuation effect. At run-time, when a function application redex is evaluated, its continuation effect is pushed on a stack of continuation effects for the duration of the function evaluation.[2] When the matching unlock operation is not located in a continuation effect, the algorithm proceeds with the remaining continuation effects on the run-time stack. The type system ensures that for each lock operation there exists a matching unlock operation. Therefore, the lockset computation algorithm is guaranteed to terminate. A lock operation succeeds only when both the lock and its future lockset are available. However, the locks in the future lockset are not prematurely acquired, as this would damage the program's degree of parallelism.

Fig. 3(a) illustrates a program where lock and unlock operations reside in different scopes. For instance, x is locked in function g, but it is unlocked in the outermost scope. Application terms are annotated with their continuation effects. For instance, the application of f is annotated with the continuation effect $[z-,\ x-]$ as it is succeeded by two unlock operations on z and x respectively. Fig. 3(b) shows the run-time state of the program when control reaches the lock operation on x: the run-time stack (which grows downwards in the figure) contains the continuation effects of f and g and the lockset computation algorithm starts off with the continuation effect of the lock operation. The algorithm adds $y+$ to the future lockset of x and then considers the continuation effects on the stack, from top to bottom. Thus, $z+$ is added to the future lockset and the matching unlock operation is found on the next element of the stack. The resulting lockset is $\{y, z\}$.

Our language provides support for conditional expressions and recursion. A shortcoming of representing effects as ordered events is that, when typing conditional expressions, it is too restrictive to require that both branches have the same effect. Consider the following example:

$$\texttt{if}\ e\ \texttt{then}\ (\texttt{lock}_{[y]}\ x;\ \ldots\ \texttt{lock}_{\emptyset}\ y;\ \ldots\ \texttt{unlock}\ y)$$
$$\texttt{else}\ (\texttt{lock}_{[x]}\ z;\ \ldots\ \texttt{lock}_{\emptyset}\ x;\ \ldots\ \texttt{unlock}\ z)$$

The lock operations of the two branches differ: the effect of the first branch is $[x+,\ y+,\ y-]$ and that of the second is $[z+,\ x+,\ z-]$. Although the overall effect of the two branches (as most programmers understand it) is the same, a simple type and effect system would have to reject this program.

Our system is able to overcome this issue by keeping track of the effects in both branches. For the example shown above, we make the effect of the conditional expression $[x+,\ y+,\ y-]\,?\,[z+,\ x+,\ z-]$. Given this effect the lockset calculation algorithm computes the lockset of the two branches separately. The resulting lockset is formulated by joining the two locksets. However, for each lock, we impose the restriction that the number of unmatched lock/unlock operations must be equal in both branches.

Additional problems need to be addressed when dealing with recursive function definitions. Consider the following example:

$$\texttt{letrec}\ f = \lambda x.\,\lambda y.\,\lambda z.$$
$$\texttt{if}\ z > 0\ \texttt{then}\ (\texttt{lock}_{\gamma}\ x;\ f\ x\ y\ (z-1);\ \texttt{unlock}\ x)$$
$$\texttt{else}\ (\texttt{lock}_{\emptyset}\ y; \ldots \texttt{unlock}\ y;)$$

In this case, if we employ the usual typing for `letrec`, the effect of f must equal the effect of its body. However, this is impossible, as the two effects cannot be structurally equivalent: in fact, the effect of f is *contained* in the effect of its body, due to the recursive call. To overcome this issue, our system assigns f a *summary* of the effect of its body. A detailed discussion of effect summaries is deferred until Sect. 4.3 but let us briefly see how our system can infer the effect of function f in the example above. Suppose that γ_f is the (unknown) effect of f. Then, the effect of *the body* of f as a function of γ_f is expressed as

$$\gamma_b(\gamma_f) = ([x+] :: \gamma_f :: [x-])\,?\,[y+,\ y-]$$

where $\gamma_1 :: \gamma_2$ denotes the appending of two effects γ_1 and γ_2. We are looking for a solution to the equation

$$\gamma_f = \mathsf{summary}(\gamma_b(\gamma_f))$$

At this point, we can start with $\gamma_0 = \emptyset$ (noticing that function f has no unmatched lock or unlock operations) and look for the limit of the sequence $\gamma_{n+1} = \mathsf{summary}(\gamma_b(\gamma_n))$ in other words, for a fixed point of the summarized function's body. We have

$$\gamma_1 = \mathsf{summary}(\gamma_b(\gamma_0)) = \mathsf{summary}([x+,\ x-]\,?\,[y+,\ y-])$$

Although we have not formally defined what function summary does, a possible (but conservative) choice here would be to "merge" the effects of the two branches in the summary. (In Sect. 4.3 we discuss how exactly this "merging" takes place and also discuss less conservative alternatives.) Therefore,

$$\gamma_1 = [x+,\ x-,\ y+,\ y-]$$

We can then proceed in the same way and take

$$\gamma_2 = \mathsf{summary}([x+,\ x+,\ x-,\ y+,\ y-,\ x-]\,?\,[y+,\ y-])$$

If we are outside function f, we don't care if inside f lock x is taken more than once. Nor do we care if x is held or not, at the moment when y is taken. We are just happy to know that x and y are taken and released. Therefore, by merging again:

$$\gamma_2 = [x+,\ x-,\ y+,\ y-] = \gamma_1$$

We reached a fixed point and we can take γ_1 as the summarized effect of function f. Therefore, the effect γ in the annotation of the first lock operation in the example is equal to $[x+,\ x-,\ y+,\ y-,\ x-]$.

[2] As we will see in Sect. 6, this is a constant time operation.

Expression	e	$::=$	$x \mid v \mid (e\ e)^{\xi} \mid (e)[r] \mid \mathtt{pop}_{\gamma}\ e$
		$\mid$	$\mathtt{newlock}\ \rho, x\ \mathtt{in}\ e \mid \mathtt{lock}_{\gamma}\ e \mid \mathtt{unlock}\ e$
		$\mid$	$\mathtt{if}\ e\ \mathtt{then}\ e\ \mathtt{else}\ e$
Value	v	$::=$	$() \mid \mathtt{true} \mid \mathtt{false} \mid f \mid \mathtt{lk}_{\iota}$
Function	f	$::=$	$\lambda x.\ e \mid \Lambda\rho.\ f \mid \mathtt{fix}\ x.\ f$
Type	τ	$::=$	$\langle\rangle \mid \mathsf{Bool} \mid \mathsf{Lk}(r) \mid \tau \xrightarrow{\gamma} \tau \mid \forall\rho.\ \tau$
Lock	r	$::=$	$\rho \mid \iota$
Calling mode	ξ	$::=$	$\mathsf{seq}(\gamma) \mid \mathsf{par}$
Operation	κ	$::=$	$+ \mid -$
Effect	γ	$::=$	$\emptyset \mid r^{\kappa}, \gamma \mid \gamma\ ?\ \gamma, \gamma$

Figure 4. Language and type syntax.

4. Formal Semantics and Metatheory

The syntax of our language is illustrated in Fig. 4, where x and ρ range over term and lock variables, respectively, and ι ranges over lock constants. In this paper, to make the presentation as simple as possible, we do not include any mutable shared state in our language. In other words, we study locks in isolation: locks do not serve any other purpose than thread synchronization (mutual exclusion). Without shared mutable references, locks may seem a bit pointless. However, our primary goal is to develop a simple and understandable type and effect system that guarantees deadlock avoidance. Including shared memory and achieving other interesting properties, such as memory safety and data race freedom, are goals which are more or less orthogonal to deadlock freedom. For one way on how to achieve them, we refer the reader to our previous work [8] and to the workshop paper [10] mentioned in the introduction.

The language core comprises of constants (`true`, `false` and () — the "unit" value), functions (f), and function application. Functions can be monomorphic ($\lambda x.\ e$), lock polymorphic ($\Lambda\rho.\ f$), and recursive ($\mathtt{fix}\ x.\ f$). The application of lock polymorphic functions is explicit ($e[r]$, where r is a metavariable ranging over lock constants and variables). The application of monomorphic functions is annotated with a *calling mode* (ξ), which is $\mathsf{seq}(\gamma)$ for normal sequential application and par for parallel application.[3] The semantics of parallel application is that, once the application term is evaluated to a redex, it is moved to a new thread of execution and the spawning thread can proceed with the remaining computation in parallel with the new thread. Conditional expressions ($\mathtt{if}\ e\ \mathtt{then}\ e_1\ \mathtt{else}\ e_2$) are standard.

The construct $\mathtt{newlock}\ \rho, x\ \mathtt{in}\ e$ allocates a fresh lock, which is initially unlocked, and associates it with variables ρ and x within expression e. The type variable ρ is bound to the type-level representation of the fresh lock and allows the type system to statically track uses of it, whereas the term variable x is bound to the fresh lock's handle. Handles can be used as arguments in operations $\mathtt{lock}_{\gamma}\ e$ and $\mathtt{unlock}\ e$, which have been explained in Sect. 3. It is worth noting that run-time locks are re-entrant, so each lock is associated with a count which is modified after each successful lock/unlock operation. As mentioned, the run-time system inspects the lock annotation γ to determine whether it is safe to lock e.

The term $\mathtt{pop}_{\gamma}\ e$ encloses a function body e and cannot exist at the source-level; it only appears during evaluation. The same applies to constant lock handles $\mathtt{lk}_{\iota}$.

The syntax of types is more or less standard; a function's type is annotated with the function's effect. Effects (γ) are sequences of events, in the way that was explained in Sect. 3. An atomic event can either be r^{+} or r^{-}, representing acquire and release operations on a lock handle of type $\mathsf{Lk}(r)$. Events also include $\gamma_1\ ?\ \gamma_2$, where γ_1 and γ_2 are the continuation effects corresponding to the two branches of a conditional expression.

[3] Notice that sequential application terms are annotated with γ, the *continuation effect*, as mentioned earlier in Sect. 3.

Lock Store	S	$::=$	$\emptyset \mid S, \iota \mapsto n; n; \epsilon; \epsilon$
Threads	T	$::=$	$\emptyset \mid T, n : e$
Configuration	C	$::=$	$S; T$
Lockset	ϵ	$::=$	$\emptyset \mid \epsilon, \iota$
Context	E	$::=$	$\Box \mid E[F]$
Frame	F	$::=$	$(\Box\ e)^{\xi} \mid (v\ \Box)^{\xi} \mid (\Box)[r] \mid \mathtt{pop}_{\gamma}\ \Box$
		$\mid$	$\mathtt{lock}_{\gamma_1}\ \Box \mid \mathtt{unlock}\ \Box \mid \mathtt{if}\ \Box\ \mathtt{then}\ e\ \mathtt{else}\ e$

Figure 5. Operational semantics syntax and evaluation context.

4.1 Operational Semantics

We define a *small-step* operational semantics for our language in Fig. 5 and 6.[4] The evaluation relation transforms *configurations*. A configuration C consists of an abstract *lock store* S and a thread map T.[5] A store S maps constant locks (ι) to tuples of the form $(n_1; n_2; \epsilon_1; \epsilon_2)$. The first two elements of the tuple are natural numbers representing the thread identifier that owns ι and the count of ι, respectively. The remaining two elements are locksets; they bear no operational significance but are necessary for the type safety proof. The first lockset (ϵ_1) represents the set of all locks in S when ι was last locked (when its n_2 went from zero to one). The second lockset (ϵ_2) represents the future lockset of ι when it was last locked.

A thread map T associates thread identifiers to expressions (i.e., threads). A *frame* F is an expression with a *hole*, represented as $\Box$. The hole indicates the position where the next reduction step can take place. A *thread evaluation context* E is defined as a stack of nested frames. Our notion of evaluation context imposes a call-by-value evaluation strategy to our language. Subexpressions are evaluated in a left-to-right order. We assume that concurrent reduction events can be totally ordered [15]. At each step, a *random* thread (n) is chosen from the thread list for evaluation. Therefore, the evaluation rules are *non-deterministic*.

When a parallel function application redex is detected within the evaluation context of a thread, a new thread is created (rule *E-SN*). The redex is replaced with the unit value in the currently executed thread and a new thread is added to the thread list, with a *fresh* thread identifier. The calling mode of the application term is changed from parallel to sequential, with an empty continuation effect. When evaluation of a thread reduces to a unit value, the thread is removed from the thread list (rule *E-T*). The sequential function application rule (*E-A*) reduces an application redex to a `pop` expression, which contains the body of the function and is annotated with the same effect as the application term. Pop expressions are used to form the run-time stack of continuation effects, explained in the example of Fig. 3(b). When the expression contained within a `pop` has been reduced to a value, then enclosing `pop` is removed and the value is returned to the context (rule *E-PP*). The rules for evaluating the application of polymorphic functions (*E-RP*) and recursive functions (*E-FX*) are standard, as well as the rules for evaluating conditionals (*E-IT* and *E-IF*). Rule *E-NG* appends to S a fresh lock ι, which is initially unlocked.

[4] The descriptions of some functions that are not defined formally in this paper, due to space restrictions, are given in the appendix. A full formalization is given in the companion technical report [9].

[5] The order of elements in comma-separated lists, e.g., in a store S or in a list of threads T, is unimportant; we consider all list permutations as equivalent. However, in sequences (e.g., effects), order is important.

$$\frac{\text{fresh } n'}{S;T,n:E[(v'\ v)^{\mathsf{par}}] \rightsquigarrow S;T,n:E[()],n':\square[(v'\ v)^{\mathsf{seq}(\emptyset)}]}\ \textit{(E-SN)} \qquad \frac{}{S;T,n:\square[()] \rightsquigarrow S;T}\ \textit{(E-T)}$$

$$\frac{}{S;T,n:E[((\lambda x.\, e_1)\ v)^{\mathsf{seq}(\gamma)}] \rightsquigarrow S;T,n:E[\mathsf{pop}_\gamma\ e_1[v/x]]}\ \textit{(E-A)} \qquad \frac{}{S;T,n:E[\mathsf{pop}_\gamma\ v] \rightsquigarrow S;T,n:E[v]}\ \textit{(E-PP)}$$

$$\frac{}{S;T,n:E[(\Lambda\rho.\, f)[\iota]] \rightsquigarrow S;T,n:E[f[\iota/\rho]]}\ \textit{(E-RP)} \qquad \frac{v' = \mathtt{fix}\ x.\, f}{S;T,n:E[(v'\ v)^{\mathsf{seq}(\gamma)}] \rightsquigarrow S;T,n:E[(f[v'/x]\ v)^{\mathsf{seq}(\gamma)}]}\ \textit{(E-FX)}$$

$$\frac{}{S;T,n:E[\mathtt{if\ true\ then}\ e_1\ \mathtt{else}\ e_2] \rightsquigarrow S;T,n:E[e_1]}\ \textit{(E-IT)} \qquad \frac{}{S;T,n:E[\mathtt{if\ false\ then}\ e_1\ \mathtt{else}\ e_2] \rightsquigarrow S;T,n:E[e_2]}\ \textit{(E-IF)}$$

$$\frac{\text{fresh } \iota \qquad S' = S, \iota \mapsto n;0;\emptyset;\emptyset}{S;T,n:E[\mathtt{newlock}\ \rho, x\ \mathtt{in}\ e_1] \rightsquigarrow S';T,n:E[e_1[\iota/\rho][\mathtt{lk}_\iota/x]]}\ \textit{(E-NG)}$$

$$\frac{\begin{array}{cc} S(\iota) = n_1;0;\epsilon_1;\epsilon_2 & S' = S[\iota \mapsto n;1;\mathsf{dom}(S);\epsilon] \\ \epsilon = \mathsf{run}(\mathsf{stack}(E[\mathsf{pop}_{\gamma_1}\ \square]),\iota,1) & \epsilon \cup \{\iota\} \subseteq \mathsf{available}(S,n) \end{array}}{S;T,n:E[\mathtt{lock}_{\gamma_1}\ \mathtt{lk}_\iota] \rightsquigarrow S';T,n:E[()]}\ \textit{(E-LK0)}$$

$$\frac{S(\iota) = n;n_2;\epsilon_1;\epsilon_2 \qquad n_2 > 0 \qquad S' = S[\iota \mapsto n;n_2+1;\epsilon_1;\epsilon_2]}{S;T,n:E[\mathtt{lock}_{\gamma_1}\ \mathtt{lk}_\iota] \rightsquigarrow S';T,n:E[()]}\ \textit{(E-LK1)}$$

$$\frac{S(\iota) = n;n_2;\epsilon_1;\epsilon_2 \qquad n_2 > 0 \qquad S' = S[\iota \mapsto n;n_2-1;\epsilon_1;\epsilon_2]}{S;T,n:E[\mathtt{unlock}\ \mathtt{lk}_\iota] \rightsquigarrow S';T,n:E[()]}\ \textit{(E-UL)}$$

Figure 6. Operational semantics.

The most interesting rule is *E-LK0*, which dynamically computes the future lockset (ϵ) of lock ι. To achieve this, function stack assembles the overall (stacked) continuation effect by concatenating the continuation effect annotations of pop expressions that are found in the stack of the evaluation context. The lockset computation is modeled by function $\mathsf{run}(\gamma, \iota, k)$, which accepts the stacked effect γ, the lock ι whose lockset is to be computed and the number k of unmatched unlock events (ι^-) in the stack. It returns a subset of the lock events (r^+) located in the stack, such that each element of the subset is locked *before* the last unmatched unlock operation of ι. Function run is defined only when all unlock events for ι are found in the stacked effect. The future lockset of ι (ϵ) is equal to $\mathsf{run}(\gamma, \iota, 1)$. Rule *E-LK0* also requires that both ι and its future lockset are available — $\epsilon \cup \{\iota\} \subseteq \mathsf{available}(S, n)$. Function $\mathsf{available}$ takes as input a lock store S and a thread identifier n and returns a set of locks, such that each element of the set can be acquired by thread n (i.e., locks whose thread identifier either equals n or their count is zero). If the availability premise holds, the lock count of ι is set to one and the thread identifier is set to n. In addition, both ϵ_1 and ϵ_2 (the last two elements of $S(\iota)$) are replaced with $\mathsf{dom}(S)$ (all locks allocated in the program) and ϵ, respectively.

The rules for acquiring or releasing a held lock (*E-LK1* or *E-UL*) require that the count of that lock is positive and that it is owned by the thread that is performing the unlock/lock operation. Otherwise, the semantics will get stuck. We will soon present a type system for this language and also the type safety formulation that guarantees that well-typed programs cannot reach a stuck state.

Note that, although rule *E-LK0* ensures that all locks in the future lockset ϵ are available before proceeding, our semantics only acquires the requested lock ι and not any of the locks in ϵ. As a possible optimization, an implementation could choose to acquire additionally some subset $\epsilon' \subseteq \epsilon$. These locks are all available at this point and an implementation might not want to recheck for their availability and more importantly risk having to wait for them at the time they are needed, in case some other thread has got hold of them until then. Pre-acquisition of locks, however, may reduce parallelism and an implementation should use it only when an analysis shows that the locks will definitely be needed, and not "too late" in the future. (Additional information could statically be placed in the effects to guide such an implementation.) The type safety of our system, stated in Sect. 5, can be proved even if the semantics pre-acquires a subset of the future lockset in this rule.

4.2 Static Semantics

The syntax of types and effects is given in Fig. 4 (on page 5). Basic types consist of the boolean and the unit type, denoted by $\langle\rangle$; lock handle types $\mathtt{Lk}(r)$ are singleton types parameterized by a type-level lock name r; and monomorphic function types carry the function's effect. Effects (γ) are used to statically track lock ownership information; they are ordered *sequences* of events, which can be either r^κ or $\gamma_1\ ?\ \gamma_2$.

The typing relation is denoted by $M;\Delta;\Gamma \vdash e : \tau\,\&\,(\gamma;\gamma')$. It takes an expression e, the typing context $M;\Delta;\Gamma$, and an input effect γ, and produces the type τ assigned to expression e as well as an output effect γ'. Here, M is a set of lock constants, Δ is a set of lock variables, and Γ is a mapping of term variables to types.

As lock operations and application terms are annotated with their continuation effect, it is natural that effects *flow backwards* through the type system: the input effect to an expression e represents the events that follow in the future of e, that is, after e is evaluated. On the other hand, the output effect represents the combined sequence of events caused by e and its future. In fact, the typing relation does not modify the input effect but rather appends to it: the input effect is always a *suffix* of the output effect, in chronological order. (This is ensured by the typing relation and the typing context well-formedness.) The typing rules are given in Fig. 7.[6] The typing rules *T-U*, *T-T*, *T-F*, *T-V*, *T-L*, *T-RF*, *T-RP* and *T-FN* are standard. Notice, that in the case of rule *T-FN*, the input effect of the function's body e_1 is empty. The typing rule for sequential function application (*T-SA*) appends the input effect γ to the function's effect γ_a and propagates the new effect to expression e_2, which in turn propagates its output effect to e_1. The output effect of the sequential function application is the output effect of expression e_1. The annotation of the application must match with the input effect γ. Rule *T-PP* acts as a bridge between the body of a function that is being executed and its calling environment, by appending the continuation effect to the effect of the function's body. The rule for parallel application (*T-PA*) is similar to the sequential application rule, except that the function's effect (γ_a) is not combined with the input effect (as the function will be evaluated in a new thread) and the function's return type must be unit. In addition, all locks in the function's effect must be released before and after the function's execution — $\forall r.\, r;0 \vdash_{ok} \gamma_a$. The relation $r;n \vdash_{ok} \gamma$ checks

[6] A complete formalization appears in the companion technical report [9].

$$\frac{M;\Delta \vdash \Gamma \quad M;\Delta \vdash \gamma}{M;\Delta;\Gamma \vdash () : \langle\rangle \,\&\, (\gamma;\gamma)}\;(\textit{T-U}) \qquad \frac{x : \tau \in \Gamma \quad M;\Delta \vdash \Gamma \quad M;\Delta \vdash \gamma}{M;\Delta;\Gamma \vdash x : \tau \,\&\, (\gamma;\gamma)}\;(\textit{T-V})$$

$$\frac{M;\Delta \vdash \Gamma \quad M;\Delta \vdash \gamma \quad \tau \equiv \tau_1 \xrightarrow{\gamma_b} \tau_2 \quad M;\Delta \vdash \tau \quad M;\Delta;\Gamma, x : \tau_1 \vdash e_1 : \tau_2 \,\&\, (\emptyset;\gamma_b)}{M;\Delta;\Gamma \vdash \lambda x.\, e_1 : \tau \,\&\, (\gamma;\gamma)}\;(\textit{T-FN})$$

$$\frac{M;\Delta \vdash \Gamma \quad M;\Delta \vdash \gamma}{M;\Delta;\Gamma \vdash \texttt{true} : \texttt{Bool} \,\&\, (\gamma;\gamma)}\;(\textit{T-T}) \qquad \frac{M;\Delta,\rho;\Gamma \vdash f : \tau \,\&\, (\gamma;\gamma)}{M;\Delta;\Gamma \vdash \Lambda\rho.\, f : \forall\rho.\,\tau \,\&\, (\gamma;\gamma)}\;(\textit{T-RF})$$

$$\frac{r \in M \cup \Delta \quad M;\Delta;\Gamma \vdash e_1 : \forall\rho.\,\tau \,\&\, (\gamma;\gamma')}{M;\Delta;\Gamma \vdash (e_1)\,[r] : \tau[r/\rho] \,\&\, (\gamma;\gamma')}\;(\textit{T-RP})$$

$$\frac{M;\Delta \vdash \Gamma \quad M;\Delta \vdash \gamma}{M;\Delta;\Gamma \vdash \texttt{false} : \texttt{Bool} \,\&\, (\gamma;\gamma)}\;(\textit{T-F}) \qquad \frac{M;\Delta \vdash \gamma \quad M;\Delta;\Gamma \vdash e : \tau \,\&\, (\emptyset;\gamma')}{M;\Delta;\Gamma \vdash \texttt{pop}_\gamma\; e : \tau \,\&\, (\gamma;\gamma' :: \gamma)}\;(\textit{T-PP})$$

$$\frac{M;\Delta \vdash \Gamma \quad M;\Delta \vdash \gamma \quad \iota \in M}{M;\Delta;\Gamma \vdash \texttt{lk}_\iota : \texttt{Lk}(\iota) \,\&\, (\gamma;\gamma)}\;(\textit{T-L})$$

$$\frac{M;\Delta;\Gamma \vdash e : \texttt{Lk}(r) \,\&\, (r^+,\gamma;\gamma')}{M;\Delta;\Gamma \vdash \texttt{lock}_\gamma\, e : \langle\rangle \,\&\, (\gamma;\gamma')}\;(\textit{T-LK}) \qquad \frac{M;\Delta;\Gamma \vdash e : \texttt{Lk}(r) \,\&\, (r^-,\gamma;\gamma')}{M;\Delta;\Gamma \vdash \texttt{unlock}\, e : \langle\rangle \,\&\, (\gamma;\gamma')}\;(\textit{T-UL})$$

$$\frac{M;\Delta;\Gamma \vdash e_1 : \tau_1 \xrightarrow{\gamma_a} \tau_2 \,\&\, (\gamma_1;\gamma') \quad M;\Delta;\Gamma \vdash e_2 : \tau_1 \,\&\, (\gamma_a :: \gamma;\gamma_1)}{M;\Delta;\Gamma \vdash (e_1\; e_2)^{\mathsf{seq}(\gamma)} : \tau_2 \,\&\, (\gamma;\gamma')}\;(\textit{T-SA})$$

$$\frac{\forall r \in \mathsf{dom}(\gamma_a).\; r;0 \vdash_{ok} \gamma_a \quad M;\Delta;\Gamma \vdash e_1 : \tau_1 \xrightarrow{\gamma_a} \langle\rangle \,\&\, (\gamma_1;\gamma') \quad M;\Delta;\Gamma \vdash e_2 : \tau_1 \,\&\, (\gamma;\gamma_1)}{M;\Delta;\Gamma \vdash (e_1\; e_2)^{\mathsf{par}} : \langle\rangle \,\&\, (\gamma;\gamma')}\;(\textit{T-PA})$$

$$\frac{M;\Delta \vdash \tau \quad \rho \notin \mathsf{dom}(\gamma) \quad \rho;0 \vdash_{ok} \gamma' \quad M;\Delta,\rho;\Gamma, x : \texttt{Lk}(\rho) \vdash e_1 : \tau \,\&\, (\gamma;\gamma')}{M;\Delta;\Gamma \vdash \texttt{newlock}\,\rho, x\;\texttt{in}\; e_1 : \tau \,\&\, (\gamma;\gamma' \setminus \rho)}\;(\textit{T-NG})$$

$$\frac{M;\Delta;\Gamma, x : \tau_a \vdash f : \tau_b \,\&\, (\gamma;\gamma) \quad \tau_a \equiv \tau_1 \xrightarrow{\gamma_a} \tau_2 \quad \tau_b \equiv \tau_1 \xrightarrow{\gamma_b} \tau_2 \quad \gamma_a = \mathsf{summary}(\gamma_b)}{M;\Delta;\Gamma \vdash \texttt{fix}\; x.\, f : \tau_a \,\&\, (\gamma;\gamma)}\;(\textit{T-FX})$$

$$\frac{M;\Delta;\Gamma \vdash e_1 : \texttt{Bool} \,\&\, (\gamma_1 \,?\, \gamma_2, \gamma;\gamma') \quad M;\Delta;\Gamma \vdash e_2 : \tau \,\&\, (\gamma;\gamma_1 :: \gamma) \quad M;\Delta;\Gamma \vdash e_3 : \tau \,\&\, (\gamma;\gamma_2 :: \gamma)}{M;\Delta;\Gamma \vdash \texttt{if}\; e_1\; \texttt{then}\; e_2\; \texttt{else}\; e_3 : \tau \,\&\, (\gamma;\gamma')}\;(\textit{T-IF})$$

Figure 7. Typing rules.

that there exist exactly n unmatched unlock events in γ for lock r (it is used at the same time to make sure that r is never released more times than it has been acquired).

The rule for typing recursive functions (*T-FX*) is the standard one, if we ignore the effects γ_a and γ_b on the function types. As mentioned in Sect. 3, it may be impossible to assign the recursive function variable x the same effect as the function body f (i.e., γ_b). The intuition here is that x must be assigned an effect γ_a that *summarizes* γ_b, and this effect can be computed as a least fixed point with the procedure that was sketched in Sect. 3. We postpone the discussion on summaries for a little longer, until Sect. 4.3.

The rule for creating new locks (*T-NG*) passes the input effect γ to e_1, the body of `let`, assigns the lock handle variable x the singleton type $\texttt{Lk}(\rho)$ and adds ρ to the lock variable context for the scope of e_1. The output effect of the lock creation construct is equal to the output effect of e_1 minus any events of the form ρ^κ. The rule also requires that ρ is unlocked before and after the execution of e_1 — $\rho;0 \vdash_{ok} \gamma'$. Rule *T-LK* prepends r^+ to the input effect and propagates the resulting effect to e_1. Notice, that the input effect must match the lock annotation (the continuation effect of the lock operation must be valid). The typing rule *T-UL* prepends r^- to the input effect and propagates the resulting effect to e_1.

The typing rule for conditional expressions (*T-IF*) propagates the input effect of the conditional expression to its branches e_2 and e_3 respectively. We know that γ is a common suffix of the output effect of e_2 and e_3. Let us assume that γ_1 and γ_2 are the prefixes of the two branches respectively. Thus, the input effect of the guard expression e_1 is $\gamma_1 \,?\, \gamma_2, \gamma$, which tells us that the type system records the effects of both branches but it does not unify them.

The typing rules *T-SA*, *T-LK* and *T-PP* ensure that the effect annotations in sequential applications, `lock` and `pop` expressions are equal to the expression's input effect. This means that, even in this language (and much more so in a language like C), programmers are not really expected to explicitly annotate such expressions: it is easy for the type and effect system to infer the annotations.

4.3 Summarizing Recursive Functions

We have already discussed why it is necessary to summarize the effects of recursive functions. However, the function $\mathsf{summary}$ can be correctly defined in different ways. In principle, any possible definition will do, as long as it satisfies Lemmata 1 and 2.

LEMMA 1 (Consistency of Summary). *Let σ be a substitution of lock variables with lock constants and γ_s be a continuation effect. If $\gamma_a = \mathsf{summary}(\gamma_b)$ then for all ι and n we have*

$$\mathsf{run}(\sigma(\gamma_b :: \gamma_s), \iota, n) \subseteq \mathsf{run}(\sigma(\gamma_a :: \gamma_s), \iota, n)$$

Before we proceed to Lemma 2, we provide an informal definition for function $\mathsf{startup}$. This function takes an effect γ and finds all unmatched lock and unlock operations in γ. It produces an effect γ' which has all the unmatched lock operations, followed by all the unmatched unlock operations. E.g.

$$\mathsf{startup}([x+,\; x-] \,?\, [y+,\; y-]) = \emptyset$$
$$\mathsf{startup}([z-,\; y+] \,?\, [x+,\; y+,\; x-,\; z-]) = [y+,\; z-]$$

We can also define the notion of compositionality for functions on effects. Informally, a function $F(\gamma)$ is *compositional* if γ can only be used as a sub-effect in the result (i.e. in the way that our type and effect system uses effects).

LEMMA 2 (Fixed Point of Summary). *Let $F(\gamma)$ be a compositional function, $\gamma_0 = \mathsf{startup}(F(\emptyset))$, and $\gamma_{n+1} = \mathsf{summary}(F(\gamma_n))$. Then there exists a k such that for all $n > k$ we have $\gamma_k = \gamma_n$.*

If a $\mathsf{summary}$ function satisfies Lemma 2, then the procedure described in Sect. 3 can be used to compute the fixed point of all recursive functions. This fixed point can be used by the type system to determine type τ_a in rule *T-FX*. Furthermore, if a $\mathsf{summary}$ function satisfies Lemma 1, then it is safe for the run-time system to use the summarized effect in the place of the real effect of a function's body. In all cases, the future lockset that will be computed based on the summary will be a superset of the future lockset that would be computed based on the body's real effect.

In our implementation, we use a conservative function $\mathsf{summary}$ that can be shown to satisfy Lemmata 1 and 2. For any effect γ, we define $\mathsf{summary}(\gamma)$ as follows. We take $\mathsf{startup}(\gamma)$ and split it in two components: γ_+, which contains the unmatched lock operations, and γ_-, which contains the unmatched unlock operations. We reorder the events in γ_+ and γ_- using any total order relation on lock variables ρ. (This *normalization* is required for ensuring that a fixed point exists — Lemma 2.) We then build a third component: γ_0, which contains one pair of $[x+, x-]$ for each lock x that is acquired at any time in γ, excluding the ones that are in γ_+. Again, we normalize γ_0 by reordering the events that it contains. Finally, we take $\mathsf{summary}(\gamma) = \gamma_+ :: \gamma_0 :: \gamma_-$.

As an example, consider the conditional statement of Sect. 3, copied here without the annotations to lock operations:

```
if e then (lock x; ... lock y; ... unlock y)
     else (lock z; ... lock x; ... unlock z)
```

The corresponding effect is:

$$\gamma = [x+, y+, y-] \,?\, [z+, x+, z-]$$

There is one unmatched lock operation (for x, which occurs in both branches of the conditional), therefore $\mathsf{startup}(\gamma) = [x+]$. We take $\gamma_+ = [x+]$ and $\gamma_- = \emptyset$. Then, we build $\gamma_0 = [y+, y-, z+, z-]$, by taking one matching pair for each of the lock operations that occur in γ and are not contained in γ_+ (these are $y+$ and $z+$, and we order lock variables lexicographically). Thus:

$$\mathsf{summary}(\gamma) = [x+, y+, y-, z+, z-]$$

More accurate summary functions can also be constructed, not merging branching effects and respecting the nested structure of lock/unlock operations. However, we are not convinced of their practical importance and, in particular, whether the future locksets $\mathsf{run}(\sigma(\gamma_a :: \gamma_s), \iota, n)$ that they produce are indeed more accurate.

As a last note here, summarization is not only necessary for dealing with recursive functions. It is useful for reducing the size of the effects of non-recursive functions, to improve the performance of the run-time system.

5. Type Safety and Deadlock Freedom

In this section we present the fundamental theorems that prove type safety for our language, together with very brief proof sketches.[7] Type safety, which in this system implies deadlock freedom, is based on proving the *preservation*, *deadlock freedom* and *progress* lemmata. Informally, a program written in our language is safe when each thread of execution can perform an evaluation step or is waiting for a lock (*blocked*). In addition, there must not exist threads that have reached a deadlocked state.

As discussed in Sect. 4.1, a thread may become stuck when it performs an ill-typed operation, or when it attempts to compute the future lockset of a malformed stack, or when it attempts to acquire a non-existing lock, or when it attempts to release a lock whose count has already reached the value zero, and so on.

Definition 1 (Thread Effect Consistency). *The following rules define* effect-consistent *threads.*

$$\frac{\iota; n_1 \vdash_{ok} \gamma \quad \epsilon_3 = \mathsf{run}(\gamma, \iota, n_1) \quad n;\gamma \vdash S \quad \epsilon_1 \cap \epsilon_3 \subseteq \epsilon_2}{n;\gamma \vdash S, \iota \mapsto n; n_1; \epsilon_1; \epsilon_2}$$

$$\frac{\iota; 0 \vdash_{ok} \gamma \quad n \neq n_1 \quad n;\gamma \vdash S}{n;\gamma \vdash S, \iota \mapsto n_1; n_2; \epsilon_1; \epsilon_2} \qquad \frac{}{n;\gamma \vdash \emptyset}$$

[7] Longer proof sketches are included in the appendix. A full formalization of our language and complete proofs are given in the companion technical report [9].

Thread effect consistency (denoted by $n;\gamma \vdash S$) ensures that any lock acquired by thread n will be released before thread n terminates. Furthermore, it establishes an exact correspondence between locks in γ and S. In particular, for each lock ι in the domain of γ, $\iota; n_1 \vdash_{ok} \gamma$ must hold, where n_1 must equal the reference count of ι in S for each thread n. Notice that only one thread can have a positive reference count for ι. It also establishes that the future lockset of an acquired lock at any program point (ϵ_3 — modulo the locations that have been created *after* the lock was initially acquired) is *always* a subset of the future lockset computed when the lock was initially acquired (ϵ_2).

Definition 2 (Thread Typing). *The following rules define* well typed *threads.*

$$\frac{}{S; M \vdash \emptyset} \qquad \frac{M;\emptyset;\emptyset \vdash e : \langle\rangle \,\&\, (\emptyset;\gamma) \quad S; M \vdash T \quad n \notin \mathsf{dom}(T) \quad n;\gamma \vdash S}{S; M \vdash T, n : e}$$

A collection of threads T is well typed w.r.t. a lock store S and a set of lock identifiers M, if for each thread $n : e$, expression e is well-typed with an empty input effect and some output effect γ and the lock store is consistent w.r.t. n and γ.

Definition 3 (Configuration Typing). *A configuration $S;T$ is* well typed *w.r.t. M (we denote this by $M \vdash S;T$) when $S;M \vdash T$ and $M = \mathsf{dom}(S)$.*

Definition 4 (Deadlocked State). *A configuration has reached a* deadlocked state *when there exist a set of threads $n_0, \ldots, n_k$, for $k > 0$, and a set of locks $\ell_0, \ldots, \ell_k$, such that each thread n_i has acquired lock $\ell_{(i+1) \bmod (k+1)}$ and is waiting for lock ℓ_i.*

Definition 5 (Not Stuck). *A configuration $S;T$ is* not stuck *when each thread in T can take one of the evaluation steps in Fig. 6 or is waiting for a lock held by some other thread.*

Given these definitions, we can now present the main results of this paper. The *progress*, *deadlock freedom* and *preservation* lemmata are formalized at the *program* level, i.e., for all concurrently executed threads. Let expression e be the initial program. The initial program configuration $S_0; T_0$ is defined by taking $S_0 = \emptyset$, and $T_0 = \{\emptyset; e\}$.

Lemma 3 (Deadlock Freedom). *If the initial configuration takes n steps, where each step is well-typed for some M, then the resulting configuration has not reached a deadlocked state.*

Proof sketch. We assume that a cyclic set of threads exists, in the sense of Def. 4. Let m be the thread that first acquires its lock ℓ_k. When thread k subsequently acquires its lock ℓ_o, we know that ℓ_k does not belong to the corresponding future lockset (otherwise the lock could not have been acquired). We show that this is a contradiction, using the effect consistency of the store and the threads' typing.

Lemma 4 (Progress). *If $S;T$ is a closed well-typed configuration with $M \vdash S;T$, then $S;T$ is not stuck.*

Proof sketch. Let $n : e$ be a thread in T. It suffices to show that e can take a step or is waiting for a lock held by some other thread. As $S;T$ is well-typed, we know that e is well typed with type $\langle\rangle$. If it is a value, the proof is trivial. Otherwise, e is of the form $E[u]$ where u is a redex, and we proceed by a case analysis on u. In each case, based on what the typing derivation gives us, we can deduce that either u can take a step, or that it is blocked.

Lemma 5 (Preservation). *Let $S;T$ be a well-typed configuration with $M \vdash S;T$. If the operational semantics takes a step $S;T \leadsto$*

S'; T', then there exists $M' \supseteq M$ such that the resulting configuration is well-typed with $M' \vdash S'; T'$.

Proof sketch. By induction on the thread evaluation relation.

LEMMA 6 (Multi-step Preservation). *Let $S_0; T_0$ be a* closed well-typed configuration *for some M_0 and assume that $S_0; T_0$ evaluates to $S_n; T_n$ in n steps. Then for all $\iota \in [0, n]$ $M_\iota \vdash S_\iota; T_\iota$ holds.*

Proof. Proof by induction on the number of steps n using Lemma 5.

THEOREM 1 (Type Safety). *If the initial configuration $S_0; T_0$ is closed and well-typed ($\emptyset \vdash S_0; T_0$) and the operational semantics takes any number of steps $S_0; T_0 \rightsquigarrow^n S_n; T_n$, then the resulting configuration $S_n; T_n$ is not stuck and T_n has not reached a deadlocked state.*

Proof. The application of Lemma 6 to the typing derivation of $S_0; T_0$ implies that for all steps from zero to n there exists an M_ι such that $M_\iota \vdash S_\iota; T_\iota$. Therefore, Lemma 3 implies that T_n has not reached a deadlocked state and Lemma 4 implies $S_n; T_n$ is not stuck.

Using an empty typing context for typing the initial configuration $S_0; T_0$ guarantees that all functions in the program are closed and that no explicit lock values ($\texttt{lk}_\iota$) are used in the source of the original program.

6. Prototype Implementation

We have implemented our approach for programs written in C using the pthreads library. Our tool uses CIL [16] to parse and analyze C source code, as well as some modules from the implementation of RELAY [23] that perform pointer analyses.[8]

As in the formal semantics, our approach guarantees deadlock freedom by combining static analysis and dynamic checks. Therefore, our tool performs a source-to-source transformation that instruments the original C code with meta-data representing future lock usage. The instrumented C program is then linked with a run-time library that provides replacements for some pthreads functions. We provide a very brief description of our tool below.

Static Analysis Our tool performs a bottom-up traversal of the program call graph and computes the effect of each function with a standard forward intra-procedural effect analysis. Effects flowing from back edges of a node must be equivalent (with respect to the unmatched lock and unlock operations) to effects flowing from front edges in the same node. Therefore, loops and goto statements can perform arbitrary locking operations, but they must not surprise their environment. Indirect calls (i.e., function pointers) are treated by computing the set of all possible aliases for each function pointer and assigning a new join effect, whose branches represent the effects of all aliased functions. The effect of recursive calls is computed in a manner similar to that described earlier for the formal language. Currently, the effect inference component of the tool is incomplete in the sense that it does not handle all C/pthreads programs. It cannot deal with non-local jumps, dynamically allocated data structures containing locks and rejects programs with arithmetic on pointers (including arrays) that contain or point to locks. Stack-allocated lock handles are also not supported. Lock handle variables cannot be directly used in the program (e.g., parameter passing or assignment) but only through the use of pointers. Lifting these limitations of the analysis is the target of future work.

[8] Our tool and the benchmark programs we use in Sect. 7 are available from `http://www.softlab.ntua.gr/~pgerakios/deadlocks/`.

Code Generation and Run-time System Our main goal for the run-time system was to minimize the overhead induced by "effect accounting". A naïve implementation of the formal semantics would simply allocate and initialize effect frames for each function call and this would be unacceptable in terms of performance. The code generation phase statically creates a *single* block of initialization code for the effect of each function and inserts effect index update instructions (i.e., a single assignment) before each call and lock operation. Therefore, the overhead imposed for such operations is minimal. Each function is also instrumented with instructions for pushing and popping effects from the run-time stack at function entry and exit points respectively. This imposes a constant cost to function calls independently of the effect's size. The run-time system extends the standard implementation of locking functions such as the pthreads functions `pthread_mutex_lock` and `pthread_cond_wait`. If a lock is already held by the requesting thread then the lock's count is simply incremented. Otherwise, the run-time system computes the future lockset of the requested lock from the current effect and verifies that all locks in the future lockset are available when the lock is acquired.

7. Performance Evaluation

In this section we describe our experimental results, aiming to demonstrate that our approach can achieve deadlock freedom with relatively low run-time overhead. The experiments were performed on a multiprocessor machine with four Intel Xeon E7340 CPUs (2.40 GHz), having a total of 16 cores and 16 GB of RAM. In the benchmarks involving network interaction, a second machine was also used with two Intel Xeon CPUs (2.80 GHz), having a total of 4 cores and 4 GB of RAM. Both machines were running Linux 2.6.26-2-amd64 and GCC 4.3.2.

We used a total of six benchmark programs of varying complexity: two written by us (these are programs from the literature which are known to exhibit deadlocks) and four which are real, publicly available applications. Except for the first program, whose only purpose is to show that our approach avoids deadlocks, the rest of the benchmarks are used to evaluate scalability as the number of threads increases, and to demonstrate that our approach not only avoids deadlocks but, in some cases, may result in better parallelism (dining philosophers).

bank transactions: a small multithreaded program simulating repeated concurrent circular transactions between two accounts that may deadlock. The program is based on the example used in the introduction of Boudol's paper [1]. Each transaction consists of a withdrawal step from account A and a deposit step to account B, each of which is protected by a lock. In addition, the whole transaction is protected by the lock account A; this creates a necessity for recursive (reentrant) locks and makes the program prone to deadlocks. The original program deadlocks with probability very close to 100%.

dining philosophers: a program implementing the obvious and deadlock-prone attempt to solve the classic multi-process synchronization problem. Each philosopher first picks up the stick on his left, then the stick on his right. The original program deadlocks with a probability that decreases as the number of philosophers increases (for five philosophers, the probability for deadlock was roughly 70%) but increases again when the number of philosophers exceeds the number of available cores. For the performance comparison that we discuss below, we only used the deadlock-free runs of the original program.

The performance of the original and the instrumented versions are shown in Fig. 8. For a given elapsed time (2 secs) we measured the total number of times that the philosophers ate (using

n	original	instrumented	improvement
5	126,536	126,961	0.34%
10	224,536	230,981	2.87%
15	284,150	298,563	5.07%
31	536,889	587,051	9.34%
63	1,080,322	1,193,509	10.48%
127	1,603,880	2,219,022	38.35%
255	1,480,183	4,220,603	185.14%

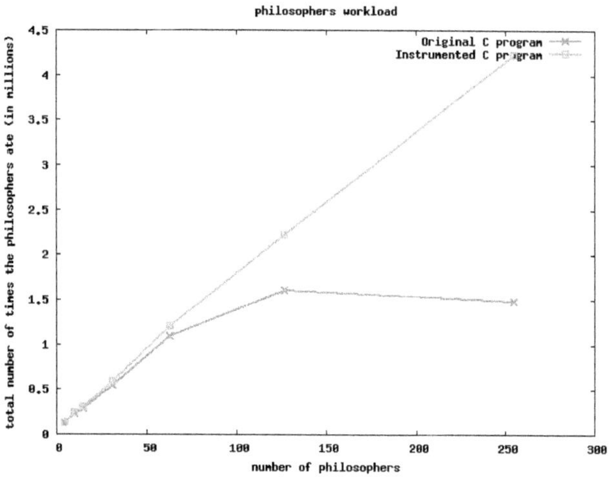

Figure 8. Performance comparison for the *dining philosophers*. We measure the total number of times that the n philosophers ate.

a per-thread random number generator that was identical in both versions). It is interesting to see that in the instrumented program, the number grows linearly with the number of philosophers, i.e., each philosopher eats for a (more or less) constant number of times during the 2 secs (this number is determined by the ratio of eating time versus sleeping time, which was chosen to be 0.1 in both programs). On the other hand, in the original program, the linear growth seems to last only as long as the number of philosophers is small and we do not run out of cores.

In the original program, it is frequent that a philosopher holds his left stick while waiting to acquire his right stick. This is far less frequent in the instrumented program, which checks that the right stick is available before granting the left stick (if the right neighbour is fast enough, he can still get to it first but this is rather very improbable). This results in a much better degree of parallelism, which clearly shows in Fig. 8.

The four remaining programs are applications whose source code is publicly available on the internet. The first two contain only one lock (therefore they cannot possibly deadlock) while the last two have multiple locks. In all programs, independently of whether deadlocks are possible or not, we were primarily concerned with measuring and comparing the performance of the original and the instrumented versions of the programs, in order to evaluate the overhead imposed by our approach.

thrhttp: a multithreaded HTTP server (implemented in 500 lines), using a single lock for synchronizing various counters which are concurrently accessed [21]. We measured the server's performance at varying loads (number of responses over number of requests) using *httperf*, an open source tool for measuring web server performance. The results were almost identical for the original and the instrumented version of *thrhttp*.

flam3: a multithreaded program which creates "cosmic recursive fractal flames", i.e., (animations consisting of) algorithmically generated images based on fractals [5]. A single lock is used to synchronize access to a shared bucket accumulator that merges computations of distinct threads. We measured the time required to generate a long sequence of fractal images, varying the number of threads that were dedicated to the task. The results again were almost identical for the original and the instrumented version of *flam3-render*.

tgrep: a multithreaded version of the utility program `grep` which is part of the SUNWdev suite of Solaris 10 [20]. The program achieves speedup by splitting the search space across threads, using multiple locks for implementing thread-safe queues, logging and counters. In our experiment, we looked for an occurrence of a six-letter word in a directory tree containing 100,000 files, with a varying number of threads dedicated to the task. The results are shown in Fig. 9. The performance difference between the original and the instrumented program is roughly between -10% and 20%. The instrumented program consistently performs better for a few working cores (2 and 4) and worse for more working cores (≥ 16).

sshfs: a filesystem client based on the SSH File Transfer Protocol [18]. It creates threads on demand so as to serve concurrent read and write requests to the filesystem, using multiple locks to synchronize data structures, logging and access to non thread-safe functions. In our experiment, we mount a remote directory over *sshfs* and start n concurrent threads, each of which is trying to download a number of large files. The total volume of data that is copied over *sshfs* is linear w.r.t. n, and this is of course reflected in our measured results in Fig. 10. Again, we notice a small improvement in the performance of the instrumented program w.r.t. the original one, which we attribute to a slightly better degree of parallelism (as in the case of the dining philosophers).

8. Further Comparison with Related Work

In Sect. 2 we mentioned type-based approaches to preventing deadlocks. All works in this category prevent deadlocks using a type system which computes a partial order of all locks in the program and checks statically that all threads adhere to this order. In most such systems [6, 14, 19, 22], this partial order is statically fixed and can not be changed at runtime. A notable exception is the type system of Boyapati *et al.* [2] which allows for some form of dynamism. Namely, it allows programmers to partition the locks into a fixed number of equivalence classes (lock levels), use recursive tree-based data structures to describe their partial order, and also perform a limited set of mutations to these data structures which can change the partial order of locks *within* a given lock level at runtime. Even in this system though, to guarantee soundness, the partial order between lock levels is fixed statically. In contrast, our system does not impose any partial order on locks at compile time, but instead naturally grants locks of different threads during runtime based on the actual program needs and lock contention.

In the rest of this section, we compare our work with other techniques and tools that deal with deadlock detection and avoidance.

Purely static approaches to deadlock detection employ flow-sensitive static analysis [4] and theorem proving [7] to identify places in the code where programs do not adhere to some global lock acquisition order for all threads. In theory, such static approaches are attractive because they do not incur run-time overhead. In practice however, adhering to a strict lock acquisition order is rarely easy and seems unsuitable for systems programming. Even in simpler application domains, experience has shown that a

n	original			instrumented			overhead
	U	S	e	U	S	e	
1	7.91	7.18	14.30	8.35	7.40	14.66	2.52%
2	8.08	7.30	9.71	9.53	8.02	9.51	−2.06%
4	8.48	7.69	7.19	7.32	7.33	6.39	−11.13%
8	9.21	9.09	5.16	10.04	9.58	5.32	3.10%
16	12.02	10.42	4.94	14.48	12.42	5.45	10.32%
32	12.72	11.23	5.32	13.84	12.89	6.34	19.17%
64	12.71	11.14	5.34	13.56	12.32	5.66	5.99%

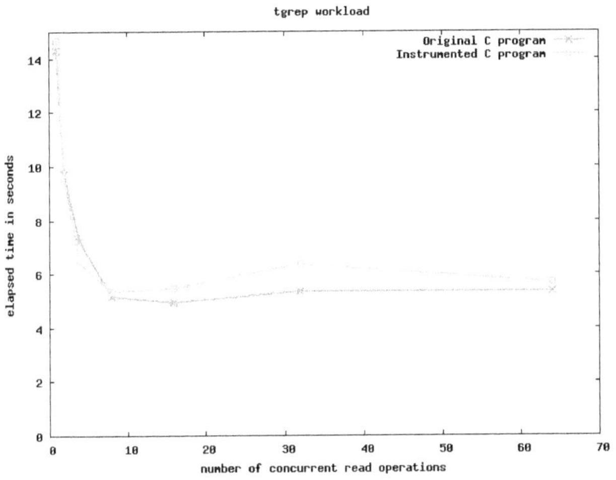

Figure 9. Performance comparison for the *tgrep* utility.

n	original			instrumented			improvement
	U	S	e	U	S	e	
1	0.00	0.48	0.57	0.00	0.53	0.57	0.00%
2	0.04	2.02	1.46	0.01	1.96	1.44	1.37%
4	0.07	6.07	2.59	0.03	5.85	2.58	0.39%
8	0.13	18.70	4.48	0.14	17.71	4.42	1.34%
16	0.27	122.53	11.97	0.27	103.75	10.95	8.52%
32	0.45	422.57	31.52	0.50	412.08	30.75	2.44%
64	0.90	1050.64	71.83	1.05	1029.45	70.20	2.27%

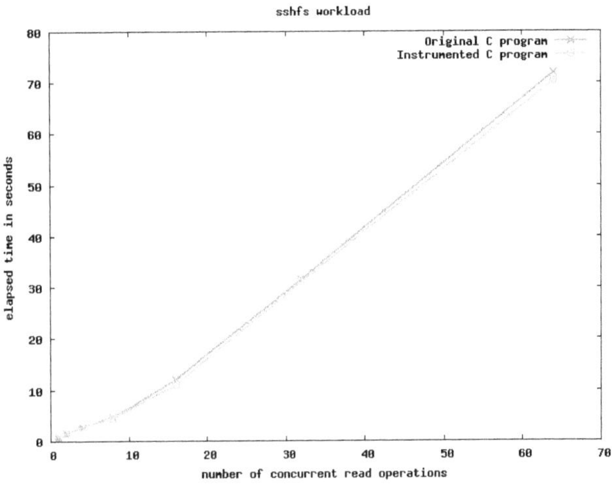

Figure 10. Performance comparison for the *sshfs*.

global lock ordering is inflexible and difficult to enforce in complex, multi-layered software written by large teams of programmers. More importantly, because purely static approaches are by definition conservative, they often reject programs unnecessarily or result in a large number of false alarms.

On the other end of the spectrum, dynamic approaches to deadlock detection [13, 17] do not suffer from false positives, but they are often inflexible because when a deadlock is detected it is quite often too late to react on or recover from it. (The programs may have already performed some irrevocable operations such as I/O.)

From approaches that combine static and dynamic techniques, besides Boudol's proposal for deadlock avoidance, a tool that is quite similar to ours is Gadara [24]. Gadara employs whole program analysis to model programs and discrete control theory to synthesize a concurrent logic that avoids deadlocks at run time [25]. Like our work, Gadara targets C/pthreads programs and is claimed to avoid deadlocks quite efficiently because it performs the majority of its deadlock avoidance computations offline. (The tool is not publicly available.) Similarly to our future locksets, Gadara uses the notion of *control places* to decide whether it is safe to admit a lock acquisition. More precisely, a lock acquisition can only proceed when all the control places associated with the lock are available. The mostly static approach followed by Gadara, as well as the lack of alias analysis, results in an over-approximation of the set of run-time locks associated with a control place.

9. Concluding Remarks

Locks are here to stay as a language construct either for programmers or for compiler writers. Deadlocks are an important problem especially for languages that employ non block-structured locking.

In this paper, we have presented a novel technique that dynamically avoids deadlock states for a lock-polymorphic lambda calculus with unstructured locking primitives. The key idea is to utilize statically computed information regarding lock usage at execution time in order to avoid deadlocks. This approach accepts a wider class of programs compared to purely static approaches based on deadlock prevention. The main drawback is the additional run-time overhead induced by the future lockset computation and blocking time (i.e., both the requested lock and its future lockset must be available). Additionally, in some cases threads may unnecessarily block because our type and effect system is conservative.

We have presented a semantics for the proposed language, a sound type and effect system that guarantees that well-typed programs cannot reach a deadlocked state, and a proof sketch for the type safety theorem and related lemmata. Most importantly, we have also shown the promise of our approach by implementing a tool for C/pthreads and evaluating it on a number of programs. Our benchmark evaluation suggests that our approach imposes only a modest run-time overhead on real applications and, in some cases, it produces remarkably increased throughput.

Acknowledgement

This research is partially funded by the programme for supporting basic research (ΠΕΒΕ 2010) of the National Technical University of Athens under a project titled "Safety properties for concurrent programming languages."

References

[1] G. Boudol. A deadlock-free semantics for shared memory concurrency. In M. Leucker and C. Morgan, editors, *Proceedings of the International Colloquium on Theoretical Aspects of Computing*, volume 5684 of *LNCS*, pages 140–154. Springer, 2009.

[2] C. Boyapati, R. Lee, and M. Rinard. Ownership types for safe programming: Preventing data races and deadlocks. In *Proceedings of the ACM SIGPLAN Conference on Object-Oriented Programming, Sys-*

tems, Languages, and Applications, pages 211–230, New York, NY, USA, Nov. 2002. ACM Press.

[3] E. G. Coffman, M. Elphick, and A. Shoshani. System deadlocks. *ACM Comput. Surv.*, 3(2):67–78, 1971.

[4] D. Engler and K. Ashcraft. RacerX: effective, static detection of race conditions and deadlocks. In *Proceedings of ACM Symposium on Operating Systems Principles*, pages 237–252, New York, NY, USA, 2003. ACM.

[5] flam3.com. Cosmic recursive fractal flames. `http://flam3.com/`.

[6] C. Flanagan and M. Abadi. Types for safe locking. In *Programming Language and Systems: Proceedings of the European Symposium on Programming*, number 1576 in LNCS, pages 91–108. Springer, 1999.

[7] C. Flanagan, K. R. M. Leino, M. Lillibridge, G. Nelson, J. B. Saxe, and R. Stata. Extended static checking for Java. In *Proceedings of the ACM SIGPLAN Conference on Programming Language Design and Implementation*, pages 234–245, New York, NY, USA, 2002. ACM.

[8] P. Gerakios, N. Papaspyrou, and K. Sagonas. Race-free and memory-safe multithreading: Design and implementation in Cyclone. In *Proceedings of the ACM SIGPLAN International Workshop on Types in Languages Design and Implementation*, pages 15–26, New York, NY, USA, 2010. ACM Press.

[9] P. Gerakios, N. Papaspyrou, and K. Sagonas. A type and effect system for deadlock avoidance in low-level languages. Technical report, National Technical University of Athens, 2010.

[10] P. Gerakios, N. Papaspyrou, and K. Sagonas. A type system for unstructured locking that guarantees deadlock freedom without imposing a lock ordering. In *Pre-proceedings of the Workshop on Programming Language Approaches to Concurrency and communication-cEntric Software (PLACES)*, 2010. An extended version of this paper is available from `http://www.softlab.ntua.gr/~pgerakios/deadlocks/`.

[11] D. Grossman, G. Morrisett, T. Jim, M. Hicks, Y. Wang, and J. Cheney. Region-based memory management in Cyclone. In *Proceedings of the ACM SIGPLAN Conference on Programming Language Design and Implementation*, pages 282–293, New York, NY, USA, 2002. ACM Press.

[12] M. Hicks, J. S. Foster, and P. Pratikakis. Lock inference for atomic sections. In *Proceedings of the First ACM SIGPLAN Workshop on Languages Compilers, and Hardware Support for Transactional Computing*, June 2006.

[13] H. Jula, D. Tralamazza, C. Zamfir, and G. Candea. Deadlock immunity: Enabling systems to defend against deadlocks. In R. Draves and R. van Renesse, editors, *Symposium on Operating Systems Design and Implementation*, pages 295–308. USENIX Association, 2008.

[14] N. Kobayashi. A new type system for deadlock-free processes. In C. Baier and H. Hermanns, editors, *CONCUR 2006*, volume 4137 of *LNCS*, pages 233–247. Springer, 2006.

[15] L. Lamport. A new approach to proving the correctness of multiprocess programs. *ACM Trans. Prog. Lang. Syst.*, 1(1):84–97, 1979.

[16] G. C. Necula, S. McPeak, S. P. Rahul, and W. Weimer. CIL: Intermediate language and tools for analysis and transformation of C programs. In *Compiler Construction: Proceedings of the International Conference*, volume 2304 of *LNCS*, pages 213–228. Springer, 2002.

[17] F. Qin, J. Tucek, Y. Zhou, and J. Sundaresan. Rx: Treating bugs as allergies — a safe method to survive software failures. *ACM Trans. Comput. Syst.*, 25(3):7/2, 2007.

[18] SSH FileSystem. `http://fuse.sourceforge.net/sshfs.html`.

[19] K. Suenaga. Type-based deadlock-freedom verification for non-block-structured lock primitives and mutable references. In G. Ramalingam, editor, *Asian Symposium on Programming Languages and Systems*, volume 5356 of *LNCS*, pages 155–170. Springer, 2008.

[20] Multithreaded `grep`. Part of Sun Microsystems' *Multithreaded Programming Guide*, available at `http://docs.sun.com/app/docs/doc/806-5257`.

[21] Multithreaded HTTP server. `http://www.xmailserver.org/thrhttp.c`.

[22] V. Vasconcelos, F. Martin, and T. Cogumbreiro. Type inference for deadlock detection in a multithreaded polymorphic typed assembly language. In A. R. Beresford and S. Gay, editors, *Post-proceedings of the Workshop on Programming Language Approaches to Concurrency and communication-cEntric Software (PLACES 2009)*, volume 17 of *EPTCS*, pages 95–109, 2010.

[23] J. W. Voung, R. Jhala, and S. Lerner. RELAY: static race detection on millions of lines of code. In *Proceedings of the joint meeting of the European Software Engineering Conference and the ACM SIGSOFT Symposium on the Foundations of Software Engineering*, pages 205–214, New York, NY, USA, 2007. ACM.

[24] Y. Wang, T. Kelly, M. Kudlur, S. Lafortune, and S. Mahlke. Gadara: Dynamic deadlock avoidance for multithreaded programs. In R. Draves and R. van Renesse, editors, *Symposium on Operating Systems Design and Implementation*, pages 281–294. USENIX Association, 2008.

[25] Y. Wang, S. Lafortune, T. Kelly, M. Kudlur, and S. Mahlke. The theory of deadlock avoidance via discrete control. In *Conference Record of the ACM SIGPLAN-SIGACT Symposium on Principles of Programming Languages*, pages 252–263, New York, NY, USA, 2009. ACM.

Appendix

A. Summary of additional functions and relations

$\mathsf{run}(\gamma, \iota, n)$ computes the future lockset for a `lock` ι operation, by traversing the continuation effect γ until n matching unlock operations for ι are found.

$\mathsf{stack}(E)$ computes the continuation effect that corresponds to the evaluation context E, by concatenating the annotations found in stacked pop expressions.

$\mathsf{available}(S, n)$ computes the set of locks that are available to thread n in the lock store S; the locks that are not currently owned by some thread other than n.

$\gamma_1 :: \gamma_2$ appends the two effects γ_1 and γ_2, so that all operations in γ_2 chronologically follow those in γ_1.

$\gamma \setminus r$ removes all occurrences of r from effect γ.

$r; n \vdash_{ok} \gamma$ checks that γ contains exactly n unmatched unlock operations for r, i.e. that the effect $\gamma_r :: \gamma$ is well balanced, where γ_r contains exactly n lock operations for r.

$M; \Delta \vdash \Gamma$ well formedness relation for typing environments.

$M; \Delta \vdash \gamma$ well formedness relation for effects.

$M; \Delta \vdash \tau$ well formedness relation for types.

$\mathsf{summary}(\gamma)$ the effect summarization function (see Sect. 4.3).

$M; \Delta; \Gamma \vdash E : \tau \xrightarrow{\gamma_a;\gamma_b} \tau' \,\&\, (\gamma_1;\gamma_2)$ typing relation for evaluation contexts; τ is the expected type for the innermost hole in E, γ_a and γ_b are the hole's input and output effects, τ' is the type of the expression computed by E, and γ_1 and γ_2 are the input and output effects.

B. Longer proof sketches for the main lemmata

LEMMA 3 (Deadlock Freedom). *If the initial configuration takes n steps, where each step is well-typed for some M, then the resulting configuration has not reached a deadlocked state.*

Proof. Let us assume that z threads have reached a deadlocked state and let $m \in [0, z-1]$, $k = (m+1) \bmod z$ and $o = (k+1) \bmod z$. According to definition of *deadlocked state*, thread m acquires lock ι_k and waits for lock ι_m, whereas thread k acquires lock ι_o and waits for lock ι_k. Assume that m is the first of the z threads that acquires a lock, so it acquires lock ι_k before thread k acquires lock ι_o.

Let us assume that $S_y; T_y$ is the configuration once ι_o is acquired by thread k for the first time, ϵ_{1y} is the corresponding lockset of ι_o (ϵ_{1y} = $\mathsf{run}(\mathsf{stack}(E[\mathsf{pop}_{\gamma_y}\ \square]), 1, \iota_o))$ and ϵ_{2y} is the set of all heap locations ($\epsilon_{2y} = \mathsf{dom}(S_y)$) at the time ι_o is acquired. Then, ι_k does not belong to ϵ_{1y}, otherwise thread k would have been blocked at the lock request of ι_o as ι_k is already owned by thread m.

Let us assume that when thread k attempts to acquire ι_k, the configuration is of the form $S_x; T_x$. According to the assumption of this lemma that all configurations are well typed so $S_x; T_x$ is well-typed as well. By inversion of the typing derivation of $S_x; T_x$, we obtain the typing derivation of thread $n_k : E_k[\mathtt{lock}_{\gamma'_k}\ \mathtt{lk}_{\iota_k}]$: $\mathtt{lock}_{\gamma'_k}\ \mathtt{lk}_{\iota_k}$ is well-typed with input-output effect $(\gamma'_k;\gamma''_k)$, where $\gamma''_k = \iota_k{}^+, \gamma'_k$, $E_k[\mathtt{lock}_{\gamma'_k}\ \mathtt{lk}_{\iota_k}]$ is well typed with input-output effect $(\emptyset;\gamma_k)$, where $\gamma_k = \iota_k{}^+, \gamma'''_k$ (for some γ'''_k), and $n_k; \gamma_k \vdash S_x$ holds. The latter derivation implies that $\mathsf{run}(\gamma_k, \iota_o, n_2) \cap \epsilon_1 \subseteq \epsilon_2$, where $S_x = S'_x, \iota_o \mapsto n_k; n_2; \epsilon_1; \epsilon_2$ (notice that n_2 is positive, $\epsilon_2 = \epsilon_{1y}$ and $\epsilon_1 = \epsilon_{2y}$ — this is immediate by the operational steps from $S_y; T_y$ to $S_x; T_x$ and rule *E-LK0*).

We have assumed that m is the first thread to lock ι_k at some step before $S_y; T_y$, thus $\iota_k \in \mathsf{dom}(S_y)$ (the store can only grow — this is immediate by observing the operational semantics rules). By the definition of function run and the definition of γ''_k we have that $\iota_k \in \mathsf{run}(\gamma_k, \iota_o, n_2) = \mathsf{run}(\gamma'''_k, \iota_o, n_2) \cup \{\iota_k\}$. Therefore, $\iota_k \in \mathsf{run}(\gamma_k, \iota_o, n_2) \cap \mathsf{dom}(S_y) \subseteq \epsilon_{1y}$, which is a contradiction. □

LEMMA 4 (Progress). *If $S; T$ is a closed well-typed configuration with $M \vdash S; T$, then $S; T$ is not stuck.*

Proof. It suffices to show that for any thread in T, a step can be performed or the thread is blocked. Let n be an arbitrary thread in T such that $T = T_1, n{:}e$ for some T_1. By inversion of the configuration typing derivation we have that $S; M \vdash T_1, n : e$, and $M = \mathsf{dom}(S)$. By inversion of the former derivation we obtain that $n; \gamma \vdash S$ and $M; \emptyset; \emptyset \vdash e : \langle\rangle \,\&\, (\emptyset;\gamma)$. If e is a value then it can only be the unit value and a step can be performed using rule *E-T*. If e is not value then e is of the form $E[u]$ (this can be shown by induction on the typing derivation of e). The application of the context decomposition lemma (proof by induction on the shape of E) to the typing derivation of $E[u]$ yields that: $M; \emptyset; \emptyset \vdash u : \tau \,\&\, (\gamma_a;\gamma_b)$ and $M; \emptyset; \emptyset \vdash E' : \tau \xrightarrow{\gamma_a;\gamma_b} \langle\rangle \,\&\, \&\, (\emptyset;\gamma)$. We proceed by a case analysis on u (we only consider the most interesting cases):

Case $(v'\ v)^{\mathsf{seq}(\gamma_a)}$: the typing derivation of u implies that v' is of the form $\lambda x.\, e'$ or $\mathtt{fix}\ x.\, e'$. In the first case rule *E-A* can be applied, whereas in the second case rule *E-FX* can be applied.

Case $\mathtt{unlock}\ v$: the typing derivation of u implies that v is a lock handle (i.e., $v = \mathtt{lk}_\iota$). It is possible to derive that $\gamma = \iota^-, \gamma'$, for some γ'. By inversion of the store typing premise ($n; \gamma \vdash S$) of the derivation for thread n we have that $\iota; n_2 \vdash_{ok} \iota^-, \gamma'$, where n_2 is the reference count of lock ι. By inversion of the latter derivation (rule *OK2*) n_2 is positive. Combined with the store typing derivation, this tells us that the thread identifier of ι is n. Therefore, a single step can be performed via rule *E-UL*.

Case $\mathtt{lock}_{\gamma_a}\ v$: the typing derivation of u implies that v is a lock handle (i.e., $v = \mathtt{lk}_\iota$). If the reference count (n_2) of lock ι is positive then the proof is similar to the case of $\mathtt{unlock}\ v$ and a step can be performed via rule *E-LK1*. If $n_2 = 0$, it is possible to derive $\gamma = \iota^+, \gamma_a :: \gamma'$ for some γ'. By inversion of the store typing premise ($n; \gamma \vdash S$) of the derivation for thread n we have that $\iota; 0 \vdash_{ok} \iota^+, \gamma_a :: \gamma'$ and that the thread identifier of ι is n. Therefore $\iota; 0 \vdash_{ok} \iota^+, \gamma_a :: \gamma'$ implies $\epsilon = \mathsf{run}(\mathsf{stack}(E[\mathsf{pop}_{\gamma_a}\ \square]), \iota, 1)$ is defined (here we are using the fact that the typing derivation implies that $\gamma_a :: \gamma' = \mathsf{stack}(E[\mathsf{pop}_{\gamma_a}\ \square])$ and also the fact than when ok is defined so is run — this can be trivially shown). Now, if $\epsilon \cup \{\iota\} \subseteq \mathsf{available}(S, n)$, then rule *E-LK0* can be applied. Otherwise, the thread is considered to be blocked *but not stuck* (see the third rule of judgement *stuck*). □

LEMMA 5 (Preservation). *Let $S; T$ be a well-typed configuration with $M \vdash S; T$. If the operational semantics takes a step $S; T \rightsquigarrow S'; T'$, then there exists $M' \supseteq M$ such that the resulting configuration is well-typed with $M' \vdash S'; T'$.*

Proof. By induction on the thread evaluation relation (we only consider the most interesting cases):

Case *E-A*: this rule is side-effect free so $S' = S$ and $T' = T$. Therefore, it suffices to show that $E[\mathsf{pop}_{\gamma_a}\ e_1[v/x]]$ is well-typed with the same effect as $E[u]$, where u equals $(v'\ v)^{\mathsf{seq}(\gamma_a)}$ and v' is equal to $\lambda x.\, e_1$. By inversion of the configuration typing we have that $M; \emptyset; \emptyset \vdash E[e] : \langle\rangle \,\&\, (\emptyset;\gamma)$. The application of the context decomposition lemma (proof by induction on the shape of E) to the typing derivation of $E[u]$ yields that: $M; \emptyset; \emptyset \vdash E : \tau'_2 \xrightarrow{\gamma_a;\gamma_b} \langle\rangle \,\&\, (\emptyset;\gamma)$ and $M; \emptyset; \emptyset \vdash e : \tau'_2 \,\&\, (\gamma_a;\gamma_b)$. By inversion of the latter derivation we have that $M; \emptyset; \emptyset \vdash v : \tau'_1 \,\&\, (\gamma_b;\gamma_b)$, and $M; \emptyset; \emptyset \vdash \lambda x.\, e_1 : \tau'_1 \xrightarrow{\gamma'_c} \tau'_2 \,\&\, (\gamma_b;\gamma_b)$, where $\gamma_b = \gamma'_c :: \gamma_a$. We can apply inversion to the latter derivation to obtain $M; \emptyset; \emptyset, x : \tau'_1 \vdash e_1 : \tau'_2 \,\&\, (\emptyset;\gamma'_c)$. The standard substitution lemma implies that $M; \emptyset; \emptyset \vdash e_1[v/x] : \tau'_2 \,\&\, (\emptyset;\gamma'_c)$ holds. The application of rule *T-PP* yields $M; \emptyset; \emptyset \vdash \mathsf{pop}_{\gamma_a}\ e_1[v/x] : \tau'_2 \,\&\, (\gamma_a;\gamma_b)$ holds. Finally, the context composition lemma yields $M; \emptyset; \emptyset \vdash E[\mathsf{pop}_{\gamma_a}\ e_1[v/x]] : \langle\rangle \,\&\, (\emptyset;\gamma)$.

Case *E-FX*: as in the previous case, this rule is side-effect free. Redex u is equal to $(\mathtt{fix}\ x.\, f\ v)^{\mathsf{seq}(\gamma_a)}$. By inversion of the configuration typing derivation we obtain $M; \emptyset; \emptyset \vdash E[e] : \langle\rangle \,\&\, (\emptyset;\gamma)$. The context decomposition lemma yields $M; \emptyset; \emptyset \vdash E : \tau'_2 \xrightarrow{\gamma_a;\gamma_b} \langle\rangle \,\&\, (\emptyset;\gamma)$ and $M; \emptyset; \emptyset \vdash e : \tau'_2 \,\&\, (\gamma_a;\gamma_b)$. By inversion of the latter derivation we have that $M; \emptyset; \emptyset \vdash v : \tau'_1 \,\&\, (\gamma_b;\gamma_b)$, and $M; \emptyset; \emptyset \vdash \mathtt{fix}\ x.\, f : \tau'_1 \xrightarrow{\gamma'_c} \tau'_2 \,\&\, (\gamma_b;\gamma_b)$, where $\gamma_b = \gamma'_c :: \gamma'_a$. By inversion of the typing derivation of $\mathtt{fix}\ x.\, f$ we obtain that $M; \emptyset; \emptyset, x : \tau'_1 \xrightarrow{\gamma'_c} \tau'_2 \vdash f : \tau'_1 \xrightarrow{\gamma''_c} \tau'_2 \,\&\, (\gamma_b;\gamma_b)$ and $\mathsf{summary}(\gamma''_c) = \gamma'_c$. The variable substitution lemma yields $M; \emptyset; \emptyset \vdash f[\mathtt{fix}\ x.\, f/x] : \tau'_1 \xrightarrow{\gamma''_c} \tau'_2 \,\&\, (\gamma_b;\gamma_b)$ holds. The effects of E can be strengthened and then weakened (proof by induction on the shape of E) so that $M; \emptyset; \emptyset \vdash E : \tau'_2 \xrightarrow{\gamma_a;\gamma''_c::\gamma_a} \langle\rangle \,\&\, (\emptyset;\gamma''_c :: \gamma')$ holds and γ' is such that $\gamma = \gamma'_c :: \gamma'$. Values, such as $f[\mathtt{fix}\ x.\, f/x]$ can be assigned any well-formed effect provided that the input effect is identical to the output effect (proof by induction on the expression typing derivation). Therefore, $M; \emptyset; \emptyset \vdash f[\mathtt{fix}\ x.\, f/x] : \tau'_1 \xrightarrow{\gamma''_c} \tau'_2 \,\&\, (\gamma''_c :: \gamma_a;\gamma''_c :: \gamma_a)$ and $M; \emptyset; \emptyset \vdash v : \tau'_1 \,\&\, (\gamma''_c :: \gamma_a;\gamma''_c :: \gamma_a)$ hold. The application of rule *T-SA* yields $M; \emptyset; \emptyset \vdash (f[\mathtt{fix}\ x.\, f/x]\ v)^{\mathsf{seq}(\gamma_a)} : \tau'_2 \,\&\, (\gamma_a;\gamma''_c :: \gamma_a)$. The application context composition lemma gives $M; \emptyset; \emptyset \vdash E[(f[\mathtt{fix}\ x.\, f/x]\ v)^{\mathsf{seq}(\gamma_a)}] : \langle\rangle \,\&\, (\emptyset;\gamma''_c :: \gamma')$. Given that $n; \gamma \vdash S$ and $\gamma'_c = \mathsf{summary}(\gamma''_c)$ hold it is possible to show that $n; \gamma''_c :: \gamma' \vdash S$. The key idea in this proof is to show that $\mathsf{summary}$ preserves unmatched lock acquisition or release operations and that the future lockset of any lock in γ'_c is a superset of the corresponding lockset in γ''_c.

Case *E-LK0*: rule *E-LK0* implies that $T' = T, n : E[()]$, where $()$ replaces u ($u = \mathtt{lock}_{\gamma_a}\ \mathtt{lk}_\iota$) in context E. It also implies that $\epsilon = \mathsf{run}(\mathsf{stack}(E[\mathsf{pop}_{\gamma_a}\ \square]), \iota, 1)$, $\epsilon \cup \{\iota\} \subseteq \mathsf{available}(S, n)$ and $S' = S[\iota \mapsto n; 1; \mathsf{dom}(S); \epsilon]$. It suffices to show that $M = \mathsf{dom}(S')$, $n; \gamma'_n \vdash S'$, $\forall n' \in \mathsf{dom}(T).\ n'; \gamma_{n'} \vdash S'$, where $\gamma_{n'}$ is the output effect of thread n' and $M; \emptyset; \emptyset \vdash E[()] : \langle\rangle \,\&\, (\emptyset;\gamma'_n)$, where γ_n is the output effect of thread n and is defined as $\gamma_n = \iota^+, \gamma'_n$.

$M = \mathsf{dom}(S')$ is immediate from $M = \mathsf{dom}(S)$ and the definition of S'. $n;\gamma'_n \vdash S'$ can be shown by a case analysis on location $\mathtt{j}$ of S'. If $\mathtt{j} \neq \iota$, then all premises of $n;\gamma_n \vdash S$ also hold for S' and γ'_n. If $\mathtt{j} = \iota$, then premise $\iota;0 \vdash_{ok} \iota^+,\gamma'_n$ implies $\iota;1 \vdash_{ok} \gamma'_n$. In addition, $\mathsf{stack}(E[\mathsf{pop}_{\gamma_a}\ \square]) = \gamma'_n$, thus $\epsilon = \mathsf{run}(\gamma'_n, \iota, 1)$. The invariant $n';\gamma_{n'} \vdash S'$ holds for all threads $n' \neq n$ as $S(\mathtt{j}) = S'(\mathtt{j})$ for all $\mathtt{j} \neq \iota$ and ι is not locked by n' in S'. By inversion of the thread typing derivation we have that: $M;\emptyset;\emptyset \vdash E[u] : \langle\rangle\,\&\,(\emptyset;\gamma)$. The application of the context decomposition lemma (proof by induction on the shape of E) to the typing derivation of $E[u]$ yields that: $M;\emptyset;\emptyset \vdash E : \langle\rangle \xrightarrow{\gamma_a;\iota^+,\gamma_a} \langle\rangle\,\&\,(\emptyset;\gamma_n)$ and $M;\emptyset;\emptyset \vdash u : \langle\rangle\,\&\,(\gamma_a;\iota^+,\gamma_a)$. The effects of E can be strengthened (proof by induction on the shape of E) so that $M;\emptyset;\emptyset \vdash E : \langle\rangle \xrightarrow{\gamma_a;\gamma_a} \langle\rangle\,\&\,(\emptyset;\gamma'_n)$ holds. Rule *T-U* implies $M;\emptyset;\emptyset \vdash () : \langle\rangle\,\&\,(\gamma_a;\gamma_a)$. The application of the context composition lemma on the derivations of E and $()$ yields $M;\emptyset;\emptyset \vdash E[()] : \langle\rangle\,\&\,(\emptyset;\gamma'_n)$. Cases *E-UL* and *E-LK1* can be shown in a similar manner. □

Extended Alias Type System using Separating Implication

Toshiyuki Maeda   Haruki Sato   Akinori Yonezawa
The University of Tokyo
{tosh,haruki,yonezawa}@yl.is.s.u-tokyo.ac.jp

Abstract

Although explicit memory management is necessary to implement low-level software such as operating systems and language runtime systems, it is prohibited by conventional strictly typed programming languages because it violates the type preservation of memory regions, a property that ensures the type safety of programs. The alias type system allows explicit memory management without the loss of type safety by statically tracking pointers and their aliases. However, it suffers from limitations in handling recursive data structures because it requires complete information about the pointer aliases. In this paper, we propose an extension of the alias type system using separating implications, which are derived from separation logic. Separating implications enable us to handle recursive data structures with incomplete aliasing information by assuming aliasing relations in a part of memory. The proposed type system is capable of expressing tail-recursive operations on recursive data structures. For example, we can implement a FIFO queue with constant-time operations; this cannot be achieved using the original alias type system.

Categories and Subject Descriptors D.3.1 [*Programming Languages*]: Formal Definitions and Theory

General Terms Languages, Security, Theory, Verification

Keywords Type system, Alias types, Separating implications, Explicit memory management

1. Introduction

Strictly typed programming languages do not allow programmers to explicitly manage memory regions. Therefore, low-level software such as operating systems and language runtime programs have not been written using strictly typed programming languages because explicit memory management is necessary to implement low-level software.

Strictly typed programming languages prohibit explicit memory management because it conflicts with the type preservation property, which ensures that the types of the allocated memory regions never change during program execution.

To investigate the relation between explicit memory management and type preservation, let us consider the following C function:

```
1: void reuse(int *p, int *q) {
2:     *(int**)p = q;
3: }
```

The memory region that stores an integer value pointed by the pointer `p` is reused to store the pointer to an integer, `q` (line 2). More specifically, the type of the pointer `p` must be updated with `int**` when the memory region is reused; thus, the type is not preserved. In general, it is not easy to ensure type safety without type preservation. For example, the function stated is not type-safe if the two pointers `p` and `q` are aliased (that is, if they point to the same memory region) because not only the type of `p` but also the type of `q` is updated accidentally.

1.1 Alias Type System and Its Drawback

The alias type system [13, 18] enables programmers to achieve both explicit memory management and type safety. It keeps track of aliasing relations between pointers by separating the type of the memory region pointed by a pointer from the type of the pointer and by tracking aliasing relations in the memory regions with the separated types. The function `reuse` is rewritten informally using the alias type system as follows:

```
1: {a ↦ int} ⊗ {b ↦ int}
2: void reuse(ptr(a) p, ptr(b) q) {
3:     *p = q;
4:     // {a ↦ ptr(b)} ⊗ {b ↦ int}
5: }
```

Line 1 denotes the store type (that is, the type of memory regions), and it implies that there are two integer values at `a` and `b`. The types of the pointers `p` and `q` are denoted by `ptr(a)` and `ptr(b)`, respectively, as shown in line 2. The type `ptr(a)` implies that it points to the address `a`. By combining the type of `p` and the store type, we know that `p` is a pointer to an integer.

In the alias type system, we also know that the two pointers `p` and `q` never point to the same memory region because the alias type system prevents all the addresses mentioned in the store type from aliasing each other. Thus, after reusing the memory region at `a`, the store type is updated without the loss of type safety, as shown in line 4.

A drawback of the original alias type system is its limited ability to handle recursive data structures, especially in the implementation of tail-recursive operations. To investigate this drawback, we first explain the treatment of recursive data structures by the original alias type system. Then, we describe the drawback.

The alias type system treats recursive data structures using existential types. For example, in the alias type system, a singly-linked list can be expressed as

$$\mathtt{List} \equiv \exists[\rho|\{\rho \mapsto \mathtt{List}\}].\mathtt{ptr}(\rho)$$

The type stated above is an existential type; it implies that the list is merely a pointer to the address ρ (the exact address of ρ is not known), and another singly-linked list exists at the address ρ. The

TLDI'11, January 25, 2011, Austin, Texas, USA.

alias type system prevents all the addresses mentioned in existential types from aliasing with other addresses.

To investigate the drawback of the original alias type system in handling recursive data structures, let us consider a program that simply traverses a singly-linked list as follows:

```
1: {ρ ↦ List}
2: while (p) { // p : ptr(ρ)
3:     unpack ρ with ρ_1;
4:     // {ρ ↦ ptr(ρ_1)} ⊗ {ρ_1 ↦ List}
5:     p = *p;
6:     // p : ptr(ρ_1)
7: }
```

Line 1 denotes the loop invariant, and it implies that there is a singly-linked list at some address ρ. In addition, let us assume that the type of the pointer `p` is `ptr`(ρ) (line 2). Line 3 performs the unpack operation on the existential type `List`. More specifically, it extracts the packed memory region from the existential type. Thus, after the unpack operation, the store type consists of the extracted memory region and the pointer to it, as shown in line 4. (It is important to note that the packed ρ is renamed as ρ_1 in order to avoid name ambiguity.) Finally, line 5 updates the variable `p`, and its type becomes `ptr`(ρ_1) (line 6).

The drawback of the original alias type system is its inability to loop back from line 6 to line 2. More specifically, although the loop invariant is satisfied with the pointer `p` and the type of the memory region at ρ_1 by instantiating ρ with ρ_1, the aliasing relations of the original memory region at ρ must be discarded. Thus, the original singly-linked list is not accessible after the `while` loop is exited.

One possible approach to overcome this drawback is to refine the loop invariant; however, this approach is not applicable to the original alias type system. For example, let us refine the loop invariant as

$$\{\rho \mapsto \texttt{ptr}(\rho_1)\} \otimes \{\rho_1 \mapsto \texttt{List}\}$$

Clearly, this invariant is not satisfied for the second iteration of the loop. Thus, for the nth iteration of the loop, the loop invariant must be of the following form:

$$\{\rho \mapsto \texttt{ptr}(\rho_1)\} \otimes \{\rho_1 \mapsto \texttt{ptr}(\rho_2)\} \otimes \ldots \otimes \{\rho_n \mapsto \texttt{List}\}$$

However, the original alias type system is not able to express the store type stated above because it cannot keep track of the aliasing relations of the n pointers, where n is unknown.

1.2 Proposed Approach: Separating Implication

To overcome the drawback of the original alias type system, we extend it using separating implications. A separating implication is derived from separation logic [10]; it is a novel store type that is written as

$$C_1 \Rightarrow C_2$$

It can be read as "if the memory regions that have the store type C_1 are added, then the combined memory regions have the store type C_2."

For example, using the proposed alias type system, the traversal of a singly-linked list can be written as follows:

```
 1: ({ρ_i ↦ List} ⇒ {ρ ↦ List}) ⊗ {ρ_i ↦ List}
 2: while (p) {
 3:     unpack ρ_i with ρ_j;
 4:     p = *p;
 5:     reserve {ρ_j ↦ List} for {ρ_i ↦ ptr(ρ_j)}
 6:     pack ρ_i;
 7:     trans ({ρ_j ↦ List} ⇒ {ρ_i ↦ List})
 8:           with ({ρ_i ↦ List} ⇒ {ρ ↦ List});
 9:     // ({ρ_j ↦ List} ⇒ {ρ ↦ List})
10:     // ⊗ {ρ_j ↦ List}
11:     // p : ptr(ρ_j)
12: }
```

Line 1 denotes the loop invariant. The separating implication in the loop invariant implies that if there is one singly-linked list at ρ_i, there is another singly-linked list at ρ, or $\rho_i = \rho$. It is important to note the extended alias type system allows implicit aliasing relations between the antecedents and consequents of separating implications, unlike the original alias type system.

In addition to the loop invariant, let us assume that the type of the pointer `p` is `ptr`(ρ), and there exists a singly-linked list at ρ before the `while` loop is entered. This assumption satisfies the loop invariant because substituting ρ_i with ρ yields the following store type, which equals $\{\rho \mapsto \texttt{List}\}$.

$$(\{\rho \mapsto \texttt{List}\} \Rightarrow \{\rho \mapsto \texttt{List}\}) \otimes \{\rho \mapsto \texttt{List}\}$$

After the loop is entered, the `unpack` operation at line 3 updates the store type as follows:

$$(\{\rho_i \mapsto \texttt{List}\} \Rightarrow \{\rho \mapsto \texttt{List}\}) \\ \otimes \{\rho_i \mapsto \texttt{ptr}(\rho_j)\} \otimes \{\rho_j \mapsto \texttt{List}\}$$

This operation is similar to that of the original alias type system.

Then, the `reserve` operation at line 5 introduces a new separating implication into the store type as follows:

$$(\{\rho_i \mapsto \texttt{List}\} \Rightarrow \{\rho \mapsto \texttt{List}\}) \\ \otimes (\{\rho_j \mapsto \texttt{List}\} \Rightarrow (\{\rho_i \mapsto \texttt{ptr}(\rho_j)\} \otimes \{\rho_j \mapsto \texttt{List}\})) \\ \otimes \{\rho_j \mapsto \texttt{List}\}$$

More specifically, it reserves a singly-linked list at ρ_j for the memory region at ρ_i. Thus, the store type $\{\rho_i \mapsto \texttt{ptr}(\rho_j)\}$ is coupled with $\{\rho_j \mapsto \texttt{List}\}$ under the supposition of $\{\rho_j \mapsto \texttt{List}\}$.

Next, the `pack` operation at line 6 restores the unpacked pointer at ρ_i to `List` as follows:

$$(\{\rho_i \mapsto \texttt{List}\} \Rightarrow \{\rho \mapsto \texttt{List}\}) \\ \otimes (\{\rho_j \mapsto \texttt{List}\} \Rightarrow \{\rho_i \mapsto \texttt{List}\}) \\ \otimes \{\rho_j \mapsto \texttt{List}\}$$

This can be regarded as the reverse of the `unpack` operation.

Finally, the `trans` operation at line 7 concatenates the two separating implications, as shown in line 9. The final store type and the type of the pointer `p` clearly satisfy the loop invariant by instantiating ρ_i with ρ_j, without the loss of any information about the memory regions. In addition, after the loop is exited, the original singly-linked list at ρ can be accessed by applying the store type $\{\rho_j \mapsto \texttt{List}\}$ to $(\{\rho_j \mapsto \texttt{List}\} \Rightarrow \{\rho \mapsto \texttt{List}\})$.

As shown in the example presented above, the extended alias type system enables us to express recursive data structures and tail-recursive operations that cannot be expressed using the original alias type system. For example, the proposed type system enables us to express a tail-recursive and destructive list append function and FIFO queues with constant-time operations.

The remainder of the paper is organized as follows. The proposed type system and the adopted imperative language are formally described in Section 2. In order to demonstrate the expressiveness of the proposed type system, several example programs are presented in Section 3. Related work is discussed in Section 4, and finally, the paper is concluded in Section 5.

2. Proposed Type System

Before we explain the proposed type system, we explain the adopted base language. The language is designed on the basis of that used by the original alias type system [18]. Careful readers may notice that the language does not contain explicit looping constructs used in Section 1. Instead, the language supports recur-

$$
\begin{array}{rcl}
v & ::= & x \mid i \mid v[c] \mid \\
 & & \texttt{fix} f[\Delta|C,\Theta](x_1:\sigma_1,\cdots,x_n:\sigma_n).I \mid \\
 & & \texttt{ptr}(\ell) \mid \langle v_1,\cdots,v_2\rangle \mid \varsigma(v) \\
\varsigma & ::= & \texttt{pack}_{[c_1,\cdots,c_n|S]\texttt{as}\exists[\Delta|C,\Theta].\tau} \mid \\
 & & \texttt{roll}_{(\texttt{rec}\ \alpha(\Delta).\tau)(c_1,\cdots,c_n)} \\
I & ::= & \iota; I \mid \texttt{ifpeq}\ v = v\ \texttt{then}\ I_1\ \texttt{else}\ I_2 \mid \\
 & & v(v_1,\cdots,v_n) \\
\iota & ::= & \texttt{new}\ \rho,x,i \mid \texttt{free}\ v \mid \texttt{let}\ x = (v).i \mid \\
 & & (v_1).i := v_2 \mid \texttt{coerce}(\gamma) \\
\gamma & ::= & \texttt{roll}_{\texttt{rec}\ \alpha(\Delta).\tau(c_1,\cdots,c_n)}(\eta) \mid \texttt{unroll}(\eta) \mid \\
 & & \texttt{pack}_{[c_1,\cdots,c_n|C]\texttt{as}\exists[\Delta|C].\tau}(\eta) \mid \\
 & & \texttt{unpack}\ \eta\ \texttt{with}\ \Delta \mid \texttt{reserve}\ C\ \texttt{for}\ C \mid \\
 & & \texttt{indicated}\ C\ \texttt{for}\ (C \Rightarrow C) \mid \\
 & & \texttt{trans}\ (C \Rightarrow C)\ \texttt{with}\ (C \Rightarrow C) \\
S & ::= & s \cdots s \\
s & ::= & \{\ell \mapsto v\} \mid \omega \mid \\
 & & \lambda\omega : C.S \quad (\omega \text{ appears exactly once in } S) \\
\mathcal{M} & ::= & (S, I)
\end{array}
$$

Figure 1. Syntax

sive functions. Loops can be represented as tail-recursive functions (several examples are presented in Section 3).

2.1 Language Syntax

Figure 1 shows the syntax of the adopted base language. $\mathcal{M}$ denotes the state of the abstract machine. The state is represented by the store S and the instruction sequence I. The store denotes the state of the allocated memory regions. More specifically, the store is a set consisting of location-value pairs ($\{\ell \mapsto v\}$), store variables (ω), and store abstractions ($\lambda\omega : C.S$).

The store abstraction $\lambda\omega : C.S$ denotes memory regions represented by S, which has a hole represented by ω. It is important to note that ω appears exactly once in S. For example, the store abstraction $\lambda\omega : C.\{\ell \mapsto v\}\omega$ denotes a memory region that stores the value v at the address ℓ. Within the abstraction, ω is treated as a store of the store type C; however, it is not available for memory accesses because it has no concrete mappings from locations to values. Therefore, ℓ is the only accessible location of the store abstraction.

The instruction sequence I is a sequence of instructions (ι) that ends with a function call or pointer comparison. The instructions consist of memory operations and coercions.

The instruction `new` ρ, x, i allocates a memory region of size i, and it binds the variable x to the pointer that points to the allocated memory region. In addition, it assigns the name ρ to the allocated memory location. On the other hand, the instruction `free` v explicitly deallocates the memory region pointed by the pointer v. The instruction `let` $x = (v).i$ loads the ith element of the tuple pointed by v, and it binds the variable x to the loaded value. The instruction $(v_1).i := v_2$ stores the value v_2 in the ith element of the tuple pointed by the pointer v_1.

The function call $v(v_1, \cdots, v_n)$ executes the instruction sequence pointed by v with the arguments $v_1, \cdots, v_n$. The pointer comparison `ifpeq` is described in Section 2.2.

The coercions (γ) are pseudo operations that only manipulate types; they have no runtime effect. They consist of operations for existential types, recursive types, and separating implications. Existential types are manipulated using `pack` and `unpack`. `pack` creates an existential package by abstracting the type constructors $c_1, \cdots, c_n$ and encapsulating the store specified by the store type C in the package. `unpack` destroys an existential package and extracts the store packed in it. Recursive types are manipulated

$$
\begin{array}{rcl}
\kappa & ::= & \texttt{Loc} \mid \texttt{Store} \mid \texttt{Small} \mid \texttt{Type} \mid \\
 & & (\kappa_1,\cdots,\kappa_n) \rightarrow \texttt{Type} \\
\beta & ::= & \rho \mid \alpha \mid \epsilon \\
\Delta & ::= & \cdot \mid \Delta, \beta : \kappa \\
c & ::= & \eta \mid \tau \mid C \\
\eta & ::= & \rho \mid \ell \\
\Theta & ::= & \cdot \mid \Theta, \eta = \eta \mid \Theta, \eta \neq \eta \\
C & ::= & a \otimes \cdots \otimes a \\
a & ::= & \{\eta \mapsto \tau\} \mid C \Rightarrow C \mid \epsilon \\
\tau & ::= & \alpha \mid \sigma \mid \langle \sigma_1,\cdots,\sigma_n\rangle \mid \\
 & & \exists[\Delta|C,\Theta].\tau \mid \texttt{rec}\ \alpha(\Delta).\tau \mid \tau(c_1,\cdots,c_n) \\
\sigma & ::= & \alpha \mid int \mid ptr(\eta) \mid \\
 & & \forall[\Delta|C,\Theta].(\sigma_1,\cdots,\sigma_n) \rightarrow \mathbf{0}
\end{array}
$$

Figure 2. Type Structure

using `roll` and `unroll`. `unroll` expands the recursive type of a memory region, whereas `roll` folds back the expanded recursive type. The operational semantics of the coercions used to manipulate separating implications are explained in Section 2.2.

Figure 2 shows the type structure of the adopted language. C is the store type that describes the shape of memory regions; it is a set consisting of location-type pairs, implications, and store type variables ϵ.

The store type $\{\eta \mapsto \tau\}$ describes the store $\{\ell \mapsto v\}$ where the type of the value v is τ. η ranges over the locations ℓ and location variables ρ. τ denotes the types of the values (the small types σ, tuple types, existential types, and recursive types). The small types σ denotes integers and pointers.

The store type of the form $C_1 \Rightarrow C_2$ corresponds to the store abstraction $\lambda\omega : C_1.S$, where the type of the store S is C_2, and the type of the store ω is C_1.

Θ denotes a set of equality constraints for the locations η. More specifically, Θ consists of equalities $\eta_1 = \eta_2$ or inequalities $\eta_1 \neq \eta_2$. In the original alias type system, the equality constraints are unnecessary because all the locations in a store type are distinguished by the type system. However, in the proposed system, the locations in the antecedent and consequent of the separating implication may be aliased. Therefore, the equality constraints are necessary to access the store within store abstractions. It is important to note that the function types and existential types are augmented with Θ.

2.2 Operational Semantics

The small-step operational semantics of the adopted language are shown in Figures 3, 4, and 5. They are virtually identical to those used in the original alias type system [18], except for the handling of stores. More specifically, we need to handle accesses to the store abstractions. In addition, we need to provide operational semantics for the coercions that manipulate the store abstractions. The notation $A[X/x]$ denotes the capture-avoiding substitution of X for x in A. $X[c_1, \cdots, c_n/\Delta]$ denotes the capture-avoiding substitution of constructors $c_1, \cdots, c_n$ for the corresponding type variables of Δ.

We explain the operational semantics of memory access operations and coercions for three cases because there are three types of stores in the adopted language.

The first and simplest case involves accessing the store of $\{\ell \mapsto v\}$. In this case, the memory access operations and coercions merely access the value v. This is virtually identical to the working of the original alias type system.

The second case is involves accessing the store of the store variable ω. In this case, the access is invalid because the store variables represent holes in the stores.

$\boxed{\mathcal{M} \longmapsto_P \mathcal{M}'}$

$$
\begin{array}{lll}
(S, \texttt{new}\,\rho, x, i; I) & \longmapsto_P & (S\{\ell \mapsto v\}, I') \\
\text{where } \ \ell \notin S, v = \langle int, \cdots, int\rangle \text{, and } I' = I[\ell/\rho][\texttt{ptr}(\ell)/x] & & \\[1em]
(S, \texttt{ifpeq}\,\texttt{ptr}(\ell_1) = \texttt{ptr}(\ell_2)\ \texttt{then}\ I_1\ \texttt{else}\ I_2) & \longmapsto_P & (S, I) \\
\text{where } I = \left\{ \begin{array}{l} I_1 \text{ when } \ell_1 = \ell_2 \\ I_2 \text{ when } \ell_1 \neq \ell_2 \end{array} \right. & & \\[1em]
(S, v(v_1, \cdots, v_n)) & \longmapsto_P & (S, \theta(I)) \\
\text{where } \begin{array}{l} v = v'[c_1, \cdots, c_m] \\ v' = \texttt{fix}f[\Delta|C, M](x_1 : \sigma_1, \cdots, x_n : \sigma_n).I \\ \theta = [c_1, \cdots, c_m/\Delta][v'/f][v_1, \cdots, v_n/x_1, \cdots, x_n] \end{array} & & \\[1em]
(S, \iota; I) & \longmapsto_P & (S', \theta(I)) \\
\text{where } \ \iota(S) \longmapsto_\iota S', \theta & &
\end{array}
$$

Figure 3. Operational Semantics

$\boxed{\iota(S) \longmapsto_\iota S', \theta}$

$$
\begin{array}{lll}
\texttt{free}\ \texttt{ptr}(\ell)(S\{\ell \mapsto v\}) & \longmapsto_\iota & S, [] \\[1em]
\texttt{let}\ x = (\texttt{ptr}(\ell)).i(S\{\ell \mapsto \langle v_1, \cdots, v_i, \cdots, v_n\rangle\}) & \longmapsto_\iota & S\{\ell \mapsto \langle v_1, \cdots, v_i, \cdots, v_n\rangle\}, [v_i/x] \\
\text{where } \ a \leq i \leq n & & \\[1em]
(\texttt{ptr}(\ell)).i := v'(S\{\ell \mapsto \langle v_1, \cdots, v_i, \cdots, v_n\rangle\}) & \longmapsto_\iota & S\{\ell \mapsto \langle v_1, \cdots, v', \cdots, v_n\rangle\}, [] \\
\text{where } \ a \leq i \leq n & & \\[1em]
\texttt{coerce}(\gamma)(S) & \longmapsto_\iota & S', \theta \\
\text{where } \ \gamma(S) \longmapsto_\gamma S', \theta & & \\[1em]
\iota(S(\lambda\omega : C.S')) & \longmapsto_\iota & S(\lambda\omega : C.S''), \theta \\
\text{where } \begin{array}{l} \cdot; \cdot \vdash \text{target}(\iota) = \mathbf{L} \\ \mathbf{L} \subseteq Dom(S') \\ \iota(S') \longmapsto_\iota S'', \theta \end{array} & &
\end{array}
$$

Figure 4. Operational Semantics: Instruction

$\boxed{\gamma(S) \longmapsto_\gamma S', \theta}$

$$
\begin{array}{lll}
\texttt{roll}_\tau(\ell)(S\{\ell \mapsto v\}) & \longmapsto_\gamma & S\{\ell \mapsto \texttt{roll}_\tau(v)\}, [] \\[1em]
\texttt{unroll}(\ell)(S\{\ell \mapsto \texttt{roll}_\tau(v)\}) & \longmapsto_\gamma & S'\{\ell \mapsto v\}, [] \\[1em]
\texttt{pack}_{[c_1, \cdots, c_n|C, \Theta]\texttt{as}\tau}(\ell)(S\{\ell \mapsto v\}S') & \longmapsto_\gamma & S\{\ell \mapsto \texttt{pack}_{[c_1, \cdots, c_n|S']\texttt{as}\tau}(v)\}, [] \\
\text{where } \ Dom(S') = Dom(C) & & \\[1em]
\texttt{unpack}\ \ell\ \texttt{with}\ \Delta(S\{\ell \mapsto \texttt{pack}_{[c_1, \cdots, c_n|S']\texttt{as}\exists[\Delta|C,\Theta].\tau}(v)\}) & \longmapsto_\gamma & S\{\ell \mapsto v\}S', [c_1, \cdots, c_n/\Delta] \\[1em]
\texttt{reserve}\ C_1\ \texttt{for}\ C_2(SS_2) & \longmapsto_\gamma & S(\lambda\omega : C_1.S_2\omega), [] \\
\text{where } \ Dom(S_2) = Dom(C_2) & & \\[1em]
\texttt{indicated}\ C_1\ \texttt{for}\ C_1 \Rightarrow C_2(S(\lambda\omega : C_1.S_2')S_1) & \longmapsto_\gamma & S(S_2'[S_1/\omega]), [] \\
\text{where } \begin{array}{l} Dom(\lambda\omega : C_1.S_2') = Dom(C_1 \Rightarrow C_2) \\ Dom(S_1) = Dom(C_1) \end{array} & &
\end{array}
$$

Figure 5. Operational Semantics: Coercions

The third and final case involves accessing the store abstraction $\lambda\omega : C.S$. The abstraction may include other stores besides ω; hence, the store S is accessed recursively. The rule at the bottom of Figure 4 represents recursive access to the store abstractions. In this rule, $Dom(S)$ denotes the accessible locations of the store S. $Dom(S)$ is defined as follows:

$$\begin{array}{lcl} Dom(\cdot) & = & \emptyset \\ Dom(s_1 \cdots s_n) & = & Dom(s_1) \oplus \cdots \oplus Dom(s_n) \\ Dom(\{\ell \mapsto v\}) & = & \{\ell\} \\ Dom(\lambda\omega : C.S') & = & Dom(S') \\ Dom(\omega) & = & \emptyset \end{array}$$

Here, $\oplus$ denotes the disjoint union of sets of locations. Additionally, target(ι) denotes the locations to be accessed by ι. Figure 6 shows the definition of target(ι).

Except for the memory access conditions described above, the operational semantics of instructions and coercions are fairly straightforward, as in the case of the original alias type system [18]. Therefore, we only explain the newly introduced instructions: `reserve`, `indicated`, `trans` and `ifpeq`.

The coercion `reserve` introduces store abstractions. For example, let us assume that the current store is

$$\{\ell_1 \mapsto \langle \mathtt{ptr}(\ell_2)\rangle\}$$

The coercion `reserve` $\{\ell_2 \mapsto \tau\}$ `for` $\{\ell_1 \mapsto \langle ptr(\ell_2)\rangle\}$ translates it as

$$(\lambda\omega : \{\ell_2 \mapsto \tau\}.\{\ell_1 \mapsto \langle \mathtt{ptr}(\ell_2)\rangle\}\omega)$$

In the store type stated above, a hole ω of the store type $\{\ell_2 \mapsto \tau\}$ is introduced by the `reserve` operation.

On the other hand, the coercion `indicated` eliminates store abstractions. For example, let us assume that the current store is

$$(\lambda\omega : \{\ell_2 \mapsto \tau\}.\{\ell_1 \mapsto \mathtt{pack}_{[|\omega]\mathtt{as}\,\tau'}(v')\})\{\ell_2 \mapsto v\}$$

where the type of v is τ. The coercion `indicated` $\{\ell_2 \mapsto \tau\}$ `for` $\{\ell_2 \mapsto \tau\} \Rightarrow \{\ell_1 \mapsto \tau'\}$ translates it as

$$\{\ell_1 \mapsto \mathtt{pack}_{[|\{\ell_2 \mapsto v\}]\mathtt{as}\,\tau'}(v')\})$$

It is important to note that the store variable can be instantiated, even though it may be packed with the coercion `pack`, as shown above.

The coercion operation `trans` is not included in Figure 5 because it can be represented by combining `reserve` and `indicated`. More specifically, `trans` $C_1 \Rightarrow C_2$ `with` $C_2 \Rightarrow C_3$ can be rewritten as follows:

$$\begin{array}{l} \mathtt{reserve}\ C_1\ \mathtt{for}\ (C_1 \Rightarrow C_2) \otimes (C_2 \Rightarrow C_3); \\ \mathtt{indicated}\ C_1\ \mathtt{for}\ C_1 \Rightarrow C_2; \\ \mathtt{indicated}\ C_2\ \mathtt{for}\ C_2 \Rightarrow C_3 \end{array}$$

For example, if we apply the coercions stated above to the store $(\lambda\omega_1 : C_1.S_2)\ (\lambda\omega_2 : C_2.S_3)$, they translate it as

$$(\lambda\omega'_1 : C_1.S_3[(S_2[\omega'_1/\omega_1])/\omega_2])$$

The instruction sequence `ifpeq` $v_1 = v_2$ `then` I_1 `else` I_2 compares the two given pointers (v_1 and v_2). If $v_1 = v_2$, `ifpeq` executes I_1; otherwise, it executes I_2. `ifpeq` is essential for accessing locations in store abstractions because it can recover the aliasing relations in the store abstractions that may be disregarded by the proposed type system. More specifically, it introduces the equality constraints Θ, as describe in Section 2.2.1.

2.2.1 Typing Rules

The important typing rules of the proposed type system are shown in Figures 7, 8, and 9; they are based on those of the original alias type system [18]. The proposed type system provides type safety by ensuring that the following theorem holds:

$$\boxed{\Delta;\Gamma \vdash \mathrm{target}(\iota) = \eta}$$

$$\frac{\iota = \mathtt{free}\ v \mid \mathtt{let}\ \_ = (v).\_ \mid (v).\_ := \_ \qquad \Delta;\Gamma \vdash v : ptr(\eta)}{\Delta;\Gamma \vdash \mathrm{target}(\iota) = \{\eta\}}$$

$$\frac{\gamma = \mathtt{roll}_{\_}(\eta) \mid \mathtt{unroll}(\eta) \mid \mathtt{pack}_{\_\mathtt{as}\_}(\eta) \mid \mathtt{unpack}\ \eta\ \mathtt{with}\ \_}{\Delta;\Gamma \vdash \mathrm{target}(\mathtt{coerce}(\gamma)) = \{\eta\}}$$

$$\frac{\gamma = \mathtt{reserve}\ \_\ \mathtt{for}\ \_ \mid \mathtt{indicated}\ \_\ \mathtt{for}\ \_}{\Delta;\Gamma \vdash \mathrm{target}(\mathtt{coerce}(\gamma)) = \{\}}$$

Figure 6. Target Location of Instruction

THEOREM 1 (Type Soundness). *If* $\vdash \mathcal{M}$*, there exists* $\mathcal{M}'$*, where* $\mathcal{M} \longmapsto^*_P \mathcal{M}'$ *and* $\vdash \mathcal{M}'$.

Well-formedness of the states of the abstract machine is defined as follows:

DEFINITION 1. $\vdash (S, I)$ *iff*

1. *There are no duplicate locations in* S*, including the packed stores.*
2. *There exists a store type* C *such that* $\cdot \vdash S : C$
3. $\cdot; C; \cdot \vdash I$

Well-formedness of the stores is defined as follows:

$$\frac{\Sigma \vdash s_1 : a_1 \quad \cdots \quad \Sigma \vdash s_n : a_n}{\Sigma \vdash s_1 \cdots s_n : a_1 \otimes \cdots \otimes a_n}$$

$$\frac{\Sigma \vdash v : \tau}{\Sigma \vdash \{\ell \mapsto v\} : \{\ell \mapsto \tau\}} \qquad \frac{}{\Sigma \vdash \omega : \Sigma(\omega)}$$

$$\frac{\Sigma, \omega : \{\eta \mapsto \tau\} \vdash S_2 : C_2}{\Sigma \vdash \lambda\omega : \{\eta \mapsto \tau\}.S_2 : \{\eta \mapsto \tau\} \Rightarrow C_2} \qquad \frac{\cdot;\cdot \vdash v : \tau}{\Sigma \vdash v : \tau}$$

$$\frac{\begin{array}{c}\cdot;\cdot \vdash \tau = (\mathtt{rec}\ \alpha(\Delta).\tau')(c_1, \cdots .c_n) : \mathtt{Type} \\ \Sigma \vdash v : \tau'[\mathtt{rec}\ \alpha(\Delta).\tau'/\alpha][c_1, \cdots, c_n/\Delta]\end{array}}{\Sigma \vdash \mathtt{roll}_\tau(v) : \tau}$$

$$\frac{\begin{array}{c}\Delta = \beta_1 : \kappa_1, \cdots, \beta_n : \kappa_n \qquad \cdot \vdash c_i : \kappa_i \\ \cdot;\cdot \vdash \Theta[c_1, \cdots, c_n/\Delta] \\ \Sigma \vdash S : C[c_1, \cdots, c_n/\Delta] \qquad \cdot;\cdot \vdash v : \tau[c_1, \cdots, c_n/\Delta]\end{array}}{\Sigma \vdash \mathtt{pack}_{[c_1, \cdots, c_n|S]\mathtt{as}\,\exists[\Delta|C,\Theta].\tau}(v) : \tau}$$

Here, Σ denotes an environment for store variables. It is important to note here that store variables (ω) do not affect disjointness of locations in S because store variables denote holes in S, not locations. In addition, instantiation of store variables preserves the disjointness because each store variable appears exactly once in S.

As shown above, the separating implication $C_1 \Rightarrow C_2$ corresponds to the store abstraction $\lambda\omega : C_1.S_2$. It is important to note that the store type of the store variable within the store abstraction must be of the form $\{\eta \mapsto \tau\}$. This limitation can be relaxed; however, it is sufficient to describe tail-recursive operations on recursive data structures. The reason why separating implications ($C_1 \Rightarrow C_2$) are not allowed is that, in the proposed language, store applications cannot be represented as the store constructs, unlike store abstractions. The reason why store type variables (ϵ) are not allowed is that, although the proposed type system keeps track of equality constraints for locations (Θ), it does not consider inclusion relations between locations and store type variables.

The typing rules for memory accesses are shown in Figure 8. Let us consider the typing rule for the instruction `let` $x = (v).i$. Two possible rules can be applied on the basis of its target location.

$\boxed{\Delta; C; \Theta; \Gamma \vdash \iota \Longrightarrow \Delta'; C'; \Theta'; \Gamma'}$

$$\frac{\Delta; \Gamma \vdash v : ptr(\eta) \qquad \Delta; \Theta \vdash C = C' \otimes \{\eta \mapsto \langle \sigma_1, \cdots, \sigma_i, \cdots, \sigma_n \rangle\} : \mathtt{Store}}{\Delta; C; \Theta; \Gamma \vdash \mathtt{let}\ x = (v).i \Longrightarrow \Delta; C; \Theta; \Gamma, x : \sigma_i} \left(\begin{array}{c} 1 \leq i \leq n \\ x \notin Dom(\Gamma) \end{array} \right)$$

$$\frac{\Delta; \Gamma \vdash v_1 : ptr(\eta) \qquad \Delta; \Gamma \vdash v_2 : \sigma \qquad \Delta; \Theta \vdash C = C' \otimes \{\eta \mapsto \langle \sigma_1, \cdots, \sigma_i, \cdots, \sigma_n \rangle\} : \mathtt{Store}}{\Delta; C; \Theta; \Gamma \vdash (v_1).i := v_2 \Longrightarrow \Delta; C' \otimes \{\eta \mapsto \langle \sigma_1, \cdots, \sigma, \cdots, \sigma_n \rangle\}; \Theta; \Gamma} \left(1 \leq i \leq n \right)$$

$$\frac{\Delta; \Theta \vdash \tau = (\mathtt{rec}\ \alpha(\Delta').\tau')(c_1, \cdots, c_n) : \mathtt{Type} \qquad \Delta; \Theta \vdash C = C' \otimes \{\eta \mapsto \tau'[\mathtt{rec}\ \alpha(\Delta').\tau'/\alpha][c_1, \cdots, c_n/\Delta']\} : \mathtt{Store}}{\Delta; C; \Theta; \Gamma; \vdash \mathtt{coerce}(\mathtt{roll}_{\tau}(\eta)) \Longrightarrow \Delta; C' \otimes \{\eta \mapsto \tau\}; \Theta; \Gamma}$$

$$\frac{\Delta; \Theta \vdash C = C' \otimes \{\eta \mapsto \tau\} : \mathtt{Store} \qquad \Delta; \Theta \vdash \tau = (\mathtt{rec}\ \alpha(\Delta').\tau')(c_1, \cdots, c_n) : \mathtt{Type}}{\Delta; C; \Theta; \Gamma; \vdash \mathtt{coerce}(\mathtt{unroll}(\eta)) \Longrightarrow \Delta; C' \otimes \{\eta \mapsto \tau'[\mathtt{rec}\ \alpha(\Delta').\tau'/\alpha][c_1, \cdots, c_n/\Delta']\}; \Theta; \Gamma}$$

$$\frac{\begin{array}{c} \Delta' = \beta_1 : \kappa_1, \cdots, \beta_n : \kappa_n \qquad \cdot \vdash c_i : \kappa_i \text{ (for } 1 \leq i \leq n) \qquad \Delta; \Theta \vdash \Theta'[c_1, \cdots, c_n/\Delta'] \\ \Delta; \Theta \vdash C = C'' \otimes \{\eta \mapsto \tau[c_1, \cdots, c_n/\Delta']\} \otimes C'[c_1, \cdots, c_n/\Delta'] : \mathtt{Store} \end{array}}{\Delta; C; \Theta; \Gamma \vdash \mathtt{coerce}(\mathtt{pack}_{[c_1, \cdots, c_n | C'[c_1, \cdots, c_n/\Delta'], \Theta'[c_1, \cdots, c_n/\Delta']] \mathtt{as} \exists [\Delta' | C', \Theta'].\tau}(\eta)) \Longrightarrow \Delta; C'' \otimes \{\eta \mapsto \exists[\Delta' | C', \Theta'].\tau\}; \Theta; \Gamma}$$

$$\frac{\Delta; \Theta \vdash C = C'' \otimes \{\eta \mapsto \exists[\Delta' | C', \Theta'].\tau\} : \mathtt{Store}}{\Delta; C; \Theta; \Gamma \vdash \mathtt{coerce}(\mathtt{unpack}\ \eta\ \mathtt{with}\ \Delta') \Longrightarrow \Delta, \Delta'; C'' \otimes \{\eta \mapsto \tau\} \otimes C'; \Theta\Theta'; \Gamma}$$

$$\frac{\Delta; \Theta \vdash C = C' \otimes C_2 : \mathtt{Store}}{\Delta; C; \Theta; \Gamma \vdash \mathtt{coerce}(\mathtt{reserve}\ \{\eta \mapsto \tau\}\ \mathtt{for}\ C_2) \Longrightarrow \Delta; C' \otimes (\{\eta \mapsto \tau\} \Rightarrow C_2 \otimes \{\eta \mapsto \tau\}); \Theta; \Gamma}$$

$$\frac{\Delta; \Theta \vdash C = C' \otimes C_1 \otimes (C_1 \Rightarrow C_2) : \mathtt{Store}}{\Delta; C; \Theta; \Gamma \vdash \mathtt{coerce}(\mathtt{indicated}\ C_1\ \mathtt{for}\ (C_1 \Rightarrow C_2)) \Longrightarrow \Delta; C' \otimes C_2; \Theta; \Gamma}$$

$$\frac{\Delta' \equiv \Delta, \rho : \mathtt{Loc} \quad C' \equiv C \otimes \{\rho \mapsto \overbrace{\langle int, \cdots, int \rangle}^{i}\} \quad \Gamma' \equiv \Gamma, x : ptr(\rho)}{\Delta; C; \Theta; \Gamma \vdash \mathtt{new}\ x, \rho, i \Longrightarrow \Delta'; C'; \Theta; \Gamma'} \left(\begin{array}{c} \rho \notin Dom(\Delta) \\ x \notin Dom(\Gamma) \end{array} \right)$$

$$\frac{\Delta; \Gamma \vdash v : ptr(\eta) \qquad \Delta; \Theta \vdash C = C' \otimes \{\eta \mapsto \tau\} : \mathtt{Store}}{\Delta; C; \Theta; \Gamma; \vdash \mathtt{free}\ v \Longrightarrow \Delta; C'; \Theta; \Gamma}$$

$$\frac{\begin{array}{c} \Delta; \Theta \vdash C = C' \otimes (C_1 \Rightarrow C_2) \qquad \Delta; \Gamma \vdash \text{target}(\iota) = \mathbf{L} \qquad \forall \eta \in \mathbf{L}.\exists \eta' \in Dom_{\Theta}(C_1 \Rightarrow C_2).\Theta \vdash \eta = \eta' \\ \Delta; C_2; \Theta; \Gamma \vdash \iota \Longrightarrow \Delta'; C_2'; \Theta'; \Gamma' \end{array}}{\Delta; C; \Theta; \Gamma \vdash \iota \Longrightarrow \Delta'; C' \otimes (C_1 \Rightarrow C_2'); \Theta'; \Gamma'}$$

Figure 8. Typing Rules for Instructions

$\boxed{\Delta; C; \Theta; \Gamma \vdash I}$

$$\frac{\Delta; C; \Theta; \Gamma \vdash \iota \Longrightarrow \Delta'; C'; \Theta'; \Gamma' \qquad \Delta'; C'; \Theta'; \Gamma' \vdash I}{\Delta; C; \Theta; \Gamma \vdash \iota; I}$$

$$\frac{\Delta; \Gamma \vdash v_1 : ptr(\eta_1) \qquad \Delta; \Gamma \vdash v_2 : ptr(\eta_2) \qquad \Delta; C; \Theta, (\eta_1 = \eta_2); \Gamma \vdash I_1 \qquad \Delta; C; \Theta, (\eta_1 \neq \eta_2); \Gamma \vdash I_2}{\Delta; C; \Theta; \Gamma \vdash \mathtt{ifpeq}\ v_1 = v_2\ \mathtt{then}\ I_1\ \mathtt{else}\ I_2}$$

$$\frac{\begin{array}{c} \Delta; \Gamma \vdash v : \forall[\cdot | C', \Theta'].(\sigma_1, \cdots, \sigma_n) \to \mathbf{0} \qquad \Delta; \Theta \vdash C = C' : \mathtt{Store} \\ \Delta; \Theta \vdash \Theta' \qquad \Delta; \Gamma \vdash v_1 : \sigma_1 \quad \cdots \quad \Delta; \Gamma \vdash v_n : \sigma_n \end{array}}{\Delta; C; \Theta; \Gamma \vdash v(v_1, \cdots, v_n)}$$

Figure 9. Typing Rules for Instruction Sequences

$\boxed{\Delta; \Gamma \vdash v : \tau}$

$$\frac{}{\Delta; \Gamma \vdash x : \Gamma(x)} \qquad \frac{}{\Delta; \Gamma \vdash i : int}$$

$$\frac{\begin{array}{c}\Delta, \Delta'; C'; \Theta'; f : \sigma_f, x_1 : \sigma_1, \cdots, x_n : \sigma_n \vdash I \\ \text{(where store type variables do not appear in} \\ \text{antecedents of separating implications in } C')\end{array}}{\begin{array}{c}\Delta; \Gamma \vdash \mathtt{fix} f[\Delta'|C', \Theta'](x_1 : \sigma_1, \cdots, x_n : \sigma_n).I : \sigma_f \\ (\sigma_f = \forall[\Delta'|C', \Theta'].(\sigma_1, \cdots, \sigma_n) \to \mathbf{0})\end{array}}$$

$$\frac{\begin{array}{c}\Delta; \Gamma \vdash v : \forall[\beta : \kappa, \Delta'|C', \Theta'].(\sigma_1, \cdots, \sigma_n) \to \mathbf{0} \\ \Delta \vdash c : \kappa\end{array}}{\Delta; \Gamma \vdash v[c] : (\forall[\Delta'|C', \Theta'].(\sigma_1, \cdots, \sigma_n) \to \mathbf{0})[c/\beta]}$$

Figure 7. Typing Rules for Values

If the target location is contained in a separating implication, the last rule of Figure 8 is applied. This rule states that we can temporarily discard the antecedent of the separating implication if the target location is accessible according to the separating implication. More specifically, this rule checks whether the target location is contained in the domain of the store type $C_1 \Rightarrow C_2$ under the equality constraints Θ. Then, it checks the instruction with the store type C_2. Finally, it checks the rest of the instruction sequence with the updated store type $C_1 \Rightarrow C_2'$. $Dom_\Theta(C)$ is defined as follows:

$$\begin{array}{lcl} Dom_\Theta(\cdot) & = & \emptyset \\ Dom_\Theta(a_1 \otimes \cdots) & = & Dom_\Theta(a_1) \oplus \cdots \\ Dom_\Theta(\{\eta \mapsto \tau\}) & = & \{\eta\} \\ Dom_\Theta(C_1 \Rightarrow C_2) & = & \{\eta \in Dom_\Theta(C_2) | \\ & & \quad \forall \eta' \in Dom_\Theta(C_1).\Theta \vdash \eta \neq \eta'\} \\ Dom_\Theta(\epsilon) & = & \emptyset \end{array}$$

If the target location is not contained in a separating implication, the second rule of Figure 8 is applied. It checks whether the pointer v points to a tuple by examining the store type. Then, it checks whether the size of the tuple satisfies the access offset i. Finally, it binds the variable x to the type of the ith element of the tuple, and it checks the rest of the instruction sequence.

The typing rule for the instruction $(v_1).i := v_2$ governs the strong update, that is, it changes the types of the memory regions. It first checks whether there exists a tuple at the location η by examining the current store type; it also checks whether the size of the tuple satisfies the specified access offset i. Then, it updates the type of the ith element of the tuple with the type of v_2, and it checks the rest of the instruction sequence with the updated tuple type. This strong update is safe because the proposed type system prevents the location η from aliasing with other locations in the store type. Strictly speaking, the proposed type system allows locations in the consequent of a separating implication to be aliased with locations in its antecedent. The aliasing relations in separating implications are handled using the last rule of Figure 8, as described above.

The typing rules for `roll` and `unroll` govern recursive types. The rule for `roll` first unrolls the given recursive type ($\mathtt{rec}\ \alpha(\Delta').\tau'$) with the given type constructors $(c_1, \cdots, c_n)$. Then, it checks whether the location η holds the unrolled type. Finally, it updates the type at the location η with the given type τ, and it checks the rest of the instruction sequence with the updated store type. The rule for `unroll` first checks whether the location η holds a recursive type. Then, it unrolls the recursive type and updates the type of the location η with the unrolled type. Finally, it checks the rest of the instruction sequence with the updated store type. It is important to note that the last rule of Figure 8 can be used before applying these rules, as in the case of memory accesses,

The typing rules for `pack` and `unpack` govern existential types. As in the case of the typing rules for recursive types, the last rule of Figure 8 can be used before applying these rules. The rule for `pack` first instantiates the packed type τ with the given type constructors $(c_1, \cdots, c_n)$, and it checks whether the location η holds the instantiated type. Next, it checks whether the current store type contains the store type to be packed. In addition, it checks whether the equality constraints specified in the given existential type are satisfied by the current equality constraints ($\Delta; \Theta \vdash \Theta'[c_1, \cdots, c_n/\Delta']$). Then, it updates the type of the location η with the existential type, and it removes the packed store from the current store type. Finally, it checks the rest of the instruction sequence with the updated store type. The rule for `unpack` first checks whether the location η holds an existential type. Next, it extracts the packed store type (C') by unpacking the existential type, and it adds the store type to the current store type. Finally, it checks the rest of the instruction sequence with the extended store type. It is important to note that the equality constraints are also extended with the packed equality constraints (Θ').

The typing rules for `reserve` and `indicated` govern separating implications. The rule for `reserve` is the introduction rule of the separating implication. It basically checks nothing; however, it states that the antecedent of the implication to be introduced must be of the form of $\{\eta \mapsto \tau\}$. The reason for this limitation is the same as explained in Section 2.2.1. Then, it checks the subsequent instruction sequence with the introduced separating implication. The rule for `indicated` is the elimination rule of the separating implication. It checks whether the antecedent of the given implication equals the given store type. Then, it extracts the consequent of the implication, and it checks the subsequent instruction sequence with the extracted store type.

The typing rules for `new` and `free` govern explicit memory allocation and deallocation. The rule for `new` first extends the current store type with the store type that corresponds to the allocated memory region. Then, it checks the rest of the instruction sequence with the extended store type. The rule for `free` first checks whether the given pointer points to the valid memory region by examining the current store type. Then, it removes the store type that corresponds to the memory region to be freed, and it checks the rest of the instruction sequence with the updated store type.

The equality constraints Θ are introduced by the typing rule for `ifpeq`, as shown in Figure 9. The rule first checks whether both the variables v_1 and v_2 are pointers. Then, it checks the instruction sequences I_1 and I_2 under the condition that $v_1 = v_2$ and $v_1 \neq v_2$, respectively. For example, let us consider a store of the type $\{\rho_1 \mapsto \tau\} \Rightarrow \{\rho_2 \mapsto \tau\}$. The proposed type system does not keep track of aliasing relations between ρ_1 and ρ_2; therefore, we need to explicitly check the aliasing relations by using `ifpeq`. At first glance, this approach may seem superfluous; however, it is essential and well suited to typical programming styles, as described in Section 3.

The typing rule for function calls is the last rule of Figure 9. It checks whether the type of the value v is the instruction type and whether the types of the values $v_1, \cdots, v_n$ are the types specified in the instruction type. It also checks whether the store type and equality constraints specified in the instruction type are satisfied by the current store type and equality constraints.

3. Examples

In this section, we present several examples in order to demonstrate the expressiveness of the proposed type system. The obvious coercions are omitted for brevity.

1 : $\texttt{fix}\ append[\rho_h, \rho_p, \rho_x, \rho_y, \epsilon|$
2 : $(\{\ell_0 \mapsto \mathit{List}\} \Rightarrow$
3 : $(\{\rho_p \mapsto \mathit{List}\} \Rightarrow \{\rho_h \mapsto \mathit{List}\})$
4 : $\otimes\{\rho_p \mapsto \langle ptr(\rho_x)\rangle\} \otimes \{\rho_x \mapsto \mathit{List}\})$
5 : $\otimes(\{\ell_0 \mapsto \mathit{List}\} \Rightarrow \{\rho_y \mapsto \mathit{List}\}) \otimes \epsilon,$
6 : $\ell_0 \neq \rho_p]$
7 : $(h : ptr(\rho_h), p : ptr(\rho_p), y : ptr(\rho_y), cont : \tau_c[\rho_h, \epsilon]).$
8 : $\texttt{let}\ x = (p).1;$
9 : $\texttt{ifpeq}\ x = \texttt{ptr}(\ell_0)\ \texttt{then}$
10 : $(p).1 := y;$
11 : $\texttt{last\_coercions};$
12 : $cont(h);$
13 : $\texttt{else}$
14 : $\texttt{unpack}\ \rho_x\ \texttt{with}\ \rho_{xs};$
15 : $\texttt{reserve}\ \{\rho_x \mapsto \mathit{List}\}\ \texttt{for}\ \{\rho_p \mapsto \langle ptr(\rho_x)\rangle\};$
16 : $\texttt{pack}_{[\rho_x|\{\rho_x \mapsto \mathit{List}\}]\texttt{as}\mathit{List}}(\rho_p);$
17 : $\texttt{trans}\ \{\rho_x \mapsto \mathit{List}\} \Rightarrow \{\rho_p \mapsto \mathit{List}\}\ \texttt{with}$
18 : $\{\rho_p \mapsto \mathit{List}\} \Rightarrow \{\rho_h \mapsto \mathit{List}\};$
19 : $append[\rho_h, \rho_x, \rho_{xs}, \rho_y, \epsilon](h, x, y, cont);$
where
20 : $\mathit{List} \equiv \exists[\rho|\{\rho \mapsto \mathit{List}\}].\langle ptr(\rho)\rangle$
21 : $\tau_c[\rho, \epsilon] \equiv \forall[|\{\ell_0 \mapsto \mathit{List}\} \Rightarrow$
22 : $\{\rho \mapsto \mathit{List}\} \otimes \epsilon].(a : ptr(\rho)) \rightarrow \mathbf{0}$
23 : $\texttt{last\_coercions} \equiv$
24 : $\texttt{reserve}\ \{\ell_0 \mapsto \mathit{List}\}\ \texttt{for}\ C_{all};$
25 : $\texttt{indicated}\ \{\ell_0 \mapsto \mathit{List}\}\ \texttt{for}$
26 : $\{\ell_0 \mapsto \mathit{List}\} \Rightarrow$
27 : $(\{\rho_p \mapsto \mathit{List}\} \Rightarrow \{\rho_h \mapsto \mathit{List}\})$
28 : $\otimes\{\rho_p \mapsto \langle ptr(\rho_y)\rangle\} \otimes \{\ell_0 \mapsto \mathit{List}\};$
29 : $\texttt{indicated}\ \{\ell_0 \mapsto \mathit{List}\}\ \texttt{for}$
30 : $\{\ell_0 \mapsto \mathit{List}\} \Rightarrow \{\rho_y \mapsto \mathit{List}\};$
31 : $\texttt{pack}_{[\rho_y|\{\rho_y \mapsto \mathit{List}\}]\texttt{as}\mathit{List}}(\rho_p);$
32 : $\texttt{indicated}\ \{\rho_p \mapsto \mathit{List}\}\ \texttt{for}$
33 : $\{\rho_p \mapsto \mathit{List}\} \Rightarrow \{\rho_h \mapsto \mathit{List}\};$

Figure 10. Tail-Recursive Append

3.1 List Append

Figure 10 shows a destructive and tail-recursive append function for null-terminated lists. It takes four arguments (shown in line 7). The argument h is a pointer to one list, and the argument y is a pointer to the other list that is destructively appended to the end of the first list. The argument p is a pointer to an element of the first list, and it is incremented each time the function is recursively called. The variable *cont* is a continuation.

As shown in line 5, the type of the lists is basically denoted by $\{\ell_0 \mapsto \mathit{List}\} \Rightarrow \{\rho_y \mapsto \mathit{List}\}$. The implication implies that the list at the location ρ_y is null-terminated. More specifically, the list can be accessed if the location ρ_y is not equal to ℓ_0, as described in the typing rules of Section 2.2.1. Here, we assume that the location ℓ_0 denotes the null pointer, that is, ℓ_0 is never available during program execution. It is important to note that this representation of null-terminated lists is more intuitive than that of the original alias type system, which uses the variant types [18].

The function first loads the pointer to the next element in the first list by using p (line 8), and it binds the variable x to it. If the pointer x is null, that is, if the end of the first list is reached, the second list is appended to the end of the first list by storing the pointer y in the last element (line 10). Then, the store type is adjusted via several coercion operations (line 11). After the coercion `reserve` (line 24), the entire store type is translated as follows (C_{all} denotes the entire store type here):

$$\begin{array}{l}\{\ell_0 \mapsto \mathit{List}\} \Rightarrow \\ \quad \{\ell_0 \mapsto \mathit{List}\} \otimes (\{\ell_0 \mapsto \mathit{List}\} \Rightarrow \\ \quad (\{\rho_p \mapsto \mathit{List}\} \Rightarrow \{\rho_h \mapsto \mathit{List}\}) \\ \quad \otimes\{\rho_p \mapsto \langle ptr(\rho_y)\rangle\} \otimes \{\ell_0 \mapsto \mathit{List}\}) \\ \quad \otimes(\{\ell_0 \mapsto \mathit{List}\} \Rightarrow \{\rho_y \mapsto \mathit{List}\}) \otimes \epsilon\end{array}$$

Then, the coercion `indicated` is performed (line 25), and the store type is translated as follows:

$$\begin{array}{l}\{\ell_0 \mapsto \mathit{List}\} \Rightarrow \\ \quad (\{\rho_p \mapsto \mathit{List}\} \Rightarrow \{\rho_h \mapsto \mathit{List}\}) \\ \quad \otimes\{\rho_p \mapsto \langle ptr(\rho_y)\rangle\} \otimes \{\ell_0 \mapsto \mathit{List}\} \\ \quad \otimes(\{\ell_0 \mapsto \mathit{List}\} \Rightarrow \{\rho_y \mapsto \mathit{List}\}) \otimes \epsilon\end{array}$$

Next, the coercion `indicated` is performed again (line 29), and the store type is translated as follows:

$$\begin{array}{l}\{\ell_0 \mapsto \mathit{List}\} \Rightarrow \\ \quad (\{\rho_p \mapsto \mathit{List}\} \Rightarrow \{\rho_h \mapsto \mathit{List}\}) \\ \quad \otimes\{\rho_p \mapsto \langle ptr(\rho_y)\rangle\} \otimes \{\rho_y \mapsto \mathit{List}\} \otimes \epsilon\end{array}$$

Now, the location ρ_p is packed (line 31), and the store type is translated as follows:

$$\begin{array}{l}\{\ell_0 \mapsto \mathit{List}\} \Rightarrow \\ \quad (\{\rho_p \mapsto \mathit{List}\} \Rightarrow \{\rho_h \mapsto \mathit{List}\}) \\ \quad \otimes\{\rho_p \mapsto \mathit{List}\} \otimes \epsilon\end{array}$$

Next, the coercion `indicated` is performed (line 32), and the store type is translated as follows:

$$\{\ell_0 \mapsto \mathit{List}\} \Rightarrow \{\rho_h \mapsto \mathit{List}\} \otimes \epsilon$$

Finally, the function returns the appended list (line 12).

If the pointer x is not null, the sublist of the first list pointed by x is unpacked (line 14). Then, the entire store type is translated as follows:

$$\begin{array}{l}(\{\ell_0 \mapsto \mathit{List}\} \Rightarrow \\ \quad (\{\rho_p \mapsto \mathit{List}\} \Rightarrow \{\rho_h \mapsto \mathit{List}\}) \\ \quad \otimes\{\rho_p \mapsto \langle ptr(\rho_x)\rangle\} \otimes \{\rho_x \mapsto \langle ptr(\rho_{xs})\rangle\} \otimes \{\rho_{xs} \mapsto \mathit{List}\}) \\ \quad \otimes(\{\ell_0 \mapsto \mathit{List}\} \Rightarrow \{\rho_y \mapsto \mathit{List}\}) \otimes \epsilon\end{array}$$

Next, the store type $\{\rho_x \mapsto \mathit{List}\}$ is reserved for $\{\rho_p \mapsto \langle ptr(\rho_x)\rangle\}$, and the location ρ_p is packed to *List* (lines 15 and 16, respectively). Then, the store type is translated as follows:

$$\begin{array}{l}(\{\ell_0 \mapsto \mathit{List}\} \Rightarrow \\ \quad (\{\rho_p \mapsto \mathit{List}\} \Rightarrow \{\rho_h \mapsto \mathit{List}\}) \\ \quad \otimes(\{\rho_x \mapsto \mathit{List}\} \Rightarrow \{\rho_p \mapsto \mathit{List}\}) \\ \quad \otimes\{\rho_x \mapsto \langle ptr(\rho_{xs})\rangle\} \otimes \{\rho_{xs} \mapsto \mathit{List}\}) \\ \quad \otimes(\{\ell_0 \mapsto \mathit{List}\} \Rightarrow \{\rho_y \mapsto \mathit{List}\}) \otimes \epsilon\end{array}$$

Next, the `trans` operation (lines 17 and 18) is performed, and the entire store type is finally translated as follows:

$$\begin{array}{l}(\{\ell_0 \mapsto \mathit{List}\} \Rightarrow \\ \quad (\{\rho_x \mapsto \mathit{List}\} \Rightarrow \{\rho_h \mapsto \mathit{List}\}) \\ \quad \otimes\{\rho_x \mapsto \langle ptr(\rho_{xs})\rangle\} \otimes \{\rho_{xs} \mapsto \mathit{List}\}) \\ \quad \otimes(\{\ell_0 \mapsto \mathit{List}\} \Rightarrow \{\rho_y \mapsto \mathit{List}\}) \otimes \epsilon\end{array}$$

Finally, the function calls itself tail-recursively (line 19). The tail-recursive call passes the type check because the entire store type satisfies the precondition of the append function by instantiating ρ_p with ρ_x and ρ_x with ρ_{xs}. In addition, its equality constraint is also satisfied because $\rho_x \neq \ell_0$, as derived from the `ifpeq` operation (line 9).

It is important to note here that the destructive list append function presented in this section is fully tail-recursive, unlike the one presented in [18]. As stated in [18], the list append function of [18] is not fully tail-recursive because each time the function calls itself recursively, it creates a new continuation by wrapping the passed continuation with several type coercions. Although the coercions can be erased at compilation time (as indicated in [18]), they cannot be omitted in the original alias type system.

At first glance, it seems to be possible to make the list append function of [18] fully tail-recursive, for example, by introducing an additional pointer that always points to the head of the original list. However, this is not the case in the original alias type system because it prohibits aliasing of locations in store types entirely. More specifically, a recursive data structure with two (or more) pointers that may point to the different elements cannot be implemented in a straightforward way.

For example, let us consider a list and a pair of pointers. In addition, let us also consider that the first pointer of the pair always points to the head of the list, and the second pointer points to one of the elements in the list. First, assume that both the pointers point to the head of the list as follows:

$$\{\rho_p \mapsto \langle ptr(\rho_h), ptr(\rho_h)\rangle\} \otimes \{\rho_h \mapsto \mathit{List}\}$$

Next, let us consider to make the second pointer point to the second element of the list. In order to obtain the location of the second element of the list, it is necessary to unpack the location ρ_h. Then, the store type is updated as follows:

$$\begin{array}{l}\{\rho_p \mapsto \langle ptr(\rho_h), ptr(\rho'_h)\rangle\}\\ \otimes\{\rho_h \mapsto \langle ptr(\rho_{h'})\rangle\} \otimes \{\rho_{h'} \mapsto \mathit{List}\}\end{array}$$

At this point, although the pointer to the first element of the list is not modified, the store type forgets that the pointer points to the list. In order to revert the type of the location ρ_h, it is necessary to pack the location ρ_h. Then, the store type is translated as follows:

$$\{\rho_p \mapsto \langle ptr(\rho_h), ptr(\rho'_h)\rangle\} \otimes \{\rho_h \mapsto \mathit{List}\}$$

Now, the store type remembers that the first pointer of the pair points to the first element of the list. However, the store type forgets that the second pointer points to the second element of the list.

On the other hand, in the proposed type system, the list and the pair of the pointers can be concisely represented using a separating implication as follows:

$$\begin{array}{l}\{\rho_p \mapsto \langle ptr(\rho_h), ptr(\rho'_h)\rangle\}\\ \otimes(\{\rho_{h'} \mapsto \mathit{List}\} \Rightarrow \{\rho_h \mapsto \mathit{List}\}) \otimes \{\rho'_h \mapsto \mathit{List}\}\end{array}$$

3.2 FIFO Queue

An implementation of a FIFO queue is shown in Figures 11 and 12. Both the functions *enqueue* and *dequeue* are constant-time functions. In these functions, we use the following type abbreviations:

$$\begin{array}{rcl}\mathit{List} & \equiv & \exists[\rho|\{\rho \mapsto \mathit{List}\}].\,\langle int, ptr(\rho)\rangle\\ \tau_c[\epsilon] & \equiv & \forall[\rho_q, \rho_h|(\{\rho_q \mapsto \mathit{List}\} \Rightarrow \{\rho_h \mapsto \mathit{List}\})\otimes\\ & & \quad\{\rho_q \mapsto \langle \mathcal{S}(0), ptr(\rho_h)\rangle\} \otimes \epsilon].\\ & & \qquad(r : int, q : ptr(\rho_q)) \to \mathbf{0}\end{array}$$

The type *List* denotes singly-linked lists of integers, and the type τ_c denotes the type of the continuations of the functions.

The queue is represented by the store type $(\{\rho_q \mapsto \mathit{List}\} \Rightarrow \{\rho_h \mapsto \mathit{List}\}) \otimes \{\rho_q \mapsto \langle \mathcal{S}(0), ptr(\rho_h)\rangle\}$. In the store type, ρ_q denotes the tail of the queue, and it contains the pointer to ρ_h, the head of the queue. If $\rho_q = \rho_h$, the queue is empty. It is important to note that if $\rho_q = \rho_h$, the implication in the store type is equivalent to $\{\rho_q \mapsto \mathit{List}\} \Rightarrow \{\rho_q \mapsto \mathit{List}\}$, which denotes an empty store.

The *enqueue* function is shown in Figure 11. It takes three arguments (line 4). The argument q is a queue to be manipulated, and the argument x is an integer value to be enqueued. The argument *cont* is a continuation of the function. The function first binds the variable h to the head of the queue (line 5). Next, it allocates a new tuple, and it binds the variable n to the pointer to the tuple (line 6). It also initializes the second field of the tuple with the pointer to the head of the queue (line 8). Then, it concatenates the allocated tuple to the tail of the queue (lines 9 and 10). Next, it reserves $\{\rho_n \mapsto \mathit{List}\}$ for $\{\rho_q \mapsto \langle int, \rho_n\rangle\}$ (line 11). Then, the entire store type is updated as follows:

$$\begin{array}{l}(\{\rho_q \mapsto \mathit{List}\} \Rightarrow \{\rho_h \mapsto \mathit{List}\})\otimes\\ (\{\rho_n \mapsto \mathit{List}\} \Rightarrow \{\rho_q \mapsto \langle int, ptr(\rho_n)\rangle\} \otimes \{\rho_n \mapsto \mathit{List}\})\otimes\\ \{\rho_n \mapsto \langle \mathcal{S}(0), ptr(\rho_h)\rangle\} \otimes \epsilon\end{array}$$

Next, it packs the tuple at the location ρ_q (line 12), and the store type is translated as follows:

$$\begin{array}{l}(\{\rho_q \mapsto \mathit{List}\} \Rightarrow \{\rho_h \mapsto \mathit{List}\})\otimes\\ (\{\rho_n \mapsto \mathit{List}\} \Rightarrow \{\rho_q \mapsto \mathit{List}\})\otimes\\ \{\rho_n \mapsto \langle \mathcal{S}(0), ptr(\rho_h)\rangle\} \otimes \epsilon\end{array}$$

Then, it concatenates the two separating implications via `trans` (lines 13 and 14) as follows:

$$\begin{array}{l}(\{\rho_n \mapsto \mathit{List}\} \Rightarrow \{\rho_h \mapsto \mathit{List}\})\otimes\\ \{\rho_n \mapsto \langle \mathcal{S}(0), ptr(\rho_h)\rangle\} \otimes \epsilon\end{array}$$

Finally, the function returns the updated queue (line 14) by instantiating ρ_q with ρ_n.

$$\begin{array}{rl}
1: & \texttt{fix}\ enqueue[\rho_h, \rho_q, \epsilon|\\
2: & \quad(\{\rho_q \mapsto \mathit{List}\} \Rightarrow \{\rho_h \mapsto \mathit{List}\})\otimes\\
3: & \quad\{\rho_q \mapsto \langle \mathcal{S}(0), ptr(\rho_h)\rangle\} \otimes \epsilon]\\
4: & \quad(q : ptr(\rho_q), x : int, cont : \tau_c[\epsilon]).\\
5: & \quad\texttt{let}\ h = (q).2;\\
6: & \quad\texttt{new}\ \rho_n, n, 2;\\
7: & \quad(n).1 := 0;\\
8: & \quad(n).2 := h;\\
9: & \quad(q).1 := x;\\
10: & \quad(q).2 := n;\\
11: & \quad\texttt{reserve}\ \{\rho_n \mapsto \mathit{List}\}\ \texttt{for}\ \{\rho_q \mapsto \langle int, \rho_n\rangle\};\\
12: & \quad\texttt{pack}_{[\rho_n|\{\rho_n \mapsto \mathit{List}\}]\mathrm{as}\mathit{List}}(\rho_q);\\
13: & \quad\texttt{trans}\ \{\rho_n \mapsto \mathit{List}\} \Rightarrow \{\rho_q \mapsto \mathit{List}\}\ \texttt{with}\\
14: & \qquad\qquad\{\rho_q \mapsto \mathit{List}\} \Rightarrow \{\rho_h \mapsto \mathit{List}\};\\
15: & \quad cont[\rho_n, \rho_h](0, n)
\end{array}$$

Figure 11. Enqueue

The *dequeue* function is shown in Figure 12. It takes two arguments (line 4). The argument q is a queue to be manipulated, and the argument *cont* is a continuation of the function. The function first binds the variable h to the head of the queue (line 5). Next, it checks whether the queue is empty (line 6). If the queue is empty, it returns the integer value -1 (line 7). Otherwise, it unpacks the first element of the queue (line 9). Then, the entire store type is translated as follows:

$$\begin{array}{l}(\{\rho_q \mapsto \mathit{List}\} \Rightarrow \{\rho_h \mapsto \langle int, ptr(\rho_n)\rangle\} \otimes \{\rho_n \mapsto \mathit{List}\})\otimes\\ \{\rho_q \mapsto \langle \mathcal{S}(0), ptr(\rho_h)\rangle\} \otimes \epsilon\end{array}$$

It is important to note that `unpacking` is possible because of the last rule of Figure 8, described in Section 2.2.1. Next, it binds the variable r to the stored integer (line 10) and the variable n to the pointer to the next element (line 11). Then, it unlinks and deallocates the first element (lines 12 and 13), and the entire store type is translated as follows:

$$\begin{array}{l}(\{\rho_q \mapsto \mathit{List}\} \Rightarrow \{\rho_n \mapsto \mathit{List}\})\otimes\\ \{\rho_q \mapsto \langle \mathcal{S}(0), ptr(\rho_n)\rangle\} \otimes \epsilon\end{array}$$

Finally, the function returns the stored integer and the updated queue (line 14) by instantiating ρ_h with ρ_n.

3.3 Deletion from a Binary Search Tree

An implementation of deletion from a binary search tree is shown in Figures 13, 14, 15, 16, and 17. The main function (*delete_bst*)

```
 1:    fix dequeue[ρ_h, ρ_q, ε|
 2:        ({ρ_q ↦ List} ⇒ {ρ_h ↦ List})⊗
 3:        {ρ_q ↦ ⟨S(0), ptr(ρ_h)⟩} ⊗ ε]
 4:        (q : ptr(ρ_q), cont : τ_c[ε]).
 5:    let h = (q).2;
 6:    ifpeq q = h then
 7:        cont[ρ_q, ρ_h](-1, q);
 8:    else
 9:        unpack ρ_h with ρ_n;
10:        let r = (h).1;
11:        let n = (h).2;
12:        (q).2 := n;
13:        free h;
14:        cont[ρ_q, ρ_n](r, q)
```

Figure 12. Dequeue

is shown in Figure 13. The auxiliary functions (*delete_aux*, *delete_aux_left*, and *delete_aux_right*) used in *delete_bst* are shown in Figures 14, 15, and 16, respectively. The *search_max* function that finds the maximum value from a binary search tree is shown in Figure 17.

The *delete_bst* function takes five arguments (shown in lines 6 and 7). The argument h is a pointer to the root node of a binary search tree, and the argument p is a pointer to a node that is to be examined in the binary search tree. The argument p' is a pointer to the parent node of the node pointed by p, and the argument i is an integer value to be deleted from the binary search tree. The argument *cont* is a continuation.

As shown in lines 33 and 34, the type of the binary search trees is defined using a variant type. The first element of the variant type denotes leaf nodes, and the second element denotes intermediate nodes. An intermediate node consists of three elements. The first element denotes an integer value stored in the node. The second and third elements denote left and right subtrees, respectively. It is important to note that, although variant types are not handled in the proposed language presented in Section 2, it should be straightforward to extend it with variant types, in the same way as in [18].

The store type of lines 2 to 5 specifies the precondition of the function in the same way as in Sections 3.1 and 3.2, except for the location $ρ_{p'}$. As shown in lines 3 and 4, the type of the value at the location $ρ_{p'}$ is denoted as a variant type. This is because there are two cases how the node pointed by p is reached from its parent node pointed by p': its left child and its right subtree. The variant type is utilized in order to handle the two cases uniformly by the single function *delete_bst*.

The function *delete_bst* first examines the node pointed by p whether it is a leaf node or an intermediate node (line 8). If the node is a leaf, the location $ρ_{p'}$ is packed (line 10), and the store type is translated as follows:

$$({ρ_{p'} ↦ Tree} ⇒ {ρ_h ↦ Tree}) ⊗ {ρ_{p'} ↦ Tree} ⊗ ε$$

Next, the coercion **indicated** is performed (lines 11 and 12), and the store type is translated as follows:

$${ρ_h ↦ Tree} ⊗ ε$$

Finally, the function returns the binary search tree pointed by h (line 13).

Otherwise, if the node is an intermediate node, the location pointed by p is unpacked (line 15). Then, the entire store type is

```
 1:    fix delete_bst[ρ_h, ρ_{p'}, ρ_p, ρ_q, ε|
 2:        ({ρ_{p'} ↦ Tree} ⇒ {ρ_h ↦ Tree})
 3:        ⊗{ρ_{p'} ↦ ⟨int, ptr(ρ_p), ptr(ρ_q)⟩
 4:                ∪ ⟨int, ptr(ρ_q), ptr(ρ_p)⟩}
 5:        ⊗{ρ_p ↦ Tree} ⊗ {ρ_q ↦ Tree} ⊗ ε]
 6:        (h : ptr(ρ_h), p : ptr(ρ_p), p' : ptr(ρ_{p'}),
 7:            i : int, cont : τ_c[ρ_h, ε]).
 8:    case p of
 9:    ( inl ⟶
10:        pack_{[ρ_p,ρ_q|{ρ_p↦Tree}⊗{ρ_q↦Tree}]asTree}(ρ_{p'});
11:        indicated {ρ_{p'} ↦ Tree} for
12:            {ρ_{p'} ↦ Tree} ⇒ {ρ_h ↦ Tree};
13:        cont(h)
14:    | inr ⟶
15:        unpack ρ_p with ρ_{pl}, ρ_{pr};
16:        let x = (p).1;
17:        if i = x then
18:            delete_aux[ρ_h, ρ_{p'}, ρ_p, ρ_q, ρ_{pl}, ρ_{pr}, ε](h, p, p', cont)
19:        else
20:            reserve {ρ_p ↦ Tree} for {ρ_q ↦ Tree}
21:                ⊗{ρ_{p'} ↦ ⟨int, ptr(ρ_p), ptr(ρ_q)⟩
22:                    ∪ ⟨int, ptr(ρ_q), ptr(ρ_p)⟩};
23:            pack_{[ρ_p,ρ_q|{ρ_p↦Tree}⊗{ρ_q↦Tree}]asTree}(ρ_{p'});
24:            trans {ρ_p ↦ Tree} ⇒ {ρ_{p'} ↦ Tree} with
25:                {ρ_{p'} ↦ Tree} ⇒ {ρ_h ↦ Tree};
26:            if i < x then
27:                let pl = (p).2;
28:                delete_bst[ρ_h, ρ_p, ρ_{pl}, ρ_{pr}, ε](h, pl, p, i, cont)
29:            else
30:                let pr = (p).3;
31:                delete_bst[ρ_h, ρ_p, ρ_{pr}, ρ_{pl}, ε](h, pr, p, i, cont)
32:    )
where
33:    Tree ≡ ⟨⟩ ∪ ∃[ρ_{pl}, ρ_{pr}|{ρ_{pl} ↦ Tree} ⊗ {ρ_{pr} ↦ Tree}].
34:        ⟨int, ptr(ρ_{pl}), ptr(ρ_{pr})⟩
35:    τ_c[ρ, ε] ≡ ∀[|{ρ ↦ Tree} ⊗ ε].(a : ptr(ρ)) → 0
```

Figure 13. Deletion from a Binary Search Tree

translated as follows:

$$({ρ_{p'} ↦ Tree} ⇒ {ρ_h ↦ Tree})$$
$$⊗{ρ_{p'} ↦ ⟨int, ptr(ρ_p), ptr(ρ_q)⟩ ∪ ⟨int, ptr(ρ_q), ptr(ρ_p)⟩}$$
$$⊗{ρ_p ↦ ⟨int, ptr(ρ_{pl}), ptr(ρ_{pr})⟩} ⊗ {ρ_{pl} ↦ Tree}$$
$$⊗{ρ_{pr} ↦ Tree} ⊗ {ρ_q ↦ Tree} ⊗ ε$$

Next, the integer value stored in the node pointed by p is examined (lines 16 and 17). If the value is equal to the value to be deleted (i), the auxiliary function *delete_aux* (shown in Figure 14) is called (line 18).

Otherwise, if the value is not equal to the value to be deleted (line 19), the coercion **reserve** first translates the store type as follows (lines 20 to 22):

$$({ρ_{p'} ↦ Tree} ⇒ {ρ_h ↦ Tree})$$
$$⊗({ρ_p ↦ Tree} ⇒ {ρ_p ↦ Tree} ⊗ {ρ_q ↦ Tree}$$
$$⊗{ρ_{p'} ↦ ⟨int, ptr(ρ_p), ptr(ρ_q)⟩ ∪ ⟨int, ptr(ρ_q), ptr(ρ_p)⟩})$$
$$⊗{ρ_p ↦ ⟨int, ptr(ρ_{pl}), ptr(ρ_{pr})⟩} ⊗ {ρ_{pl} ↦ Tree}$$
$$⊗{ρ_{pr} ↦ Tree} ⊗ ε$$

Next, the location $ρ_{p'}$ is packed (line 23), and the entire store type is translated as follows:

$$({ρ_{p'} ↦ Tree} ⇒ {ρ_h ↦ Tree})$$
$$⊗({ρ_p ↦ Tree} ⇒ {ρ_{p'} ↦ Tree})$$
$$⊗{ρ_p ↦ ⟨int, ptr(ρ_{pl}), ptr(ρ_{pr})⟩} ⊗ {ρ_{pl} ↦ Tree}$$
$$⊗{ρ_{pr} ↦ Tree} ⊗ ε$$

```
 1 :  fix delete_aux[ρ_h, ρ_p', ρ_p, ρ_q, ρ_pl, ρ_pr, ε]
 2 :    ({ρ_p' ↦ Tree} ⇒ {ρ_h ↦ Tree})
 3 :    ⊗{ρ_p' ↦ ⟨int, ptr(ρ_p), ptr(ρ_q)⟩
 4 :              ∪ ⟨int, ptr(ρ_q), ptr(ρ_p)⟩}
 5 :    ⊗{ρ_p ↦ ⟨int, ptr(ρ_pl), ptr(ρ_pr)⟩} ⊗ {ρ_pl ↦ Tree}
 6 :    ⊗{ρ_pr ↦ Tree} ⊗ {ρ_q ↦ Tree} ⊗ ε]
 7 :    (h : ptr(ρ_h), p : ptr(ρ_p), p' : ptr(ρ_p'),
 8 :      cont : τ_c[ρ_h, ε]).
 9 :  case p' of
10 :  ( inl ⟶
11 :     delete_aux_left[ρ_h, ρ_p', ρ_p, ρ_q, ρ_pl, ρ_pr, ε]
12 :        (h, p, p', cont)
13 :  | inr ⟶
14 :     delete_aux_right[ρ_h, ρ_p', ρ_p, ρ_q, ρ_pl, ρ_pr, ε]
15 :        (h, p, p', cont)
16 :  )
```

Figure 14. Auxiliary Function for Deletion from a Binary Search Tree (1 of 3)

Then, the two separating implications are concatenated via `trans` (lines 24 and 25) as follows:

$$\begin{aligned}&(\{\rho_p \mapsto \mathit{Tree}\} \Rightarrow \{\rho_h \mapsto \mathit{Tree}\})\\ &\otimes\{\rho_p \mapsto \langle int, ptr(\rho_{pl}), ptr(\rho_{pr})\rangle\} \otimes \{\rho_{pl} \mapsto \mathit{Tree}\}\\ &\otimes\{\rho_{pr} \mapsto \mathit{Tree}\} \otimes \epsilon\end{aligned}$$

Finally, the function determines which subtree should be examined next (line 26), and calls itself tail-recursively (lines 28 and 31).

The *delete_aux* function (shown in Figure 14) does almost nothing but call one of the two auxiliary functions (*delete_aux_left* or *delete_aux_right*), depending on how the node pointed by p is reached from its parent node (line 9). If it is in the left subtree of the parent node, *delete_aux_left* is called (lines 11 and 12). Otherwise, *delete_aux_right* is called (lines 14 and 15).

The *delete_aux_left* function (shown in Figure 15) first examines whether the left subtree of the node pointed by p is a leaf or not (lines 8 and 10). If it is a leaf, the function stores the pointer to the right subtree in the parent node pointed by p' (line 12), and frees the node pointed by p and the leaf (lines 13 and 14). Next, the location $\rho_{p'}$ is packed (line 15), and the store type is translated as follows:

$$(\{\rho_{p'} \mapsto \mathit{Tree}\} \Rightarrow \{\rho_h \mapsto \mathit{Tree}\}) \otimes \{\rho_{p'} \mapsto \mathit{Tree}\} \otimes \epsilon$$

Then, the coercion `indicated` is performed (lines 16 and 17), and the entire store type is translated as follows:

$$\{\rho_h \mapsto \mathit{Tree}\} \otimes \epsilon$$

Finally, the function returns the binary search tree pointed by h (line 18). It is important to note that the continuation *cont* is the one passed to *delete_bst*, that is, it directly returns to the caller of *delete_bst*.

If the left subtree is an intermediate node, the function examines whether the right subtree is a leaf or not (lines 9 and 20). If the right subtree is a leaf, the function does the same as lines 12 to 18, except that the function stores the pointer to the left subtree in the parent node (line 22).

Otherwise, if both of the subtrees are intermediate nodes, the coercion `reserve` (line 30 and 31) first translates the entire store type as follows:

$$\begin{aligned}&(\{\rho_{p'} \mapsto \mathit{Tree}\} \Rightarrow \{\rho_h \mapsto \mathit{Tree}\})\\ &\otimes(\{\rho_p \mapsto \mathit{Tree}\} \Rightarrow \{\rho_p \mapsto \mathit{Tree}\} \otimes \{\rho_q \mapsto \mathit{Tree}\}\\ &\quad\otimes\{\rho_{p'} \mapsto \langle int, ptr(\rho_p), ptr(\rho_q)\rangle\})\\ &\otimes\{\rho_p \mapsto \langle int, ptr(\rho_{pl}), ptr(\rho_{pr})\rangle\} \otimes \{\rho_{pl} \mapsto \mathit{Tree}\}\\ &\otimes\{\rho_{pr} \mapsto \mathit{Tree}\} \otimes \epsilon\end{aligned}$$

```
 1 :  fix delete_aux_left[ρ_h, ρ_p', ρ_p, ρ_q, ρ_pl, ρ_pr, ε]
 2 :    ({ρ_p' ↦ Tree} ⇒ {ρ_h ↦ Tree})
 3 :    ⊗{ρ_p' ↦ ⟨int, ptr(ρ_p), ptr(ρ_q)⟩}
 4 :    ⊗{ρ_p ↦ ⟨int, ptr(ρ_pl), ptr(ρ_pr)⟩} ⊗ {ρ_pl ↦ Tree}
 5 :    ⊗{ρ_pr ↦ Tree} ⊗ {ρ_q ↦ Tree} ⊗ ε]
 6 :    (h : ptr(ρ_h), p : ptr(ρ_p), p' : ptr(ρ_p'),
 7 :      cont : τ_c[ρ_h, ε]).
 8 :  let pl = (p).2;
 9 :  let pr = (p).3;
10 :  case pl of
11 :  ( inl ⟶
12 :     (p').2 := pr;
13 :     free p;
14 :     free pl;
15 :     pack_[ρ_pr, ρ_q | {ρ_pr ↦ Tree} ⊗ {ρ_q ↦ Tree}] as Tree (p');
16 :     indicated {ρ_p' ↦ Tree} for
17 :       {ρ_p' ↦ Tree} ⇒ {ρ_h ↦ Tree};
18 :     cont(h)
19 :  | inr ⟶
20 :     case pr of
21 :     ( inl ⟶
22 :        (p').2 := pl;
23 :        free p;
24 :        free pr;
25 :        pack_[ρ_pl, ρ_q | {ρ_pl ↦ Tree} ⊗ {ρ_q ↦ Tree}] as Tree (p');
26 :        indicated {ρ_p' ↦ Tree} for
27 :          {ρ_p' ↦ Tree} ⇒ {ρ_h ↦ Tree};
28 :        cont(h)
29 :     | inr ⟶
30 :        reserve {ρ_p ↦ Tree} for {ρ_q ↦ Tree}
31 :          ⊗{ρ_p' ↦ ⟨int, ptr(ρ_p), ptr(ρ_q)⟩};
32 :        pack_[ρ_p, ρ_q | {ρ_p ↦ Tree} ⊗ {ρ_q ↦ Tree}] as Tree (ρ_p');
33 :        trans {ρ_p ↦ Tree} ⇒ {ρ_p' ↦ Tree} with
34 :            {ρ_p' ↦ Tree} ⇒ {ρ_h ↦ Tree};
35 :        reserve {ρ_pl ↦ Tree} for ·;
36 :        search_max[ρ_pl, ρ_pl, {ρ_pr ↦ Tree} ⊗ ε
37 :            ⊗({ρ_p ↦ Tree} ⇒ {ρ_h ↦ Tree})
38 :            ⊗{ρ_p ↦ ⟨int, ptr(ρ_pl), ptr(ρ_pr)⟩}]
39 :          (pl, min_int,
40 :            fix cont'[|{ρ_pr ↦ Tree} ⊗ ε
41 :              ({ρ_p ↦ Tree} ⇒ {ρ_h ↦ Tree})
42 :              ⊗{ρ_p ↦ Tree} ⊗ {ρ_pl ↦ Tree}](m : int).
43 :            (p).1 := m;
44 :            delete_bst[ρ_h, ρ_p, ρ_pl, ρ_pr, ε](h, pl, p, m, cont)
45 :          )
46 :     )
47 :  )
```

Figure 15. Auxiliary Function for Deletion from a Binary Search Tree (2 of 3)

Next, the location $\rho_{p'}$ is packed (line 32) as follows:

$$\begin{aligned}&(\{\rho_{p'} \mapsto \mathit{Tree}\} \Rightarrow \{\rho_h \mapsto \mathit{Tree}\})\\ &\otimes(\{\rho_p \mapsto \mathit{Tree}\} \Rightarrow \{\rho_{p'} \mapsto \mathit{Tree}\})\\ &\otimes\{\rho_p \mapsto \langle \mathit{int}, \mathit{ptr}(\rho_{pl}), \mathit{ptr}(\rho_{pr})\rangle\} \otimes \{\rho_{pl} \mapsto \mathit{Tree}\}\\ &\otimes\{\rho_{pr} \mapsto \mathit{Tree}\} \otimes \epsilon\end{aligned}$$

Then, the coercion **trans** (lines 33 and 34) translates the entire store type as follows:

$$\begin{aligned}&(\{\rho_p \mapsto \mathit{Tree}\} \Rightarrow \{\rho_h \mapsto \mathit{Tree}\})\\ &\otimes\{\rho_p \mapsto \langle \mathit{int}, \mathit{ptr}(\rho_{pl}), \mathit{ptr}(\rho_{pr})\rangle\} \otimes \{\rho_{pl} \mapsto \mathit{Tree}\}\\ &\otimes\{\rho_{pr} \mapsto \mathit{Tree}\} \otimes \epsilon\end{aligned}$$

Next, the coercion **reserve** (line 35) introduces a seemingly useless separating implication that is necessary to call *search_max* (shown in Figure 17) as follows:

$$\begin{aligned}&(\{\rho_p \mapsto \mathit{Tree}\} \Rightarrow \{\rho_h \mapsto \mathit{Tree}\})\\ &\otimes\{\rho_p \mapsto \langle \mathit{int}, \mathit{ptr}(\rho_{pl}), \mathit{ptr}(\rho_{pr})\rangle\} \otimes \{\rho_{pl} \mapsto \mathit{Tree}\}\\ &\otimes\{\rho_{pr} \mapsto \mathit{Tree}\} \otimes \epsilon\\ &\otimes(\{\rho_{pl} \mapsto \mathit{Tree}\} \Rightarrow \{\rho_{pl} \mapsto \mathit{Tree}\})\end{aligned}$$

Then, it calls *search_max* in order to get the maximum value in the left subtree (lines 36 to 45), and the value is stored in the node pointed by p (line 43). Finally, it calls *delete_bst* tail-recursively in order to delete the maximum value from the left subtree (line 44).

The *delete_aux_right* function (shown in Figure 16) is almost the same as *delete_aux_left* except for that it is used when the node pointed by p is in the right subtree of the parent node pointed by p'. More specifically, if one of the subtrees of the node pointed by p is a leaf, the pointer to the other subtree is stored to the third element of the parent node pointed by p' (lines 12 and 22), instead of the second element.

search_max is a tail-recursive function that returns the maximum value stored in a binary search tree (shown in Figure 17). It first examines the tree pointed by p whether the tree is a leaf or not (line 5). If the tree is a leaf, the coercion **indicated** translates the store type as follows (lines 7 and 8):

$$\{\rho_h \mapsto \mathit{Tree}\} \otimes \epsilon$$

Finally, the function returns the integer value m (line 9). It is important to note here that the second argument of the function holds the maximum value in the tree pointed by h, excluding the subtree pointed by p.

Otherwise, the location ρ_p is unpacked (line 11), and the entire store type is translated as follows:

$$\begin{aligned}&(\{\rho_p \mapsto \mathit{Tree}\} \Rightarrow \{\rho_h \mapsto \mathit{Tree}\})\\ &\otimes\{\rho_p \mapsto \langle \mathit{int}, \mathit{ptr}(\rho_{pl}), \mathit{ptr}(\rho_{pr})\rangle\}\\ &\otimes\{\rho_{pl} \mapsto \mathit{Tree}\} \otimes \{\rho_{pr} \mapsto \mathit{Tree}\} \otimes \epsilon\end{aligned}$$

Next, the coercion **reserve** translates the store type as follows (lines 14 and 15):

$$\begin{aligned}&(\{\rho_p \mapsto \mathit{Tree}\} \Rightarrow \{\rho_h \mapsto \mathit{Tree}\})\\ &\otimes(\{\rho_{pr} \mapsto \mathit{Tree}\} \Rightarrow \{\rho_p \mapsto \langle \mathit{int}, \mathit{ptr}(\rho_{pl}), \mathit{ptr}(\rho_{pr})\rangle\}\\ &\quad\otimes\{\rho_{pl} \mapsto \mathit{Tree}\} \otimes \{\rho_{pr} \mapsto \mathit{Tree}\})\\ &\otimes\{\rho_{pr} \mapsto \mathit{Tree}\} \otimes \epsilon\end{aligned}$$

Then, the location ρ_p is packed as follows (line 16):

$$\begin{aligned}&(\{\rho_p \mapsto \mathit{Tree}\} \Rightarrow \{\rho_h \mapsto \mathit{Tree}\})\\ &\otimes(\{\rho_{pr} \mapsto \mathit{Tree}\} \Rightarrow \{\rho_p \mapsto \mathit{Tree}\}) \otimes \{\rho_{pr} \mapsto \mathit{Tree}\} \otimes \epsilon\end{aligned}$$

Now, the **trans** operation (lines 17 and 18) is performed, and the entire store type is finally translated as follows:

$$(\{\rho_{pr} \mapsto \mathit{Tree}\} \Rightarrow \{\rho_h \mapsto \mathit{Tree}\}) \otimes \{\rho_{pr} \mapsto \mathit{Tree}\} \otimes \epsilon$$

Finally, the function calls itself tail-recursively (line 19) by instantiating ρ_p with ρ_{pr}.

```
 1 :  fix delete_aux_right[ρ_h, ρ_p', ρ_p, ρ_q, ρ_pl, ρ_pr, ε|
 2 :    ({ρ_p' ↦ Tree} ⇒ {ρ_h ↦ Tree})
 3 :    ⊗{ρ_p' ↦ ⟨int, ptr(ρ_q), ptr(ρ_p)⟩}
 4 :    ⊗{ρ_p ↦ ⟨int, ptr(ρ_pl), ptr(ρ_pr)⟩} ⊗ {ρ_pl ↦ Tree}
 5 :    ⊗{ρ_pr ↦ Tree} ⊗ {ρ_q ↦ Tree} ⊗ ε]
 6 :    (h : ptr(ρ_h), p : ptr(ρ_p), p' : ptr(ρ_p'),
 7 :      cont : τ_c[ρ_h, ε]).
 8 :  let pl = (p).2;
 9 :  let pr = (p).3;
10 :  case pl of
11 :  ( inl ⟶
12 :    (p').3 := pr;
13 :    free p;
14 :    free pl;
15 :    pack[ρ_pr, ρ_q | {ρ_pr ↦ Tree} ⊗ {ρ_q ↦ Tree}] as Tree(p');
16 :    indicated {ρ_p' ↦ Tree} for
17 :      {ρ_p' ↦ Tree} ⇒ {ρ_h ↦ Tree};
18 :    cont(h)
19 :  | inr ⟶
20 :    case pr of
21 :    ( inl ⟶
22 :      (p').3 := pl;
23 :      free p;
24 :      free pr;
25 :      pack[ρ_pl, ρ_q | {ρ_pl ↦ Tree} ⊗ {ρ_q ↦ Tree}] as Tree(p');
26 :      indicated {ρ_p' ↦ Tree} for
27 :        {ρ_p' ↦ Tree} ⇒ {ρ_h ↦ Tree};
28 :      cont(h)
29 :    | inr ⟶
30 :      reserve {ρ_p ↦ Tree} for {ρ_q ↦ Tree}
31 :        ⊗{ρ_p' ↦ ⟨int, ptr(ρ_p), ptr(ρ_q)⟩};
32 :      pack[ρ_p, ρ_q | {ρ_p ↦ Tree} ⊗ {ρ_q ↦ Tree}] as Tree(ρ_p');
33 :      trans {ρ_p ↦ Tree} ⇒ {ρ_p' ↦ Tree} with
34 :        {ρ_p' ↦ Tree} ⇒ {ρ_h ↦ Tree};
35 :      reserve {ρ_pl ↦ Tree} for ·;
36 :      search_max[ρ_pl, ρ_pl, {ρ_pr ↦ Tree} ⊗ ε
37 :          ⊗({ρ_p ↦ Tree} ⇒ {ρ_h ↦ Tree})
38 :          ⊗{ρ_p ↦ ⟨int, ptr(ρ_pl), ptr(ρ_pr)⟩}]
39 :      (pl, min_int,
40 :        fix cont'[|{ρ_pr ↦ Tree} ⊗ ε
41 :          ({ρ_p ↦ Tree} ⇒ {ρ_h ↦ Tree})
42 :          ⊗{ρ_p ↦ Tree} ⊗ {ρ_pl ↦ Tree}](m : int).
43 :        (p).1 := m;
44 :        delete_bst[ρ_h, ρ_p, ρ_pl, ρ_pr, ε](h, pl, p, m, cont)
45 :        )
46 :    )
47 :  )
```

Figure 16. Auxiliary Function for Deletion from a Binary Search Tree (3 of 3)

$$
\begin{array}{l}
\texttt{fix}\ \mathit{search\_max}[\rho_h, \rho_p, \epsilon| \\
\quad (\{\rho_p \mapsto \mathit{Tree}\} \Rightarrow \{\rho_h \mapsto \mathit{Tree}\}) \\
\quad \otimes\{\rho_p \mapsto \mathit{Tree}\} \otimes \epsilon] \\
\quad (p : \mathit{ptr}(\rho_p), m : \mathit{int}, \mathit{cont} : \tau_c'[\rho_h, \epsilon]). \\
\texttt{case}\ p\ \texttt{of} \\
(\ \texttt{inl} \longrightarrow \\
\quad \texttt{indicated}\ \{\rho_p \mapsto \mathit{Tree}\}\ \texttt{for} \\
\qquad \{\rho_p \mapsto \mathit{Tree}\} \Rightarrow \{\rho_h \mapsto \mathit{Tree}\}; \\
\quad \mathit{cont}(m) \\
|\ \texttt{inr} \longrightarrow \\
\quad \texttt{unpack}\ \rho_p\ \texttt{with}\ \rho_{pl}, \rho_{pr}; \\
\quad \texttt{let}\ x = (p).1; \\
\quad \texttt{let}\ pr = (p).3; \\
\quad \texttt{reserve}\ \{\rho_{pr} \mapsto \mathit{Tree}\}\ \texttt{for}\ \{\rho_{pl} \mapsto \mathit{Tree}\} \\
\qquad \otimes\{\rho_p \mapsto \langle \mathit{int}, \mathit{ptr}(\rho_{pl}), \mathit{ptr}(\rho_{pr})\rangle\}; \\
\quad \texttt{pack}_{[\rho_{pl}, \rho_{pr} | \{\rho_{pl} \mapsto \mathit{Tree}\} \otimes \{\rho_{pr} \mapsto \mathit{Tree}\}]\,\mathrm{as}\,\mathit{Tree}}(\rho_p); \\
\quad \texttt{trans}\ \{\rho_{pr} \mapsto \mathit{Tree}\} \Rightarrow \{\rho_p \mapsto \mathit{Tree}\}\ \texttt{with} \\
\qquad \{\rho_p \mapsto \mathit{Tree}\} \Rightarrow \{\rho_h \mapsto \mathit{Tree}\}; \\
\quad \mathit{search\_max}[\rho_h, \rho_{pr}, \epsilon](pr, x, \mathit{cont}) \\
) \\
\mathit{where} \\
\tau_c'[\rho, \epsilon] \equiv \forall[|\{\rho \mapsto \mathit{Tree}\} \otimes \epsilon].(m : \mathit{int}) \rightarrow \mathbf{0}
\end{array}
$$

Figure 17. Search Maximum Value from a Binary Search Tree

It is important to note that, in a strict sense, the implementation of deletion from a binary search tree shown in this section is not fully tail-recursive because it creates a continuation as an argument for *search_max* in *delete_aux_left* and *delete_aux_right*. However, the implementation only takes constant space regardless of the size of a binary search tree because *search_max* is tail-recursive and does not call any other function except for the continuation.

4. Related Work

Linear types [16, 17] are type systems based on linear logic. They statically detect values that are used exactly once, and they deallocate their memory regions immediately after they are used. Linear types have two drawbacks from the view point of explicit memory management. First, many common data structures using pointer aliasing cannot be expressed using linear type systems because they effectively prohibit pointer aliasing of linear values, unlike alias type systems. Quasi-linear types [6] relax this limitation by taking the order of evaluation into consideration. Second, although they achieve explicit memory deallocation, explicit memory reuse is not allowed because they do not support the strong updating of memory regions, unlike alias type systems. One advantage of linear type systems is their ability to infer types. On the other hand, alias type systems currently require type annotations by programmers.

Region-based memory management [5, 14, 15] is another approach to memory management, which does not rely on garbage collection. Region-based memory management involves the division of memory allocations into groups called regions and the static management of pointers among them. By adopting the region-based memory management technique described in [5], programmers can reclaim regions explicitly; however, such a technique does not provide type inferencing mechanisms, as in the case of alias type systems. Region-base memory management has two drawbacks. First, the memory management unit is coarse, as compared to that of linear and alias type systems. Therefore, the ability to explicitly manage memory is limited. Second, it does not support explicit memory reuse, as in the case of linear type systems.

Shape analysis [11, 12] involves the extraction of shape invariants, that is, approximated structures built with memory regions and pointers among them. Although shape analysis can be used to explicitly deallocate memory regions [4], it is sometimes inadequate for explicit memory management because it does not determine whether memory regions can be explicitly reused. In addition, effective shape analysis approaches [3, 7] suffer from limitations in handling generic recursive data structures. This is because the detection of aliasing relations in programs is undecidable [9]. On the other hand, the proposed type system handles recursive data structures efficiently and precisely at the cost of coercions and type annotations by programmers. The workload of the programmers can be reduced by incorporating shape analysis.

Separation logic [10] is an extension of Hoare logic, which permits reasoning for low-level imperative programs that use shared mutable data structures. It is a substructural logic that can describe heap-allocated memory regions and pointers among them. It is known that the concept of the separating conjunction in separation logic is closely related to the original alias type system [10, 18]. The present study is the first elucidation of the application of separating implications to the alias type system; moreover, we have demonstrated its effectiveness. Separation logic is more expressive than the proposed type system; however, it requires manual proofs that are relatively complex, as opposed to the insertion of coercions in the proposed type system. Although decision procedures for restricted separation logic have been investigated [1, 2, 8], they do not handle separating implications.

5. Conclusion

In this paper, we proposed an extension of the alias type system [18] using separating implications, which are derived from separation logic [10]. The original alias type system allows programmers to write explicit memory management code by tracking aliasing relations in memory regions. However, it suffers from limitations in expressing tail-recursive operations on recursive data structures because it requires complete information about the aliasing relations. In the proposed type system, the separating implications relax the limitations by allowing implicit pointer aliases between the antecedents and the consequents of the implications. Further, we presented examples to demonstrate the expressiveness of the proposed type system. The proposed type system enables us to describe a tail-recursive and destructive list append function, a FIFO queue with constant-time operations, and an implementation of deletion from a binary search tree that only takes constant space.

Acknowledgments

This work has been partially supported by CREST of JST (Japan Science and Technology Agency).

References

[1] J. Berdine, C. Calcagno, and P. W. O'Hearn. A decidable fragment of separation logic. In *Proc. of FSTTCS 2004*, pages 97–109, 2004.

[2] J. Berdine, C. Calcagno, and P. W. O'Hearn. Symbolic execution with separation logic. In *Proc. of APLAS 2005*, pages 52–68, 2005.

[3] J. Berdine, C. Calcagno, B. Cook, D. Distefano, P. W. O'Hearn, T. Wies, and H. Yang. Shape analysis for composite data structures. In *Proc. of CAV 2007*, pages 178–192, 2007.

[4] S. Cherem and R. Rugina. Compile-time deallocation of individual objects. In *Proc. of ISMM 2006*, pages 138–149, 2006.

[5] K. Crary, D. Walker, and J. G. Morrisett. Typed memory management in a calculus of capabilities. In *Proc. of POPL 1999*, pages 262–275, 1999.

[6] N. Kobayashi. Quasi-linear types. In *Proc. of POPL 1999*, pages 29–42, 1999.

[7] O. Lee, H. Yang, and K. Yi. Automatic verification of pointer programs using grammar-based shape analysis. In *Proc. of ESOP 2005*, pages 124–140, 2005.

[8] H. H. Nguyen, C. David, S. Qin, and W.-N. Chin. Automated verification of shape and size properties via separation logic. In *Proc. of VMCAI 2007*, pages 251–266, 2007.

[9] G. Ramalingam. The undecidability of aliasing. *ACM Transactions on Programming Languages and Systems*, 16(5):1467–1471, 1994.

[10] J. C. Reynolds. Separation logic: a logic for shared mutable data structures. In *Proc. of LICS 2002*, pages 55–74, 2002.

[11] M. Sagiv, T. Reps, and R. Wilhelm. Solving shape-analysis problems in languages with destructive updating. *ACM Transactions on Programming Languages and Systems*, 20(1):1–50, January 1998.

[12] M. Sagiv, T. Reps, and R. Wilhelm. Parametric shape analysis via 3-valued logic. In *Proc. of POPL 1999*, pages 105–118, 1999.

[13] F. Smith, D. Walker, and G. Morrisett. Alias types. *Lecture Notes in Computer Science*, 1782:366–381, 2000.

[14] M. Tofte and J.-P. Talpin. Implementation of the typed call-by-value lambda-calculus using a stack of regions. In *Proc. of POPL 1994*, pages 188–201, 1994.

[15] M. Tofte and J.-P. Talpin. Region-based memory management. *Information and Computation*, 132:109–176, 1997.

[16] D. N. Turner, P. Wadler, and C. Mossin. Once upon a type. In *Proc. of FPCA 1995*, pages 1–11, 1995.

[17] P. Wadler. Linear types can change the world! In *Proc. of PROCOMET 1990*, pages 347–359, 1990.

[18] D. Walker and G. Morrisett. Alias types for recursive data structures. *Lecture Notes in Computer Science*, 2071:177–206, 2001.

Type Safety from the Ground Up

Chris Hawblitzel
Microsoft Research

Abstract

Type safety is the most common mechanism for securely running untrusted code from the Internet. When the untrusted code is written in a type-safe language like JavaScript, Java, or C#, the language's type system guarantees that the code cannot damage the user's computer (without the user's permission). This guarantee, however, rests on the correct enforcement of type safety, and a typical computer system has many components that must be trusted to enforce type safety. A bug in any one of these components could break security entirely: a buggy compiler could emit unsafe code, a buggy garbage collector could turn integers into unsafe pointers, a buggy operating system could overwrite a thread's context with untyped data, and a buggy device driver could instruct a device to overwrite typed memory with untyped data.

This talk will describe work on the Verve operating system [8], which uses typed assembly language (TAL) [6] and automated theorem proving to ensure type safety across all components of a computer system, including the garbage collector, the operating system, the device drivers, and all compiler-generated assembly language code. Verve consists of about 35,000 lines of safe C# code, compiled to typed assembly language, running on top of 1500 lines of assembly language, verified with the Z3 automated theorem prover [2]. For example, the operating system's scheduler is C# code compiled to TAL, while the operating system's low-level context switching and interrupt handling is verified assembly language code. Similarly, the Ethernet driver's packet processing is C# compiled to TAL, while the verified assembly language ensures that devices are managed safely (via verified interaction with PCI) and device memory access is safe (via verified programming of an I/O memory management unit). Finally, the run-time system is split into components that the TAL type system can express (including array-store checks and run-time casts), and components that are verified with theorem proving (in particular, the garbage collector). This splitting is similar to other operating systems designed for high assurance [1, 4, 5, 7], but Verve adds a higher degree of static safety verification: every assembly language instruction is statically verified, either with type checking or theorem proving, to preserve type safety.

Because Verve relies on two separate static checkers (TAL and Z3), it does not yet achieve the goal of unified, foundational certification as pursued by the FLINT project [3]. This talk will discuss ongoing work to move closer to this goal, by expressing both Verve's low-level state and a TAL type system in a unified language (Coq). Although this work is preliminary, it has already uncovered several bugs in the specification used to verify Verve's 1500 lines of assembly language. (These bugs were too-strong preconditions and too-weak postconditions; luckily, the specification bugs didn't result in bugs in the code itself.)

Verve's source code is available at the following URL (in the "verify" directory):

`http://www.codeplex.com/singularity`

Categories and Subject Descriptors D.2.4 [*SOFTWARE ENGINEERING*]: Software/Program Verification

General Terms Verification

Keywords Operating system, run-time system, verification, type safety

Acknowledgments

This is joint work with Jean Yang, Gregory Malecha, Juan Chen, Ross Tate, and Erez Petrank.

References

[1] J. Criswell, N. Geoffray, and V. Adve. Memory safety for low-level software/hardware interactions. In *Proceedings of the Eighteenth Usenix Security Symposium*, August 2009.

[2] L. M. de Moura and N. Bjørner. Z3: An efficient SMT solver. In *TACAS*, pages 337–340, 2008.

[3] X. Feng, Z. Shao, Y. Dong, and Y. Guo. Certifying low-level programs with hardware interrupts and preemptive threads. In *PLDI*, pages 170–182, 2008.

[4] T. Hallgren, M. P. Jones, R. Leslie, and A. P. Tolmach. A principled approach to operating system construction in Haskell. In *ICFP*, pages 116–128, 2005.

[5] G. Klein, K. Elphinstone, G. Heiser, J. Andronick, D. Cock, P. Derrin, D. Elkaduwe, K. Engelhardt, R. Kolanski, M. Norrish, T. Sewell, H. Tuch, and S. Winwood. seL4: Formal verification of an OS kernel. In *Proc. 22nd ACM Symposium on Operating Systems Principles (SOSP)*, pages 207–220, Big Sky, MT, USA, Oct. 2009. ACM.

[6] G. Morrisett, D. Walker, K. Crary, and N. Glew. From System F to typed assembly language. In *POPL '98: 25th ACM Symposium on Principles of Programming Languages*, pages 85–97, Jan. 1998.

[7] D. Williams, P. Reynolds, K. Walsh, E. G. Sirer, and F. B. Schneider. Device driver safety through a reference validation mechanism. In *OSDI*, 2008.

[8] J. Yang and C. Hawblitzel. Safe to the last instruction: Automated verification of a type-safe operating system. In *PLDI*, 2010.

TLDI'11, January 25, 2011, Austin, Texas, USA.
ACM 978-1-4503-0484-9/11/01.

AuraConf: A Unified Approach to Authorization and Confidentiality

Jeffrey A. Vaughan
University of California, Los Angeles

Abstract

This paper introduces AuraConf, the first programming language with a unified means to specify access-control and confidentially policies. In concert with a proof-carrying access control mechanism, AuraConf allows confidentially policies to be specified declaratively using types and enforced via cryptography. Programs written in AuraConf enjoy a formal security guarantee via noninterference. Additionally, the language definition introduces a novel type system where the typechecker may use resources (i.e., private keys) and knowledge of an object's provenance (i.e., how a ciphertext was computed) to guide analysis.

Categories and Subject Descriptors F.3.3 [*Studies of Program Constructs*]: Type structure

General Terms Languages, Security, Theory

Keywords Dependent types, information flow, cryptography

1. Introduction

Language based security research has made great strides in addressing the complementary problems of enforcing access-control restrictions and preventing unintentional disclosure of confidential data. Indeed, ongoing research into access-control logics and proof-carrying access control [1, 9, 14, 20] have realized an expressive, flexible framework for describing and enforcing authorization policies. A largely orthogonal body of research uses information flow analysis to detect unsafe, in a precise sense, uses of confidential information within a program. Such techniques can ensure that secrets are appropriately encrypted—manually by the programmer [3, 15, 22, 23, 33] or automatically by the language framework [5, 39]—before (e.g.) transmission on an insecure network.

Information flow analysis (with encryption) and proof-carrying access control represent first-rate, language-based approaches to mitigating different security problems. Because programs may deal both with confidential data and access-controlled resources, it is natural to ask: *Can these techniques be combined?*

Yes. This paper introduces AuraConf, a programing language that provides direct support for both proof-carrying access control and information flow with automatic encryption. The specific goals of this design are as follows.

- To establish a natural connection between information-flow analysis for policy specification and cryptography for policy enforcement.
- To unify these confidentiality mechanisms with proof-carrying access-control techniques as realized in Aura.
- To provide technical mechanisms for anomaly detection, including audit of relevant security events and static discovery of security errors via typing.

AuraConf is built as an extension to the Aura [20, 37, 38] programming language. Plain Aura is a platform for programming with access control and audit. Programs construct proofs of their access-control rights at runtime, and such proofs are consumed and logged by procedures that perform secure operations. Dependent types provide a precise way to connect access-control predicates with specific data values. And, mutually distrusting principals may use digitally signed propositions to introduce new access-control policies.

Aura is a solid foundation for the present work because its design explicitly captures core notations of proof-carrying access control. Additionally, Aura's expressive type system provides many components, including weak dependent types and a monadic programing style that, as we will discuss, are useful for reasoning about confidentiality. Aura is, for these reasons, a practical framework to investigate the general question of how to unify language-based approaches to confidentiality and authorization.

Mixing an informative type system with encryption, as done in AuraConf, is an enabling technology for trustworthy application development. For instance, consider a distributed streaming-movie service. Developers of such a system must address a variety of security-focused issues.

- *Authorization Policy:* Who can access a movie? When can access-rights may be transferred between users?
- *Confidentiality Policy:* What data is secret? Movie ratings and reviews, or only the bits encoding videos?
- *Enforcement and Audit Mechanisms:* What data should be encrypted? When should encryption occur? When runtime decryption failures occur, what does this mean?

While Aura provides mechanisms for answering only the authorization-policy questions, AuraConf provides a framework in which all the issues may be addressed. Confidentiality policies are specified as types, and the language ensure that confidential information is automatically encrypted at system boundaries. Decryption failures are always accompanied by a proof-object indicating system components that may be faulty or malicious; note the mechanisms used to allow precise audit of such anomalous, confidentiality-related events are defined in terms of Aura's existing access-control features.

TLDI'11, January 25, 2011, Austin, Texas, USA.

The mixture of encryption with an expressive type system exposes a fundamental tension. Type systems gain power—the ability to prevent errors and uphold invariants—by exploiting precise information about a program's terms. In contrast, the point of encryption is to obscure information in certain contexts.

This tension has several technical manifestations. First, typing is relative; each principal has its own, local notion of what is well-typed. This is desirable because it accounts for the following real phenomenon. To Alice all arbitrary, unknown bit strings are plausibly encrypted messages for Bob—elements of the AuraConf type **int for** Bob. In contrast Bob can tell which bit strings are well-formed at that type, and which are garbage.

Second, typing exhibits a hysteretic, or path dependent, effect. When Alice creates a new ciphertext for Bob, she transforms a perfectly legible piece of abstract syntax into an opaque binary blob. In order for type preservation to hold during this process, Alice's computation must annotate the ciphertext and, as a side-effect, record information to validate the annotation in the future.

Third, resolving the above issues requires a precise treatment of public keys, both at compile time and at runtime. Discussing key availability at different hosts requires ideas from modal type theories [21, 27]. Ensuring that needed keys are available dynamically requires type-and-effect analysis [26, 36]. (In principle other techniques could be used, but the concepts involved are essential.)

The AuraConf language resolves the tensions indicated above and helps programmers both handle confidential data and manage access-control credentials. Meeting these goals requires three substantial technical contributions:

- The design of AuraConf including the confidentiality type constructor **for** and a sophisticated type system that enforces both key-management and code-mobility constraints.
- A mechanized proof that AuraConf satisfies type safety and that type checking is decidable.
- A mechanized proof showing AuraConf programs protect confidential data; more precisely, they satisfy noninterference.

The rest of this paper is structured as follows. Section 2 describes AuraConf's new constructs informally, and Section 3 presents a sample program exercising these features. Section 4 summarizes the formal language definition and metatheory. Section 5 discusses AuraConf from the perceptive of conventional information flow. Section 6 reviews related work and Section 7 concludes.

2. Overview of AuraConf

This section provides an informal introduction to AuraConf's new features.

Access control in Aura

The core Aura language [20, 38] is designed to add support for authorization policy specification, runtime enforcement, and audit to a functional programming language. Aura security policies are expressed as propositions in an authorization logic. Aura's type system cleanly integrates standard data types (like integers) with proofs of authorization logic propositions, and programs manipulate authorization proofs just as they might other values.

In Aura, the proposition A **says** P denotes "Principal A says (or endorses) proposition P." Aura authorization proofs serve as *evidence* of access-control decisions, and programs must present appropriate proofs in order to access resources. Evidence is composed of a mix of cryptographic signatures, which capture principals' "utterances," and standard rules of logical deduction.

Aura has ML-like evaluation semantics, characterized by call-by-value reduction and effectful operators. Its static semantics are substantially more novel and are based on *weak dependent types* that can express a variety of useful propositions. For instance, the proposition

```
Alice says ((P: Prop) → Bob says P → P)
```

means that principal Alice will endorse any proposition that Bob endorses. This proposition, which may be pronounced "Bob speaks for Alice," means that Alice is delegating *all* of her authority to Bob. In contrast, the proposition

```
Alice says ((s: Song) → isJazz s →
              Bob says (MayPlay Bob s) → MayPlay Bob s)
```

describes a more limited form of delegation, where Alice delegates some, but not all, of her authority to Bob (only her rights to play jazz songs). The latter proposition follows the principle of least privilege and represents a safer, more secure form of delegation than the former. The ability to express such restricted delegation is an advantage of Aura compared with simpler authorization logics containing only polymorphism.

The Aura runtime system automatically logs proofs used for access-grants, and logged evidence enables useful post-hoc analysis of the authorization decisions made during a system's execution.

Confidential Computations and the For-Monad

AuraConf integrates the mechanisms described above with features for specifying and automatically enforcing confidentiality constraints.

In AuraConf secrets are protected with an indexed confidentiality monad. A confidential integer intended only for Alice can be given type (**int for** Alice). As expected, values of this type are constructed using the following monadic return operator.

```
return Alice 42 : int for Alice
```

This expression evaluates by encrypting 42 with Alice's public key, yielding a blob of ciphertext, written $\mathcal{E}$(Alice, 42, 0x2b63), with an additional annotation that will be discussed shortly. The number 0x2b63 represents a random value inserted by the encryption algorithm to ensure that encrypting identical plaintexts does not yield identical ciphertexts. Code running on any host should be able to perform the **return** operation, as it uses only Alice's public key and needs no access to private keys. A program running with Alice's private key may decrypt and declassify the ciphertext as follows.

```
run (return Alice 42) : int
```

Additionally, when given a value of type **int for** Alice, AuraConf programs can use a bind operator to produce a new encrypted computation, also for Alice, based on the existing secret.

```
bind (int for Alice)
     (return Alice 42)
     (λ{Alice} x: int . return Alice (x * 2))
  : int for Alice
```

When Alice runs the resulting encrypted computation, she will decrypt the 42 before supplying it to the decryption of the function. For now, it's ok to ignore the {Alice} component of the λ; this is an effect annotation and will be defined and discussed later.

As illustrated above, for-monad operators treat their arguments lazily. Imagine for the moment that we could use homomorphic encryption [16, 31] to allow for-bound computations to be applied eagerly. (I am not aware, by the way, of any practically efficient homomorphic encryption scheme.) An eager for-bind would permit curious adversaries to probe encrypted objects using functions that diverge on known inputs. Giving the for-monad lazy semantics eliminates this timing channel.

While the dynamic semantics of encryption are straightforward, they pose a substantial problem for typechecking. Consider a machine running on Bob's behalf that performs the above encryption for Alice. A sound type system should satisfy subject reduction and be able to relate ciphertext $\mathcal{E}$(Alice, 42, 0x2b63) with type **int for** Alice. But the entire point of encryption is to ensure that users other than Alice cannot meaningfully inspect the ciphertext, and Bob cannot decompose or examine the newly created object.

AuraConf resolves this tension as follows. Ciphertexts may be annotated with one of two forms of typing metadata. First, the term

```
cast ℰ(Alice, 42, 0x2b63) to (int for Alice)
  : int for Alice
```

is a *true cast*—a form of type coercion allowed only when semantic evidence indicates that the cast is "correct." A true cast typechecks when the ciphertext is a known value with known provenance. Whenever Bob's program creates a ciphertext, it records a *fact* associating the new ciphertext with the appropriate type. As evaluation proceeds, programs accumulate a context of facts which are used to typecheck known ciphertexts. We assume fact contexts are part of a host's local state and are not shared between different principals. True casts are also permitted when the typechecker can *statically* access an appropriate decryption key. Thus the above cast can be typechecked on Bob's machine, where it originated, as well as on Alice's machine, where it will be used. Evaluating a **return** yields a ciphertext annotated with a true cast.

True casts alone are insufficient for writing some protocols. Consider two programs, running with Bob and Charlie's authority respectively, jointly constructing an **int for** Alice using the **return** and **bind** operators. In particular, Charlie's program may need to **bind** a ciphertext previously created by Bob. Because facts are not shared between different principals, and because Charlie cannot access Alice's private key, there's no way Charlie will be able to typecheck the ciphertext annotated with a true cast. Instead, Charlie's program will need to work with a justified cast,

```
cast c to (int for Alice) blaming p : int for Alice
```

where p is a proof that ciphertext c has the correct form. Concretely,

```
p : (Bob says (c isa (int for Alice))).
```

Proposition constructor **isa** is a built-in constant with the job of witnessing these justified casts.

In combination, true and justified casts allow us to reason about ciphertexts, even those which cannot be decrypted in a particular context. Subject reduction ensures that (for suitable fact contexts) decryption never fails for true-cast ciphertexts. Furthermore, while justified casts may lead to decryption failures, such failures are accompanied by signed **isa** proofs that can be used to assign blame. Observe that the justified cast mechanism and the very notion of blame rest Aura's ability to capture principal intent via **says** types.

Casting allows the programmer to assign a precise type to ciphertext. Conversely, **asbits** strips a ciphertext's annotation, resulting in a term with the following less informative type.

```
asbits (cast(ℰ(Alice, 42, 0x2b63)) to (int for Alice))
  : bits
```

Type **bits** classifies naked ciphertexts, and this term reduces to

```
ℰ(Alice, 42, 0x2b63) : bits.
```

3. Examples

This section shows sample AuraConf programs. For illustration, we use modules—a feature that is not part of the formal language definition. Additionally, Figure 2 uses syntactic sugar for writing recursive functions; AuraConf supports general recursion (via a datatype-base encoding) but does not have this convenient syntax.

```
(* Interface providing a basic networking API *)
Signature NetIO

  assert OkToSend: prin → Type → Prop;
  val  attempt_acquire_strong_credential :
         (b: prin) →
         Maybe ((a: prin) →
         (T: Type) →
         pf (b says OkToSend a T) →
         pf (Kernel says OkToSend a T))

  val recv: (T: Type) → T

  val send: (T: Type) → (a: prin) → T →
               pf (Kernel says (OkToSend a T)) → Unit
End Signature
```

Figure 1: A simple communications library.

Figure 1 defines a simple networking interface. The functions send and recv are intended to send and receive data values. In addition to data to transmit, send consumes a proof that the system (that is the principal Kernel) permits the operation. Concretely

```
send int Bob 42 p
```

sends the data value 42 to principal Bob when p is an appropriate access-control proof. Note that both confidential and non-confidential values may be transmitted over any channel.

Assertion OkToSend and function attempt_acquire_strong_credential define an access control policy for the send function. This function allows client b to request a proof object permitting arbitrary network writes.

Suppose that a program running with Alice's authority needs to build a secret message that will eventually be read by Bob after being processed, and possibly for-bound, by Charlie. We can write this program as follows.

```
Module Sender Of Alice
  open NetIOImp

   let msg at ⊥=
         let x at Bob = return 312 as (int for Bob) in
         let y at ⊥= asbits x in
           cast y to (int for Bob)
                 blaming (say Alice (y isa (int for Bob)))
     in
   send (int for Bob) Charlie msg (get_cred msg)

End Sender
```

The program creates an annotated ciphertext for Bob—with the form of a true cast—strips its annotation with **asbits**, and creates a justified cast suitable for sending. The true cast is stored in x, whose **at** Bob annotation reflects that the true cast may only be typed in certain contexts—those where Bob's key or relevant facts are available. In contrast, y and msg may be interpreted anywhere; this is reflected by the **at** ⊥ annotations. Finally, the get_cred function is assumed to return a proof granting permission to send. Even this simple program relies on the harmonious interaction of several language features: both **casts**, **asbits**, **return**, **isa**, and **let at**.

The Sender module is annotated with **Of** Alice, indicating that it defines code that will be typechecked and run on behalf of principal Alice. In the terminology of Section 4, the module's top-level terms must be typechecked with statically available key and effect label

```
Module NetworkedStore Of Server

(* Use the a module which implements the NetIO interface. *)
open NetIOImp: NetIO;

(* The type of network requests to this server *)
data request: Type {
| r_put: (a: prin) → (id: Nat) → String for a → request
| r_get: prin → Nat → request }

(* The Map datatype stores for each principal a natural-
   number-indexed set of confidential Strings. *)
data Map: Type {
| m_intro : ((a: prin) → Nat →
        Maybe (String for a)) → Map }

let empty_map: Map =
    m_intro (λa: prin. λid: Nat. nothing (String for a))

let lookup: Map → (a: prin) →
        Nat → Maybe (String for a) =
  λm: Map. λa: prin. λn: Nat.
  match m with Maybe (String for a) {
  | m_intro → λf: ((a: prin) → Nat →
            Maybe (String for a)). f a n }

let insert : Map → (a: prin) → Nat →
        (String for a) → Map =
  λm: Map. λa: prin. λid: Nat. λmsg: String for a.
    m_intro (λa': prin. λ id': Nat.
          if a = a'
          then
            match eqnat id id' with
                Maybe (String for a') {
            | true → ⟨just (String for a) msg:
                    Maybe(String for a')⟩
            | false → lookup m a' id' }
          else lookup m a' id')

(* A helper function that lets that lets us compose functions of
   type T → S with the for monad. Bind alone only works
   with T → (S for a) functions. *)
let for_lift : (T: Type) → (S: Type) → (a: prin) →
        (T → S) → T for a → S for a =
  λT: Type. λS: Type. λa: prin. λf: T → S.
    λx: T for a.
      bind y = x
        in (return (f y) as (S for a)) as (S for a)

(* rewrite_cred uses say and a proof signed by the kernel to
 * produce a new, more useful proof access-control proof. *)
let rewrite_cred : ((a: prin) → (T: Type) →
            pf (self says OkToSend a T) →
            pf (Kernel says OkToSend a T)) -{self}→
        ((a: prin) → (T: Type) →
            pf (Kernel says OkToSend a T)) =
  λ{self} p1: ((a: prin) → (T: Type) →
          pf (self says OkToSend a T) →
          pf (Kernel says OkToSend a T)).
    let p2: pf (self says ((b: prin) →
            (S: Type) → OkToSend b S)) =
          say ((b: prin) → (S: Type) → OkToSend b S) in
    let p3: (b: prin) → (S: Type) →
            pf (self says (OkToSend b S)) =
        λb:prin. λS:Type.
          bind p2
            (λp2': self says (
                (b:prin) → (S:Type) → OkToSend b S).
              return (bind p2'
                  (λp2'': (b:prin) → (S:Type) →
                            OkToSend b S.
                    return self (p2'' b S))))
      in
    λc: prin. λU: Type. p1 c U (p3 c U)

(* attempt_acquire_credential gets a proof allowing access to the send
   function and rewrites it into a useful form using rewrite_cred. *)
let attempt_acquire_credential : Unit -{self}→ Maybe ((a: prin) →
    (T: Type) → pf (Kernel says OkToSend a T)) =
    λ{self} x: Unit.
      match ( attempt_acquire_strong_credential self ) with
          Maybe ((a: prin) → (T: Type) →
              pf (Kernel says OkToSend a T)) {
      | just → λ{self} p: (a: prin) → (T: Type) →
                  pf (self says OkToSend a T) →
                  pf (Kernel says OkToSend a T).
            just ((a: prin) → (T: Type) →
                    pf (Kernel says OkToSend a T))
                ( rewrite_cred p)
      | nothing → nothing ((a: prin) → (T: Type) →
                    pf (Kernel says OkToSend a T)) }

(* The main server loop. This reads input requests from the network
   and stores or retrieves confidential values as needed. *)
let server_loop : ((a: prin) → (T: Type) →
            pf (Kernel says OkToSend a T)) →
            Map → Unit =
  λp: (a: prin) → (T: Type) →
        pf (Kernel says OkToSend a T).
  fun rec: Map → Unit =
    λm: Map. rec
      match recv request with Map {
      | r_put → λa: prin. λid: Nat.
              λmsg: String for a. insert m a id msg
      | r_get → λa: prin. λid: Nat.
            let u: Unit =
              match lookup m a id with Unit {
              | just → λmsg: String for a.
                    send (String for a) a
                        ( for_lift String String
                              a time_stamp msg)
                        (p a (String for a))
              | nothing → send (String for a) a
                        (String a "not found")
                        (p a (String for a)) }
            in m }
    in rec end

(* This code starts the server loop after acquiring necessary
   credentials. If such credentials are not available, it fails. *)
match attempt_acquire_credential unit with Unit {
| just → λp: ((a: prin) → (T: Type) →
            pf (Kernel says OkToSend a T)).
          server_loop p empty_map
| nothing → unit }

End Module
```

Figure 2: Code for confidential storage server.

both equal to singleton world Alice. Furthermore, the code must be run with authority Alice.

Figure 2 illustrates a larger program that uses the NetIO interface to implement a storage server. Clients use the NetworkedStore program to store encrypted objects. Each principal has a storage area with a set of slots indexed by natural numbers. A request of form r_put Alice 3 v instructs the server to store value v (of type String **for** Alice) in principal Alice's third storage cell. This value can be retrieved with request r_get Alice 3. The server allows anyone to store or retrieve data from any storage location, even those belonging to another principal. Confidentiality of slot contents is maintained by the use of **for**-types and encryption. It is also possible to add a layer of proof-based access-control to limit access to ciphertexts.

At the heart of this example is the server_loop function. This reads incoming requests from the network and adds values to, or finds values in, the store. In the case of an r_get request, the loop adds a time stamp to the retrieved value (Line 111). Note that whether or not returned values are timestamped does not affect the type of the resulting object; in general the ability to compose computations with ciphertexts allows the server's behavior to change without breaking existing interfaces. This composition is made possible by function for_lift which is defined using **bind** (Lines 43–48).

The storage server must acquire access-control proofs and rewrite them into useful forms. Function attempt_acquire_credential (Lines 78–91) attempts to get a proof, which permits liberal use of send, from the network module's attempt_acquire_strong_credential function. Success yields a proof with the form of a delegation:

(a: **prin**) → (T: **Type**) → **pf** (Server **says** OkToSend a T) → **pf** (Kernel **says** OkToSend a T).

We read this proposition as delegation because it transforms an access control statement by Server into a statement by Kernel; that is, Server principal is "speaking for" Kernel. This is rewritten to a simpler form using rewrite_cred (Lines 52–52). Function rewrite_cred uses **say** to create a fresh (Server **says** ...) proof and compose it with the delegation above. Evaluating **say** requires Server's private key, and this fact is recorded as a latent effect in rewrite_cred 's type. The following section discusses effects annotations is more detail.

4. Language Definition

This section describes the definition and metatheory of AuraConf.

In type-safe languages such as AuraConf, a conservative algorithm identifies and rejects programs that might go wrong—that is crash—at runtime. There are many ways that a program can crash, such as by accessing a memory location out of scope or jumping to an invalid instruction sequence. AuraConf's type system, like Aura's or ML's, rules out these particular errors. However, an AuraConf program could potentially go wrong in several other ways, and the type system must address the following two challenges just to ensure soundness.

Challenge 1

Ensure decryption failures—in which a ciphertext cannot be decrypted to a well-typed plaintext—only occur where a proof can be used to assign blame. Failures without such proofs constitute undefined behavior.

Challenge 2

Ensure that running programs only (attempt to) use private keys that are actually available at runtime. Programs that require unavailable keys for decryption or signing are stuck.

Worlds

W, V, U	::=	$\bot$	Bottom world (no keys)
	|	t	Singleton worlds
	|	$\top$	Top world (all keys)

Terms

t ::=	...	(Standard functional programming)
|	$(x{:}t) \to_{\{W\}} t$	Implication, quantification, and function arrow
|	$\lambda_{\{W\}} x{:}t.\ t$	Abstraction
|	a **for** P	Type of encrypted data
|	$\mathcal{E}(a, e, n)$	Ciphertext ($n \in \mathbb{N}$)
|	$\textbf{return}_{\textbf{f}}\ e$ **as** t	Private data e with type t
|	$\textbf{bind}_{\textbf{f}}\ x = e_1$ **in** e_2 **as** t	Private computation
|	$\textbf{run}_{\textbf{f}}\ e$	Extract private data
|	**cast** e **to** t **blaming** p	Cast using type-evidence
|	**cast** e **to** t	Empirical cast
|	**fail** p	Decryption-failed exception
|	a **says** P	Proposition "a affirms P"
|	**say** a P	Direct affirmation
|	$\textbf{return}_s\ a\ e$	Affirmation when given proof
|	$\textbf{bind}_{\textbf{s}}\ e_1\ e_2$	Says composition

Figure 3: AuraConf Syntax

We address the first challenge by constraining the canonical forms of **for** types. Enforcing these constraints requires that types and terms have (loosely) consistent meanings to typecheckers with different capabilities, i.e. different access to private keys. AuraConf's type system accomplishes this using ideas based on modal type systems for distributed computing [21, 27, 28].

We address the second challenge by statically tracking the use of **say** and **run**, the only operators that use private keys, and ensuring that required keys will be accessible at runtime. To do so, we blend ideas from modal type systems with those from type-and-effect analysis [26, 36].

Types, propositions, and core Aura We pause to briefly summarize important features of core Aura's language design. Vaughan [37] describes this in detail.

Following the Curry-Howard correspondence [12, 19], Aura propositions are expressed as programming language types. For instance Aura's → type constructor can express several different concepts. Intuitively, (s: Song) → P → Q is analogous to the universally quantified formula $\forall s \in Song.\ P \Rightarrow Q$. Proofs of propositions are given a programming-language terms. For instance, λx: P. x is a proof of P → P.

At the same time → can be interpreted as an ML-style function arrow. Thus the factorial function might have type **int** → **int**. A kinding relation keeps track of whether → should be interpreted as logical implication or as function arrow. The kind **Prop** classifies propositions while the kind **Type** classifies computations. Aura supports general recursion for **Type**s, and the **Type**-**Prop** distinction is needed to prevent diverging computations from being unsoundly confused with valid proofs. Logical consistency of Aura's **Prop** fragment is a corollary of a strong normalization result by Jia and Zdancewic [22].

Syntax AuraConf's syntax is summarized in Figure 3, and includes the new operators introduced in Section 2. Not shown are standard functional-programming constructs, like pattern matching, and some access-control structures, like the Aura's **says** modality. While all terms are members of a single syntactic class, we will use the metavariables p, P, e, T, and a to indicate places where proofs, propositions, computational expressions, computational types, and principals are expected. To enable the type-and-effect analysis described above, abstractions and arrows are labeled with *worlds* that summarize latent uses of private keys.

Syntactically, the set of worlds is the set of terms augmented with distinguished top and bottom elements. AuraConf's static semantics identify only some worlds as well formed: namely principal constants, variables of type **prin**, $\top$, and $\bot$. We define a partial order on worlds,

$$\frac{}{\bot \sqsubseteq W} \qquad \frac{}{W \sqsubseteq W} \qquad \frac{}{W \sqsubseteq \bot}$$

and can visualize the lattice of well-formed worlds as follows.

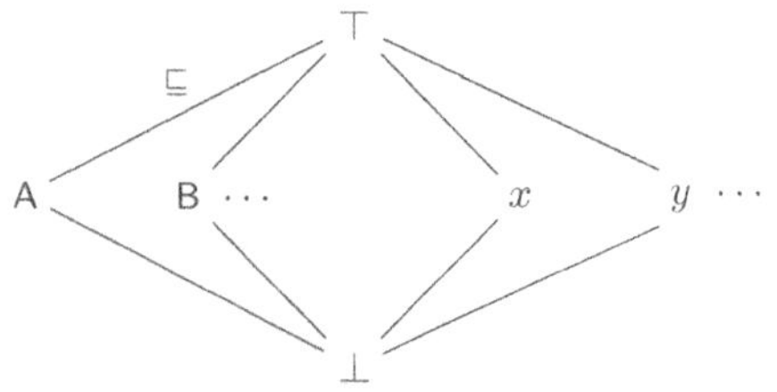

Intuitively $W \sqsubseteq U$ when U describes more private keys than W. World $\top$ represents the set of all private keys. Generalizing worlds to arbitrary principal sets would work formally, but is less appealing from an implementation perspective.

The special term **fail** p represents fatal exceptions caused by decryption failures. Argument p represents a proof to be blamed for the exception.

Static Semantics AuraConf's static semantics is based on Aura's, but with several substantial changes.

The static semantics are defined terms of several auxiliary judgments:

Term e_1 equals e_2 in E	*converts* $E\ e_1\ e_2$
e is a value	*value* e
W is a world constant	*simple* W
T has simple inhabitants	*atomic* $\Sigma\ T$
Approximate typing	$E \mathrel{|\!\!\sim} e : T$

The value relation holds for free variables, computations suspended by $\mathsf{return_f}$ or $\mathsf{bind_f}$, and usual values like lambda abstractions and constants. Judgment *atomic* $\Sigma\ T$ is intended to hold when T is **prin** or T is an inductive type that defines an enumeration, such as bool. The other auxiliary relations are discussed later in this section.

AuraConf typechecks programs using the following main judgments:

Well-formed/typed...	
... signature	$\Sigma \vdash \diamond$
... type environment	$\Sigma; \mathcal{F}; W \mid \vdash E$
... world (V)	$\Sigma; \mathcal{F}; W \mid E; V \vdash \diamond$
... worlds (V and U)	$\Sigma; \mathcal{F}; W \mid E; V; U \vdash \diamond$
... term	$\Sigma; \mathcal{F}; W \mid E; V; U \vdash t : s$
... match branches	$\Sigma; \mathcal{F}; W \mid E; V; U; s; \mathit{args} \vdash \mathit{brns} : t$

The typing relation (well-typed term) is complex. How do we read this judgment?

Facts, worlds, and the typing judgment Meta-variable $\mathcal{F}$ is a fact context as described in Section 2. It's formally defined by the grammar

Fact Contexts

$$\mathcal{F} \quad ::= \quad \cdot \mid \mathcal{F}, \mathcal{E}(a, e, n) : t.$$

Intuitively, typechecking uses the fact context to associate typing information with newly created ciphertexts. This is important, because ciphertexts are not generally amenable to inspection. Intuitively, F grows during evaluations and allows the runtime typechecker to to take advantage of information not statically available.

World W, the *statically available key*, describes which key is available for use by the typechecker. We will only consider singleton and bottom worlds here; typechecking a program with $W = \top$ corresponds to having all private keys available at once—a well-defined but unlikely scenario. Together the fact context and statically available key determine a hard limit on the typechecker's ability to reason about ciphertext.

World V, the *soft decryption limit*, is a formal upper limit describing which decryption keys or facts should be used when typechecking a particular term. Intuitively the keys used to check a term are $W \sqcap V$. The soft decryption limit is necessary to deal with mobile code. Consider what happens when Alice creates a string **for** Bob. She is building an object containing a subterm, say s, that Bob must decrypt and typecheck as string. However, Bob must check s without the benefit of Alice's private key and using a different fact context. (Because s might be a computation containing nested binds Bob's task is non-trivial.) To account for this, Alice's typing derivation uses $V =$ Bob when checking s, thus ensuring Bob can understand s without Alice's private information or state. Typechecking a top-level program takes places with $V = \top$, indicating no restriction on key or fact use.

The interaction between fact context, statically available key and soft decryption limit can be better understood by examining simplified versions of typing rules for true casts and return. (Unabridged versions of these rules may be found in figure 4; all rules including those elided here are given in author's thesis [37].) WF-TM-FORRET has form

$$\frac{\_; \mathcal{F}; W|\_; a; \_ \vdash e : t \qquad a \sqsubseteq V \qquad \cdots}{\_; \mathcal{F}; W|\_; V; \_ \vdash \mathsf{return_f}\ e\ \mathsf{as}\ (t\ \mathsf{for}\ a) : t\ \mathsf{for}\ a} \ .$$

This rule is packaging expression e for consumption by principal a. The first premise checks that e is classified by t under soft decryption limit a—this will ensure that the derivation will work even when a does not have access to the facts in $\mathcal{F}$ or a private key indicated by W. Having checked e under this restriction it's ok to conclude that $\mathsf{return_f}\ e\ \mathsf{as}\ (t\ \mathsf{for}\ a)$ has type $t\ \mathsf{for}\ a$ in a less restricted context, where soft decryption limit V is greater than a.

Observe that elements right of the vertical bar differed between WF-TM-FORRET's premise and conclusion, but symbols on the bar's left stayed the same. In general, symbols left of the bar are parameters of the relation and are held constant throughout an entire derivation tree. Symbols right of the bar are indices and may change within a derivation.

The statically available key is used directly in rule WF-TM-CASTDEC.

$$\frac{b \sqsubseteq W \qquad b \sqsubseteq V \qquad \_; \mathcal{F}; W|\_; V; \_ \vdash e : t}{\_; \mathcal{F}; W|\_; V; \_ \vdash \mathsf{cast}\ \mathcal{E}(b, e, n)\ \mathsf{to}\ (t\ \mathsf{for}\ b) : t\ \mathsf{for}\ b}$$

Here an annotated ciphertext encrypted for b is type checked by decrypting and recursively typechecking its contents. Premise $b \sqsubseteq W$ checks that the statically available key is sufficient to perform the decryption. WF-TM-CASTDEC may only be applied when current soft decryption limit V is greater than b. This last point is important. Together with setting the soft decryption limit to a in WF-TM-FORRET, it ensures that impossible decryptions are not required to later typecheck data packaged by correct programs.

Finally, WF-TM-CASTFACT has form

$$\frac{(\mathcal{E}(a, e, n) : t\ \mathsf{for}\ b) \in F \qquad b \sqsubseteq V}{\_; \mathcal{F}; W|\_; V; \_ \vdash \mathsf{cast}\ \mathcal{E}(a, e, n)\ \mathsf{to}\ (t\ \mathsf{for}\ b) : t\ \mathsf{for}\ b} \ .$$

This says that an annotated piece of ciphertext can have type t **for** b when a fact indicates the type. As above, soft decryption limit V must be greater than b. Critically, it's not necessary that $b \sqsubseteq W$—

$$\boxed{\Sigma; \mathcal{F}; W|E; V; U \vdash e : t}$$

$$\frac{\Sigma; \mathcal{F}; W|E; V; U \vdash \diamond}{\Sigma; \mathcal{F}; W|E; V; U \vdash \textsf{Type} : \textsf{Kind}} \ \textsc{wf-tm-Type}$$

$$\frac{\begin{array}{ccc} \Sigma; \mathcal{F}; W|E; \bot; \bot \vdash u_1 : k_1 & \Sigma; \mathcal{F}; W|E; V; U \vdash \diamond & \Sigma; \mathcal{F}; W|E; V; U_0 \vdash \diamond \\ \Sigma; \mathcal{F}; W|E, x : u_1 \ \textsf{at} \ \bot; \bot; \bot \vdash u_2 : k_2 & k_2 \in \{\textsf{Type}, \textsf{Prop}, \textsf{Kind}\} & k_1 \in \{\textsf{Type}, \textsf{Prop}\} \vee u_1 \in \{\textsf{Type}, \textsf{Prop}\} \end{array}}{\Sigma; \mathcal{F}; W|E; V; U \vdash (x : u_1) \rightarrow_{\{U_0\}} u_2 : k_2} \ \textsc{wf-tm-Arr}$$

$$\frac{\Sigma; \mathcal{F}; W|E; V; U \vdash \diamond \qquad (x : t \ \textsf{at} \ V_0) \in E \qquad V_0 \sqsubseteq V}{\Sigma; \mathcal{F}; W|E; V; U \vdash x : t} \ \textsc{wf-tm-Var}$$

$$\frac{\begin{array}{ccc} \Sigma; \mathcal{F}; W|E; \bot; \bot \vdash u_1 : k_1 & \Sigma; \mathcal{F}; W|E; V; U_0 \vdash \diamond & \Sigma; \mathcal{F}; W|E, x : u_1 \ \textsf{at} \ \bot; V; U_0 \vdash f : u_2 \\ \Sigma; \mathcal{F}; W|E; V; U \vdash (x : u_1) \rightarrow_{\{U_0\}} u_2 : k & k \in \{\textsf{Type}, \textsf{Prop}\} & k_1 \in \{\textsf{Type}, \textsf{Prop}\} \vee u_1 \in \{\textsf{Type}, \textsf{Prop}\} \end{array}}{\Sigma; \mathcal{F}; W|E; V; U \vdash \lambda_{\{U_0\}} x : u_1.\ f : (x : u_1) \rightarrow_{\{U_0\}} u_2} \ \textsc{wf-tm-Abs}$$

$$\frac{\begin{array}{c} \Sigma; \mathcal{F}; W|E; V; U \vdash e_1 : (x : t_2) \rightarrow_{\{U_0\}} u \\ \Sigma; \mathcal{F}; W|E; \bot; U_2 \vdash e_2 : t_2 \qquad \Sigma; \mathcal{F}; W|E; V; U \vdash t_2 : k_2 \qquad \Sigma; \mathcal{F}; W|E; V; U \vdash \{e_2/x\}u : k_u \\ U_0 \sqsubseteq U \qquad \left(\begin{array}{c} (\mathit{value}\ e_2 \wedge U_2 = \bot) \vee (k_u = \textsf{Type} \wedge x \notin \mathit{fv}(u) \wedge U_2 = U) \\ \vee\ (k_2 \in \{\textsf{Prop}, \textsf{Kind}\} \wedge x \notin \mathit{fv}(u) \wedge U_2 = U) \end{array} \right) \end{array}}{\Sigma; \mathcal{F}; W|E; V; U \vdash e_1\ e_2 : \{x/e_2\}u} \ \textsc{wf-tm-App}$$

$$\frac{\begin{array}{cc} \Sigma; \mathcal{F}; W|E; V_1; U \vdash e_1 : t_1 & \Sigma; \mathcal{F}; W|E; V; V_1 \vdash \diamond \\ \Sigma; \mathcal{F}; W|E; \bot; \bot \vdash t_1 : k \quad \Sigma; \mathcal{F}; W|E, x : t_1 \ \textsf{at} \ V_1; V; U \vdash e_2 : t & k \in \{\textsf{Type}, \textsf{Prop}\} \quad V_1 \sqsubseteq V \end{array}}{\Sigma; \mathcal{F}; W|E; V; U \vdash \textsf{let}\ x \ \textsf{at} \ V_1 = e_1 \ \textsf{in} \ e_2 : t} \ \textsc{wf-tm-LetAt}$$

$$\frac{\begin{array}{ccc} \Sigma; \mathcal{F}; W|E; b; U \vdash e_1 : t_1 \ \textsf{for} \ b & \Sigma; \mathcal{F}; W|E; b \vdash \diamond & \Sigma; \mathcal{F}; W|E; \bot; \bot \vdash t_1 : \textsf{Type} \\ \Sigma; \mathcal{F}; W|E; \bot; \bot \vdash t \ \textsf{for} \ b : \textsf{Type} \quad \Sigma; \mathcal{F}; W|E; V \vdash \diamond & \Sigma; \mathcal{F}; W|E, x : t_1 \ \textsf{at} \ b; b; b \vdash e_2 : t \ \textsf{for} \ b & b \sqsubseteq V \end{array}}{\Sigma; \mathcal{F}; W|E; V; U \vdash \textsf{bind}_{\textsf{f}}\ x = e_1 \ \textsf{in} \ e_2 \ \textsf{as} \ (t \ \textsf{for} \ b) : t \ \textsf{for} \ b} \ \textsc{wf-tm-ForBind}$$

$$\frac{\mathit{value}\ a \qquad \Sigma; \mathcal{F}; W|\cdot; \bot; \bot \vdash a : \textsf{prin} \qquad \Sigma; \mathcal{F}; W|\cdot; \bot; \bot \vdash P : \textsf{Prop} \qquad \Sigma; \mathcal{F}; W|E; V; U \vdash P : \textsf{Prop}}{\Sigma; \mathcal{F}; W|E; V; U \vdash \textsf{sign}(a, P) : a \ \textsf{says} \ P} \ \textsc{wf-tm-Sign}$$

$$\frac{\Sigma; \mathcal{F}; W|E; V; U \vdash \diamond}{\Sigma; \mathcal{F}; W|E; V; U \vdash \textsf{prin} : \textsf{Type}} \ \textsc{wf-tm-Prin}$$

Figure 4: Selected typing rules for AuraConf

this rule enables typing checking of ciphertexts without decryption and without principal b's private key.

AuraConf typing contexts track a soft decryption limit for each bound variable. This is necessary to ensure that a substitution property—replacing variables with appropriate values maintains a term's type—holds. Formally, AuraConf environments are defined by the following grammar.

Environments
$$E \ ::= \ \cdot \mid E, x{:}t \ \textsf{at} \ W \mid E, x{\sim}(t_1 = t_2){:}u \ \textsf{at} \ W$$

Equalities in the environment enable type refinement as in core Aura [20].

The typing relation's final new metavariable, U, is the judgment's *effect label*. This summarizes the keys that are necessary to successfully execute a piece of code. Effect label $U = \bot$ indicates that an expression is *pure*—that it can execute with no private keys. For instance, **say** signs a proposition. It's typed as follows:

$$\frac{\begin{array}{c} \Sigma; \mathcal{F}; W|E; \bot; \bot \vdash P : \textsf{Prop} \\ \Sigma; \mathcal{F}; W|E; \bot; \bot \vdash a : \textsf{prin} \qquad a \sqsubseteq U \qquad \cdots \end{array}}{\Sigma; \mathcal{F}; W|E; V; U \vdash \textsf{say}\ a\ P : \textsf{pf}\ a \ \textsf{says} \ P}$$

Premise $a \sqsubseteq U$ records that **say** uses a's key. Additionally AuraConf typing maintains the invariant that type-level terms, such as a **says** P, are pure. Checking the rule's premises with bottom effect label helps to enforce this condition. For a comparison, consider the rule

$$\frac{\begin{array}{c} \Sigma; \mathcal{F}; W|E; \bot; \bot \vdash P : \textsf{Prop} \\ \Sigma; \mathcal{F}; W|E; \bot; \bot \vdash a : \textsf{prin} \qquad \cdots \end{array}}{\Sigma; \mathcal{F}; W|E; V; U \vdash \textsf{sign}(a, P) : \textsf{pf}\ a \ \textsf{says} \ P},$$

which types previously created signatures. Because no new signatures are built by **sign**, typing does not require $a \sqsubseteq U$, or otherwise constrain effect label U.

It's important to understand the distinction between a judgment's soft decryption limit and effect label. The soft decryption limit controls access to a private key used *statically* for type checking. In contrast, the effect label describes keys used *dynamically* for decryption and signing. It's appealing to attempt to conflate these, but my attempts to do so were imprecise, inelegant, or plain incorrect. The difficulties arise from several considerations. Consider the application $f(\lambda x.e)$ where f does not apply $\lambda x.e$. (Function f

$$\frac{\Sigma;\mathcal{F};W|E;V;U \vdash \diamond}{\Sigma;\mathcal{F};W|E;V;U \vdash \mathsf{bits} : \mathsf{Type}}\ \textsc{wf-tm-Bits}$$

$$\frac{\Sigma;\mathcal{F};W|E;\bot;\bot \vdash P : \mathsf{Prop} \quad \Sigma;\mathcal{F};W|E;V;U \vdash \diamond \quad \Sigma;\mathcal{F};W|E;\bot;\bot \vdash a : \mathsf{prin} \quad a \sqsubseteq U \quad \mathit{value}\ a}{\Sigma;\mathcal{F};W|E;V;U \vdash \mathsf{say}\ a\ P : \mathsf{pf}\ (a\ \mathsf{says}\ P)}\ \textsc{wf-tm-Say}$$

$$\frac{\Sigma;\mathcal{F};W|E;V;\bot \vdash t : \mathsf{Type} \quad \Sigma;\mathcal{F};W|E;V;\bot \vdash a : \mathsf{prin} \quad \Sigma;\mathcal{F};W|E;V;U \vdash \diamond \quad \mathit{value}\ t \quad \mathit{value}\ a}{\Sigma;\mathcal{F};W|E;V;U \vdash t\ \mathsf{for}\ a : \mathsf{Type}}\ \textsc{wf-tm-For}$$

$$\frac{\Sigma;\mathcal{F};W|E;V;U \vdash \diamond}{\Sigma;\mathcal{F};W|E;V;U \vdash \mathcal{E}(t_1, t_2, n) : \mathsf{bits}}\ \textsc{wf-tm-Enc} \qquad \frac{\Sigma;\mathcal{F};W|E;V;U \vdash \diamond \quad E \mathrel{|\!\!\sim} e : t\ \mathsf{for}\ a}{\Sigma;\mathcal{F};W|E;V;U \vdash \mathsf{asbits}\ e : \mathsf{bits}}\ \textsc{wf-tm-AsBits}$$

$$\frac{\Sigma;\mathcal{F};W|E;a;a \vdash e : t \quad \Sigma;\mathcal{F};W|E;V;U \vdash \diamond \quad \Sigma;\mathcal{F};W|E;\bot;\bot \vdash t\ \mathsf{for}\ a : \mathsf{Type} \quad a \sqsubseteq V}{\Sigma;\mathcal{F};W|E;V;U \vdash \mathsf{return}_{\mathsf{f}}\ e\ \mathsf{as}\ (t\ \mathsf{for}\ a) : t\ \mathsf{for}\ a}\ \textsc{wf-tm-ForRet}$$

$$\frac{\Sigma;\mathcal{F};W|E;V;U \vdash t\ \mathsf{for}\ b : \mathsf{Type} \quad \Sigma;\mathcal{F};W|E;V;U \vdash e : \mathsf{bits} \quad \mathit{value}\ e}{\Sigma;\mathcal{F};W|E;V;U \vdash e\ \mathsf{isa}\ t\ \mathsf{for}\ b : \mathsf{Prop}}\ \textsc{wf-tm-Isa}$$

$$\frac{\Sigma;\mathcal{F};W|E;V;U \vdash e : t\ \mathsf{for}\ a \quad a \sqsubseteq V \quad a \sqsubseteq U}{\Sigma;\mathcal{F};W|E;V;U \vdash \mathsf{run}_{\mathsf{f}}\ e : t}\ \textsc{wf-tm-ForRun}$$

$$\frac{\Sigma;\mathcal{F};W|E;V;U \vdash e : t_1 \quad \Sigma;\mathcal{F};W|E;V;U \vdash t_2 : \mathsf{Type} \quad \mathit{converts}\ E\ t_1\ t_2}{\Sigma;\mathcal{F};W|E;V;U \vdash \langle e : t_2 \rangle : t_2}\ \textsc{wf-tm-CastConv}$$

$$\frac{(\mathcal{E}(a, e, n) : t\ \mathsf{for}\ b) \in \mathcal{F} \quad \Sigma;\mathcal{F};W|E;\bot;\bot \vdash t\ \mathsf{for}\ b : \mathsf{Type} \quad \Sigma;\mathcal{F};W|E;V;U \vdash \diamond \quad b \sqsubseteq V}{\Sigma;\mathcal{F};W|E;V;U \vdash \mathsf{cast}\ \mathcal{E}(a, e, n)\ \mathsf{to}\ (t\ \mathsf{for}\ b) : t\ \mathsf{for}\ b}\ \textsc{wf-tm-CastFact}$$

$$\frac{\begin{array}{c}\Sigma;\mathcal{F};W|\cdot;b;b \vdash e : t \\ \Sigma;\mathcal{F};W|\cdot;\bot;\bot \vdash t\ \mathsf{for}\ b : \mathsf{Type} \quad \Sigma;\mathcal{F};W|E;V;U \vdash \diamond \quad \Sigma;\mathcal{F};W|\cdot;b \vdash \diamond \quad b \sqsubseteq V \quad b \sqsubseteq W\end{array}}{\Sigma;\mathcal{F};W|E;V;U \vdash \mathsf{cast}\ \mathcal{E}(b, e, n)\ \mathsf{to}\ (t\ \mathsf{for}\ b) : t\ \mathsf{for}\ b}\ \textsc{wf-tm-CastDec}$$

$$\frac{\begin{array}{c}\Sigma;\mathcal{F};W|E;V;U \vdash p : \mathsf{pf}\ (a\ \mathsf{says}\ (e\ \mathsf{isa}\ t\ \mathsf{for}\ b)) \\ \Sigma;\mathcal{F};W|E;V;U \vdash e : \mathsf{bits} \quad \Sigma;\mathcal{F};W|E;\bot;\bot \vdash t\ \mathsf{for}\ b : \mathsf{Type} \quad \mathit{value}\ e\end{array}}{\Sigma;\mathcal{F};W|E;V;U \vdash \mathsf{cast}\ e\ \mathsf{to}\ (t\ \mathsf{for}\ b)\ \mathsf{blaming}\ p : t\ \mathsf{for}\ b}\ \textsc{wf-tm-CastJust}$$

Fig. 4: Selected typing rules for AuraConf (cont.)

may, however, do other interesting things with $\lambda x.e$, such as store it in a data structure.) We want the type system to require a sufficient soft decryption limit to analyze e's embedded ciphertexts. In contrast, e's latent effects are not forced and we would like the application to check with $\bot$ effect label. It's unclear how a single annotation can accommodate both views; using a separate soft decryption limit and effect label resolves this. More generally, the type system treats soft decryption limits like Jia and Walker's [21] **at** modality, while the effect labels are inspired by standard type-and-effect systems. Technically, these analyses are quite different and it's unsurprising that to reap the benefits of both requires incorporating mechanisms inspired by each.

Signatures, worlds, environments, branches, and conversion. The judgments for type signatures and branches follow core Aura and are not reproduced here. Every branch of a pattern match must share the same effect label. Types declared in signatures must be pure and check with $W = V = \bot$ and $\mathcal{F} = \cdot$.

Definitions of environment, world, and worlds well-formedness are more novel and are detailed in Figure 5.

The well-formed environment relation checks that all world annotations are themselves well-formed. Additionally, type-level variables (i.e., those classified by **Type** or **Prop**) may only be annotated with world $\bot$. The well-formed environment relation also ensures that the statically available key is a *simple world*—either a principal constant or $\bot$. Intuitively this ensures statically available keys may be interpreted as key constants.

The well-formed world relation always accepts $\top$ and $\bot$. If the world wraps a term, it must be value of type **prin**. The well-formed worlds relation checks that two worlds, typically a soft decryption limit and effect label, are well-formed.

Finally, *converts* $E\ e_1\ e_2$ holds when e_1 and e_2 are equal according to constraints in environment E. This relation is of course reflexive, symmetric, and transitive; the key rule is

$$\frac{x {\sim} (s = t){:}k \in E}{\mathit{converts}\ E\ s\ t}\ ,$$

which uses equality assumptions in the environment. Such equalities are introduced by a conditional operator,

$$\frac{\begin{array}{c}\Sigma;\mathcal{F};W|E, x{\sim}(v_1 = v_2){:}k;V;U \vdash e_1 : t \\ \Sigma;\mathcal{F};W|E;V;U \vdash e_2 : t \quad \ldots\end{array}}{\Sigma;\mathcal{F};W|E;V;U \vdash \mathsf{if}\ v_1 = v_2\ \mathsf{then}\ e_1\ \mathsf{else}\ e_2 : t}\ .$$

$\boxed{\mathit{simple}\ W}$

$$\frac{}{\mathit{simple}\ \bot} \qquad \frac{a \in \{\mathsf{A}, \mathsf{B}, \mathsf{C} \ldots\}}{\mathit{simple}\ a}$$

$\boxed{\Sigma; \mathcal{F}; W| \vdash E}$

$$\frac{\mathit{simple}\ W}{\Sigma; \mathcal{F}; W| \vdash \cdot}$$

$$\frac{\begin{array}{c}\Sigma; \mathcal{F}; W| \vdash E \quad \Sigma; \mathcal{F}; W|E; V \vdash \diamond \quad \Sigma; \mathcal{F}; W|E; \bot; \bot \vdash t : k \\ x \text{ fresh} \quad (k \in \{\mathsf{Type}, \mathsf{Prop}\}) \vee (t \in \{\mathsf{Type}, \mathsf{Prop}\} \wedge V = \bot)\end{array}}{\Sigma; \mathcal{F}; W| \vdash E, x : t \ \mathsf{at}\ V}$$

$$\frac{\begin{array}{c}\Sigma; \mathcal{F}; W| \vdash E \quad \Sigma; \mathcal{F}; W|E; \bot; U \vdash e_1 : t \\ \Sigma; \mathcal{F}; W|E; \bot; U \vdash e_2 : t \quad \mathit{atomic}\ \Sigma\ t \quad x \text{ fresh} \quad \mathit{value}\ e_1 \\ \mathit{value}\ e_2 \quad \Sigma; \mathcal{F}; W|E; \bot; \bot \vdash t : \mathsf{Type} \quad \Sigma; \mathcal{F}; W|E; V \vdash \diamond\end{array}}{\Sigma; \mathcal{F}; W| \vdash E, x \sim (e_1 = e_2) : t \ \mathsf{at}\ V}$$

$\boxed{\Sigma; \mathcal{F}; W|E; V \vdash \diamond}$

$$\frac{\Sigma; \mathcal{F}; W| \vdash E}{\Sigma; \mathcal{F}; W|E; \bot \vdash \diamond} \qquad \frac{\Sigma; \mathcal{F}; W|E; \bot; \bot \vdash a : \mathsf{prin} \quad \mathit{value}\ a}{\Sigma; \mathcal{F}; W|E; a \vdash \diamond}$$

$$\frac{\Sigma; \mathcal{F}; W| \vdash E}{\Sigma; \mathcal{F}; W|E; \top \vdash \diamond}$$

$\boxed{\Sigma; \mathcal{F}; W|E; V; U \vdash \diamond}$

$$\frac{\Sigma; \mathcal{F}; W|E; V \vdash \diamond \quad \Sigma; \mathcal{F}; W|E; U \vdash \diamond}{\Sigma; \mathcal{F}; W|E; V; U \vdash \diamond}$$

Figure 5: Major auxiliary judgments for AuraConf's static semantics. The predicate *atomic* $\Sigma\ t$, used here but not defined, indicates that t is an inductive type whose elements can easily be tested for equality [37].

(The Coq definition of *converts* includes an extra argument to allow for later language extensions; this is elided.) Conversion also includes congruence rules. For instance, under assumption $x =$ **self**, term x **says** P converts to **self says** P. Equalities only mention atomic values, and conversion only alters the "value" parts of a type—convertible types always have the same shape up to embedded data values. Many standard presentations of dependently typed languages use implicit conversions, which may occur anywhere in a type derivation, but Aura requires an explicit source-code cast. This is appealing because it yields an algorithmic type system.

New and modified language constructs Moving from Aura to AuraConf requires broad changes to the static semantics. Here we will examine the most interesting aspects of the new static semantics, using simplified typing rules.

Variables and binding with soft decryption limits Application, abstraction, and variable expressions are changed when moving from Aura to AuraConf. This is necessary to work with soft decryption limits and effect labels.

The variable rule is

$$\frac{\Sigma; \mathcal{F}; W|E; V; U \vdash \diamond \qquad (x : t \ \mathsf{at}\ V_0) \in E \qquad V_0 \sqsubseteq V}{\Sigma; \mathcal{F}; W|E; V; U \vdash x : t} \ .$$

From an AuraConf perspective the important part is the premise $V_0 \sqsubseteq V$. Elsewhere, we ensure that whenever some value v is substituted for x that value is well typed with soft decryption limit V_0.

A function's type is annotated with its body's suspended effects. The typing rule looks like

$$\frac{\begin{array}{c}\Sigma; \mathcal{F}; W|E; V; U_0 \vdash \diamond \\ \Sigma; \mathcal{F}; W|E, x : u_1 \ \mathsf{at}\ \bot; V; U_0 \vdash f : u_2 \qquad \cdots\end{array}}{\Sigma; \mathcal{F}; W|E; V; U \vdash \lambda_{\{U_0\}} x{:}u_1.\ f : (x{:}u_1) \rightarrow_{\{U_0\}} u_2} \ .$$

The rule could be generalized by allowing latent effect label U_0 to depend on x. This was omitted in the interest of simplicity. Dependent effects can still be written; they must reference variables quantified at a surrounding abstraction. To avoid annotating every abstraction with a soft decryption limit, this rule binds x at bottom.

Lambda abstractions are used at applications. The essence of application typing is as follows.

$$\frac{\begin{array}{c}\Sigma; \mathcal{F}; W|E; V; U \vdash e_1 : (x{:}t_2) \rightarrow_{\{U_0\}} u \\ \Sigma; \mathcal{F}; W|E; \bot; U_2 \vdash e_2 : t_2 \\ (\mathit{value}\ e_2 \wedge U_2 = \bot) \vee (x \notin \mathit{fv}(u) \wedge U_2 = U) \\ U_0 \sqsubseteq U \qquad \cdots\end{array}}{\Sigma; \mathcal{F}; W|E; V; U \vdash e_1\ e_2 : \{x/e_2\}u}$$

Application ensures that argument e_2 is typeable with bottom soft decryption limit; this matches with abstraction typing. Because evaluating the abstraction may trigger latent effect U_0, we require $U_0 \sqsubseteq U$. When e_2 is not a value—which implies e_1's type is not dependent—e_2 may also have have an effect label up to U.

So far we've only seen a way to introduce variables **at** $\bot$. The **let at** construct allows us to reason about variables with different soft decryption limits. This construct's typing rule is summarized by

$$\frac{\begin{array}{c}\Sigma; \mathcal{F}; W|E; V_1; U \vdash e_1 : t_1 \\ \Sigma; \mathcal{F}; W|E, x : t_1 \ \mathsf{at}\ V_1; V; U \vdash e_2 : t \qquad V_1 \sqsubseteq V \qquad \cdots\end{array}}{\Sigma; \mathcal{F}; W|E; V; U \vdash \mathsf{let}\ x\ \mathsf{at}\ V_1 = e_1\ \mathsf{in}\ e_2 : t} \ .$$

Here e_1 is checked with soft decryption limit V_1 and is bound to x in e_2. In e_2's environment, x is typed **at** V_1. The restriction $V_1 \sqsubseteq V$ is necessary to prevent **let at**s from raising the soft decryption limit and allowing the unsafe use of facts or statically available keys. While **let at** could be defined as a derived form, based on an enhanced abstraction form, the independent construct simplifies function definition and breaks the language into simple, orthogonal pieces.

The ciphertext and the for monad The AuraConf type system always interprets unannotated ciphertexts as unintelligible blobs.

$$\frac{\Sigma; \mathcal{F}; W|E; V; U \vdash \diamond}{\Sigma; \mathcal{F}; W|E; V; U \vdash \mathcal{E}(t_1, t_2, n) : \mathsf{bits}}$$

As discussed above, more precise typings may be given to ciphertexts annotated with true casts or justified casts.

The main operators for working with confidential values are **return**, **run**, and **bind**. The **return** operator packages an expression as a confidential computation and is typed as follows.

$$\frac{\Sigma; \mathcal{F}; W|E; a; a \vdash e : t \qquad a \sqsubseteq V \qquad \cdots}{\Sigma; \mathcal{F}; W|E; V; U \vdash \mathsf{return}_{\mathsf{f}}\ e\ \mathsf{as}\ (t\ \mathsf{for}\ a) : t\ \mathsf{for}\ a} \ .$$

Because e will eventually be run with a's authority it is type checked with soft decryption limit and effect label a. Typically $W \not\sqsubseteq a$ so setting the soft decryption limit to a prevents statically available key W from being used when checking e—important because W will not be on hand when a's program needs to check e. Likewise effect label a rules out inappropriate occurrences of **say** or **run$_{\mathsf{f}}$**. Typing for **bind$_{\mathsf{f}}$** works analogously; see rule WF-TM-FORBIND.

$\boxed{E \mid\!\sim e : t}$

$$\frac{(x : t\,\textbf{at}\,V) \in E}{E \mid\!\sim x : t}\ \text{GE-TM-VAR}$$

$$\frac{}{E \mid\!\sim \mathcal{E}(a, e, n) : \textbf{bits}}\ \text{GE-TM-ENC}$$

$$\frac{\begin{array}{c} value\ \textbf{cast}\ e\ \textbf{to}\ t\ \textbf{for}\ a\ [\ \textbf{blaming}\ p\ ] \qquad E \mid\!\sim e : \textbf{bits} \\ \forall x \in \text{vars}(p, t\ \textbf{for}\ a). \exists t_x, V_x.(x : t_x\ \textbf{at}\ V_x) \in E \end{array}}{E \mid\!\sim \textbf{cast}\ e\ \textbf{to}\ t\ \textbf{for}\ a\ [\ \textbf{blaming}\ p\ ] : t\ \textbf{for}\ a}\ \text{GE-TM-CAST}$$

Figure 6: Approximate typing judgment used by WF-TM-ASBITS

The $\textbf{run}_\mathfrak{f}$ operator decrypts and evaluates annotated ciphertexts. It's typed by:

$$\frac{\Sigma; \mathcal{F}; W|E; V; U \vdash e : t\ \textbf{for}\ a \qquad a \sqsubseteq V \qquad a \sqsubseteq U}{\Sigma; \mathcal{F}; W|E; V; U \vdash \textbf{run}_\mathfrak{f}\ e : t}$$

The premise $a \sqsubseteq U$ forces effect label U to record that the $\textbf{run}_\mathfrak{f}$ uses a's private key. Premise $a \sqsubseteq V$ prevents problems with nested occurrences of $\textbf{run}_\mathfrak{f}$. For example when a evaluates $\textbf{run}_\mathfrak{f}\ (\textbf{run}_\mathfrak{f}\ e_1)$ to $\textbf{run}_\mathfrak{f}\ e_2$, term e_2 might be contain true-casts for a. Hence V must be greater than a to ensure preservation.

Finally, **asbits** transforms an annotated ciphertext with **for** type into a bare ciphertext with type **bits**. This operator is typed as follows.

$$\frac{\Sigma; \mathcal{F}; W|E; V; U \vdash \diamond \qquad E \mid\!\sim e : t\ \textbf{for}\ a}{\Sigma; \mathcal{F}; W|E; V; U \vdash \textbf{asbits}\ e : \textbf{bits}}$$

The first premise maintains the invariant that the typing judgment's subjects are well-formed. The second premise uses a liberal over-approximation of typing to check that e is almost a t **for** a. The approximation, formalized in Figure 6, types variables and bare encryptions as usual, but always trusts the annotation on true or justified casts. (The square-bracket notation in GE-TM-CAST defines a rule that works for both flavors of cast.) It's sound to use the approximation here because **asbits** dynamically discards casts, returning the underlying ciphertexts; **asbits** launders bad **for**s into good **bits**. The typing rule is desirable because the typing of **asbits** e is independent of the facts context and statically available key, a useful property for defining mobile code.

Dynamic semantics The dynamic semantics for AuraConf makes precise the notion of a program's authority, realistically models the state necessary to perform (pseudo-)randomized cryptography, and enables reasoning about dynamically created ciphertexts.

The evaluation judgment is written

$$\Sigma; \mathcal{F}_0; W \vdash \{\!|e, n|\!\} \mapsto \{\!|e', n'|\!\}\ \text{learning}\ \mathcal{F}.$$

This says that an expression e running with W's authority—with the private keys described by world W—steps to e'. Expression e may, as described below, dynamically invoke the type checker, so the evaluation relation contains a signature Σ and fact context $\mathcal{F}_0$ for this purpose. Natural number n represents the initial seed of a randomization vector for encryption; the step updates it to n'.[1] Finally $\mathcal{F}$ is a fact context, with zero or one elements, containing facts about freshly created ciphertexts.

[1] Note that literally using a stream of sequential numbers as inputs to the encryption algorithm may not be secure for some protocols. Instead we should view such uses of n as actually looking up the nth number in a sequence of (pseudo-)random numbers.

In general AuraConf's evaluation relation subsumes Aura's. For intuition, when $e \mapsto e'$ in Aura,

$$\Sigma; \mathcal{F}_0; \textbf{self} \vdash \{\!|e, n|\!\} \mapsto \{\!|e', n|\!\}\ \text{learning}\ \cdot$$

holds in AuraConf. Figure 7 lists the evaluation rules for new operators.

Rules STEP-FORRET and STEP-FORBIND introduce new ciphertexts. In each case the current randomization seed, n is inserted into the ciphertext and the seed is incremented. Additionally a fact describing the ciphertext is learned. While STEP-FORRET is simple, STEP-FORBIND looks more complicated. The latter builds an expression using **let at** that can be run by the destination machine and that performs necessary decryptions.

Rule STEP-FORRUN-OK, STEP-FORRUN-ILLTYPED, and STEP-FORRUN-JUNK attempt to decrypt and typecheck an annotated ciphertext, signaling an error as needed.

Figure 7 elides several congruence rules. They are all similar to STEP-APP-CONGL, which copies its premise's new facts and randomization seed.

Basic metatheory and soundness AuraConf satisfies two important properties: syntactic soundness and noninterference. Syntactic soundness guarantees that all well-typed programs have a well-defined evaluation semantics. Noninterference [4, 40], states that a program's outputs are not affected (up to a natural equivalence induced by cryptography) by inputs intended to be secret. AuraConf's type system has several non-standard aspects; consequently, the technical statements and proofs of these properties are novel.

All properties of AuraConf are formalized as constructive proofs in the Coq proof assistant.[2] Such formalization is particularly important for large languages and security-focused languages; AuraConf is both.

Stating preservation and progress requires defining when a term has reached an exceptional state. This is intended to occur only after a decryption failure, and identifies a proof to be used when diagnosing the failure. We write e blames p when $(\textbf{fail}\ p)$ is a subterm of e, not located under a $\textbf{return}_\mathfrak{f}$ or a $\textbf{bind}_\mathfrak{f}$. In Coq this is defined as an inductive predicate over the syntax of terms.

Preservation states that if a well-typed term steps the result has the same type, or else a decryption error has been detected and a proof identified for blame assignment.

LEMMA 1 (Preservation). *Assume* $\Sigma; \mathcal{F}_0; W|E; V; U \vdash e : t$ *and* $\Sigma \vdash \diamond$. *Then* $\Sigma; \mathcal{F}_0; W \vdash \{\!|e, n|\!\} \mapsto \{\!|e', n'|\!\}$ *learning* $\mathcal{F}$ *implies either* $\Sigma; \mathcal{F}_0 +\!\!+ \mathcal{F}; W|E; V; U \vdash e' : t$ *or there exists* p *such that* e' blames p.

Notation $\mathcal{F}_0 +\!\!+ \mathcal{F}$ denotes a fact context containing the elements of $\mathcal{F}$ and $\mathcal{F}_0$.

The above lemma misses an important aspect of evaluation. Running an AuraConf program doesn't simply reduce an input term to a result; it also generates a sequence of new facts. There are terms that typecheck under bad fact contexts, but get stuck at evaluation. Thus we must ensure that newly generated facts are, in the following sense, semantically valid.

DEFINITION 1 (valid$_\Sigma$ $\mathcal{F}$). *We write* valid$_\Sigma$ $\mathcal{F}$ *when both the following hold. First,* $\Sigma \vdash \diamond$. *Second, for every* $\mathcal{E}(a, e, n) : t\ \textbf{for}\ b$ *in* $\mathcal{F}$ *it is the case that* $a = b$ *and* $\Sigma; \cdot; b|\cdot; b; b \vdash e : t$.

Intuitively this predicate holds when decrypting each ciphertext in a fact context would validate the declared types. Certain bogus facts, say `"hello"` : **int**, aren't harmful to soundness, and are ignored. The empty fact context is trivially valid.

[2] Coq scripts are available from the author's webpage, `http://www.cs.ucla.edu/~jeff/`.

$\boxed{\Sigma; F_0; W \vdash \{\!|e_1, n_1|\!\} \mapsto \{\!|e_2, n_2|\!\} \text{ learning } F}$

$$\frac{\textit{value } v}{\Sigma; F_0; W \vdash \{\!|\textbf{let } x \textbf{ at } V = v \textbf{ in } e, n|\!\} \mapsto \{\!|\{v/x\}e, n|\!\} \text{ learning } \cdot} \ \textsc{step-LetAt}$$

$$\frac{}{\begin{array}{l}\Sigma; F_0; W \vdash \{\!|\textbf{return}_\mathbf{f}\ e \textbf{ as } (t \textbf{ for } a), n|\!\} \mapsto \{\!|\textbf{cast } \mathcal{E}(a, e, n) \textbf{ to } (t \textbf{ for } a), n+1|\!\} \\ \qquad \text{learning } \mathcal{E}(a, e, n) : t \textbf{ for } a\end{array}} \ \textsc{step-ForRet}$$

$$\frac{\textit{value } v}{\begin{array}{l}\Sigma; F_0; W \vdash \{\!|\textbf{bind}_\mathbf{f}\ x = v \textbf{ in } e \textbf{ as } t \textbf{ for } a, n|\!\} \\ \qquad \mapsto \{\!|\textbf{cast } \mathcal{E}(a, \textbf{let } x \textbf{ at } a = (\textbf{run}_\mathbf{f}\ v) \textbf{ in } (\textbf{run}_\mathbf{f}\ e), n) \textbf{ to } (t \textbf{ for } a), n+1|\!\} \\ \qquad \text{learning } \mathcal{E}(a, \textbf{let } x \textbf{ at } a = (\textbf{run}_\mathbf{f}\ v) \textbf{ in } (\textbf{run}_\mathbf{f}\ e), n) : t \textbf{ for } a\end{array}} \ \textsc{step-ForBind}$$

$$\frac{\textit{value}(\textbf{cast } \mathcal{E}(a, e, m) \textbf{ to } t\ [\ \textbf{blaming } p\ ])}{\Sigma; F_0; W \vdash \{\!|\textbf{asbits cast } \mathcal{E}(a, e, m) \textbf{ to } t\ [\ \textbf{blaming } p\ ], n|\!\} \mapsto \{\!|\mathcal{E}(a, e, m), n|\!\} \text{ learning } \cdot} \ \textsc{step-AsBits}$$

$$\frac{\textit{value}(\textbf{cast } \mathcal{E}(a, e, m) \textbf{ to } t\ [\ \textbf{blaming } p\ ]) \qquad \Sigma; F_0; W|\cdot; a; a \vdash e : t \qquad a \sqsubseteq W}{\Sigma; F_0; W \vdash \{\!|\textbf{run}_\mathbf{f}\ (\textbf{cast } \mathcal{E}(a, e, m) \textbf{ to } t\ [\ \textbf{blaming } p\ ]), n|\!\} \mapsto \{\!|e, n|\!\} \text{ learning } \cdot} \ \textsc{step-ForRun-Ok}$$

$$\frac{\textit{value}(\textbf{cast } \mathcal{E}(a, e, m) \textbf{ to } t \textbf{ blaming } p) \qquad \Sigma; F_0; W|\cdot; a; a \nvdash e : t \qquad a \sqsubseteq W}{\Sigma; F_0; W \vdash \{\!|\textbf{run}_\mathbf{f}\ (\textbf{cast } \mathcal{E}(a, e, m) \textbf{ to } t \textbf{ blaming } p), n|\!\} \mapsto \{\!|\textbf{fail } p, n|\!\} \text{ learning } \cdot} \ \textsc{step-ForRun-IllTyped}$$

$$\frac{\textit{value}(\textbf{cast } \mathcal{E}(a, e, m) \textbf{ to } (t \textbf{ for } b) \textbf{ blaming } p) \qquad b \sqsubseteq W \qquad a \neq b}{\Sigma; F_0; W \vdash \{\!|\textbf{run}_\mathbf{f}\ (\textbf{cast } \mathcal{E}(a, e, m) \textbf{ to } (t \textbf{ for } b) \textbf{ blaming } p), n|\!\} \mapsto \{\!|\textbf{fail } p, n|\!\} \text{ learning } \cdot} \ \textsc{step-ForRun-Junk}$$

$$\frac{\Sigma; F_0; W \vdash \{\!|e_1, n|\!\} \mapsto \{\!|e_1', n'|\!\} \text{ learning } F}{\Sigma; F_0; W \vdash \{\!|e_1\ e_2, n|\!\} \mapsto \{\!|e_1'\ e_2, n'|\!\} \text{ learning } F} \ \textsc{step-App-CongL}$$

Figure 7: Selected AuraConf evaluation rules.

Importantly $\text{valid}_\Sigma\ \mathcal{F}$ is not defined as a typing judgment because its truth, in general, may only be ascertained with access to every principal's private key. Such a property is useless when implementing a typechecker. Thus it is better to consider validity as a semantic property existing beside but distinct from AuraConf's type system.

The following lemma shows facts generated during reduction are valid.

LEMMA 2 (New Fact Validity). *Assume that* $\Sigma \vdash \diamond$ *holds and* $\Sigma; \mathcal{F}_0; W|E; V; U \vdash e : t$. *Then* $\text{valid}_\Sigma\ \mathcal{F}_0$ *and* $\Sigma; \mathcal{F}_0; W \vdash \{\!|e, n|\!\} \mapsto \{\!|e', n'|\!\}$ *learning* $\mathcal{F}$ *implies* $\text{valid}_\Sigma\ \mathcal{F}$.

Additionally, AuraConf has a decidable typing relation. Decidability is of independent theoretic interest, but matters in particular because evaluating $\textbf{run}_\mathbf{f}$ dynamically invokes the type checker. Were typing undecidable, $\textbf{run}_\mathbf{f}$ could instead conservatively approximate; otherwise the progress lemma would not hold.

LEMMA 3 (Decidability). *Suppose* $\Sigma \vdash \diamond$; *then it is decidable if that* $\Sigma; \mathcal{F}; W|E; V; U \vdash e : t$. *Furthermore, it is also decidable if there exists any* S *such that* $\Sigma; \mathcal{F}; W|E; V; U \vdash e : t$.

The AuraConf statement of progress follows. Note that it describes the behavior of terms that are well-typed using a valid fact context. Additionally, any simple world greater than U and V—that is with the private keys specified by the soft decryption limit and effect label—has enough authority to step a program without getting stuck.

LEMMA 4 (Progress). *Assume Conjecture 3 holds. Assume also that* $\Sigma \vdash \diamond$, $\text{valid}_\Sigma\ \mathcal{F}_0$, *and* $\Sigma; \mathcal{F}_0; W_0|E; V; U \vdash e : t$. *Now suppose* W *is a simple world where* $U \sqsubseteq W$ *and* $V \sqsubseteq W$. *Then either* e *is a value, or there exist* e', n', *and* $\mathcal{F}$ *where* $\Sigma; \mathcal{F}_0; W \vdash \{\!|e, n|\!\} \mapsto \{\!|e', n'|\!\}$ *learning* $\mathcal{F}$.

$\boxed{W \vdash t_1 \simeq t_2}$

$$\frac{}{W \vdash x \simeq x} \ \textsc{sim-Var}$$

$$\frac{W \vdash t_{11} \simeq t_{12} \qquad W \vdash t_{21} \simeq t_{22}}{W \vdash (t_{11}\ t_{21}) \simeq (t_{12}\ t_{22})} \ \textsc{sim-App}$$

$$\frac{a \sqsubseteq W \qquad W \vdash e_1 \simeq e_2}{W \vdash \mathcal{E}(a, e_1, n_1) \simeq \mathcal{E}(a, e_2, n_2)} \ \textsc{sim-Decrypt}$$

$$\frac{a \not\sqsubseteq W \qquad b \not\sqsubseteq W}{W \vdash \mathcal{E}(a, e_1, n_1) \simeq \mathcal{E}(b, e_2, n_2)} \ \textsc{sim-Opaque}$$

Figure 8: Selected rules from the definition of similar terms.

Lemmas 1, 2, and 4 together imply that AuraConf is sound.

Noninterference Noninterference properties, which state that a program's secret inputs do not influence its public outputs, are a common way of defining security for programming languages [4, 39, 40]. Such properties are formalized by saying programs which differ only in their secret components are *similar* and showing that similar terms reduce to similar values. The following develops a noninterference property for AuraConf.

AuraConf similarity is defined relative to particular set of keys used to analyze ciphertexts. Figure 8 gives the key rules from the definition of similarity. Most often, two terms are related when they are identical, as in SIM-VAR, or share a top-level constructor with similar subterms, as in SIM-APP. The figure elides a tedious quantity of rules implementing this scheme. Similarity is more interesting for ciphertexts. Rule SIM-DECRYPT finds two ciphertexts similar when they are encrypted with the same key, can be decrypted by W (captured by premise $a \sqsubseteq W$), and have similar payloads. This formalizes the idea that encrypting similar terms should yield similar results. Finally, SIM-OPAQUE states two ciphertexts are similar when neither can be decrypted. This captures the intuition that ciphertexts are black boxes, immune to analysis without a key. We implicitly assume ciphertexts are (randomly) padded such that ciphertext length cannot be used at a side channel. A faithful implementation will require care to properly handle AuraConf's rich data structures.

The following lemma gives AuraConf's noninterference property. It considers running two terms, e_1 and e_2, that step without error under authority W. If the terms are similar at W (or any higher world W_0), the resulting terms, e_1' and e_2', are similar as well. That is, running a program twice with two different confidential inputs yields results that cannot be distinguished without a sufficiently privileged private key.

THEOREM 1 (Noninterference). *Assume that both* $\Sigma \vdash \diamond$ *and* $\Sigma; \mathcal{F}_1; W|\cdot; V; U \vdash e_1 : k_1$. *Pick* W_0 *and* e_2 *where* $W_0 \vdash e_1 \simeq e_2$ *and* $W \sqsubseteq W_0$. *If*

- $\Sigma; W; \mathcal{F}_1 \vdash \{\!|e_1, n_1|\!\} \mapsto \{\!|e_1', n_1'|\!\}$ *learning* $\mathcal{F}_1'$,
- $\Sigma; W; \mathcal{F}_2 \vdash \{\!|e_2, n_2|\!\} \mapsto \{\!|e_2', n_2'|\!\}$ *learning* $\mathcal{F}_2'$,
- *there is no p such that* e_1' blames p, *and*
- *there is no p such that* e_2' blames p,

then $W_0 \vdash e_1' \simeq e_2'$.

5. Discussion

Information-flow and Aura Information-flow analyses [32] inspired this paper's goal of augmenting Aura to handle confidential data. However, while these techniques influenced and informed the design of AuraConf, they cannot be directly applied.

In standard information-flow systems, programmers use *labels* to express confidentiality and integrity constraints on data, and the language's typing judgment is specialized to deal with these labels [40]. Well-typed terms are correct by construction; they satisfy noninterference. (However, increasingly expressive information-flow languages often satisfy variously weakened versions of the property.) Most conventional information-flow languages are limited by a focus on closed systems: the programmer must, for example, manually encrypt confidential data leaving the program with an unsafe *declassification* operator.

Aura can encode this style of of information flow analysis [22]. However, this encoding makes also makes "closed world" assumptions—attackers are assumed to respect Aura's runtime invariants and confidential data is not protected by cryptography. This work provides a means for programmers to rule out implementation errors on a single host, but, unlike AuraConf, does not directly address distributed aspects of confidentiality. Similar information flow encodings are possible in Fine [35], and Haskell [24].

In previous work with Zdancewic [39], I described an information-flow language, SImp, suitable for programming in open systems. SImp resolves the mismatch between policy specification and enforcement by connecting information flow labels directly with public key cryptography. Policies and data may be combined into *packages* that use digital signatures and encryption to ensure only principals with appropriate keys may access data.

SImp policies are specified by annotating data values and heap locations with semantically rich *labels*. Labels are lists of security sublabels with owner, confidentiality, and integrity components. Sublabel $o : \overline{r}\,!\,\overline{w}$ means owner o certifies that any principal in set $\overline{r}$ may read from the associated location, and any principal in set $\overline{w}$ may write. Full labels allow (groups of) principals to read or write when each sublabel is satisfied. This is a variant of Myers and Liskov's [29] decentralized label model (DLM).

Although SImp's design influenced AuraConf, its technical mechanisms could not be adopted wholesale. Information-flow analysis with DLM labels, the basis for SImp, provides a very different model of declarative information security than Aura. In particular Aura's **says** monad decorates propositions to express *endorsement*, while SImp's integrity sublabels described tainted data. While intuitively related, these concepts demand different treatments. It is unclear how to understand DLM owners in Aura. Additionally, interpreting the semantics of a DLM label—that is, calculating its effective reader and writer sets—requires knowledge of the global delegation relation, or "acts-for hierarchy," information that cannot be reliably obtained in Aura's distributed setting. SImp's design did provide direct inspiration for several aspects of AuraConf, including declarative policy specification, a key-based notion of identity, and automatic encryption.

On Noninterference AuraConf's noninterference property (Lemma 1) is weak in the following sense. It discusses what happens when a pair of terms with different secrets successfully take a step, but does not deal with the situation in which one steps successfully and the other fails. The reason is subtle. Consider the following definitions and terms:

```
data Singleton : bits → Type
{ | inject : (t: bits) → Singleton t }

ok: Singleton ℰ(a, "hi", 1) → Prop
e1 ≡ ok( inject (ℰ(a, "hi", 1)) )
e2 ≡ ok( inject (ℰ(a, "hi", 2)) )
```

Terms e_1 and e_2 represent differently randomized encryptions of the same string. It's intuitively appealing that these are similar for purposes of noninterference, and indeed $\mathsf{a} \vdash e_1 \simeq e_2$. However term e_1 is well-typed, but e_2 is not. Terms like these can cause $\mathbf{run_f}$ to show different failure behavior when applied to similar terms. Consequently, Lemma 1's definition of noninterference is an example of termination-insensitive noninterference [4].

Termination insensitivity is required because AuraConf and its metatheory have the following three properties. First, the language can express singleton types on ciphertexts—useful in general and necessary for **isa** propositions. Second, it features a typesafe decryption operator that works at arbitrary types—a design goal. Third, the similarity relation is aligned with standard Dolev-Yao [1983] cryptanalysis. While it's possible to alter one of these properties to induce a stronger form of noninterference, such a change appears counterproductive.

6. Related Work

Modal logics provide a framework to describe the way in which a proposition holds. Common modalities can specify that a sentence is necessarily vs. possibly true or that a condition will be met eventually vs. from-now-on. In the vernacular of Kripke structures this is a technique for reasoning about different worlds, a terminology that AuraConf borrows [17]. Pfenning and Davies [30] introduced a constructive, type-theoretic treatment of modal logic. Their account focuses on the logical foundations of the system. Jia and Walker [21] studied a similar theory from a distributed-programming perspective, interpreting modal operators as specifying the locations at which code may run. While Pfenning discusses three judgments: truth, validity and possibility, Jia presents an indexed judgment form that can describe a large quantity of locations. Murphy's [27] dissertation describes a full-scale programming language based on these ideas.

The systems above have an absolute static semantics. That is, although executing code may depend on location or resource availability, checking that a type (or proposition) is well-formed can happen anywhere. AuraConf's ability to make typing more precise using statically available keys appears novel.

One intended semantics for AuraConf implements objects of form **sign**(a, P) as digital signatures and objects like $\mathcal{E}$(a, e, n) as ciphertext. All cryptography occurs at a lower level of abstraction than the language definition. This approach has previously been used to implement or model declarative information flow policies [25, 39]. An alternative approach is to treat keys as types or first class objects and to provide encryption or signing primitives in the language [3, 15, 23, 33]. Such approaches typically provide the programmer with additional flexibility but complicate the programming model; in contrast, a goal of AuraConf is to free the programmer from such explicit key management.

Askarov and Sabelfeld [5] describe both approaches to information flow and give a translation of a high-level language with a declassification operator into a low-level language that implements declassification via publication of specific cryptographic keys. Similarly to this paper, Askarov and Sabelfeld's work uses an algebraic model of randomized cryptography to demonstrate that noninterference is preserved when secrets are encrypted. Their model can describe declassification directly, something not done here, and it would be interesting to extend the analysis of AuraConf to account for intentional declassification.

Sumii and Pierce [34] studied λ_{seal}, an extension to lambda calculus with terms of form $\{e\}_{e'}$, meaning e sealed-by e', and a corresponding elimination form. Unlike AuraConf, λ_{seal} makes seal (i.e. key) generation explicit in program text. Additionally, λ_{seal} includes black-box functions that analyze sealed values, but cannot be disassembled to reveal the seal (key). It is unclear how to implement these functions using cryptography.

Heintze and Riecke's [18] SLam calculus is an information flow lambda calculus in which the right to read a closure corresponds to the right to apply it. This sidesteps the black-box function issue from λ_{seal}. In SLam, some expressions are marked with the function writer's authority. This differs from AuraConf's notion of dynamic authority which describes the program's available keys.

We use the algebraic Dolev-Yao model to study the connection between information flow and cryptography. Laud and Vene [23] examined this problem using a computational model of encryption. More recently, Smith and Alpízar [33] extended this work to include a model of decryption. They prove noninterference for a simple language without declassification (or packing) and a two-point security lattice.

Abadi and Rogaway [2] proved that Dolev-Yao analysis is sound with respect to computational cryptographic analysis in a setting similar to Vaughan and Zdancewic's [39]. However, there are several significant differences between these approaches. In particular, Abadi and Rogaway do not discuss public key cryptography, which we use extensively. Backes and Pfitzmann [6] with Waidner [7] have also investigated the connection between symbolic and computational models of encryption. They define a Dolev-Yao style library and show that protocols proved secure with respect to library semantics are also secure with respect to computational cryptographic analysis. Likewise Barthe et al. [8] have published a Coq formalization of several cryptographic algorithms, including ElGamal digital signatures. These techniques and artifacts might provide an excellent foundation for further rigorous analysis of AuraConf.

7. Conclusions and Future Work

AuraConf's treatment of cryptography includes several novel elements. Because AuraConf uses statically available keys and fact contexts to augment compile-time typechecking, it places unusual demands on its type system. In particular, the very notion of well-typedness is dependent on which keys are available statically, and it is challenging to predict where a term can typecheck. Additionally, evaluation can also use private keys, and programs will get stuck if run in the wrong context. AuraConf answers "where can a term be typechecked?" and "where can it be run?" by combining, in a new way, ideas from modal type theory and type-and-effect analysis.

AuraConf trades increased complexity for increased ability to detect and debug security problems both statically via type checking and dynamically via audit. It appears possible to reduce complexity by giving up certain features, such as higher-order confidential data or static detection of some key-management bugs. It would be interesting to explore and evaluate these and other points in the design space.

Currently AuraConf provides a fail-stop semantics: decryption failures lead to an uncatchable, fatal exception. It would be better to handle these errors programmatically, and a variety of techniques could be brought to bear. Most promising, AuraConf could be extended with a general purpose exception mechanism like ML's or Java's. Doing this properly requires merging exceptions with effects analysis with higher-order types, a topic of active research [10, 11]. A more readily implementable scheme might make $\mathbf{run}_{\mathbf{f}}$ return a discriminated union.

AuraConf's worlds provide a simple model of key management. Programs may be run and typechecked using zero or one statically available keys. The typing judgment additionally allows $\top$ to represent "all keys" in effect labels and soft decryption limits. However worlds are treated primarily as lattice elements and it appears interesting to define worlds using a richer structure, such as sets of keys or DLM-inspired labels. This generalization would require making (hopefully) straightforward modifications to the language metatheory and, more interestingly, carefully designing an expressive and practical security lattice.

Acknowledgments

This work was initiated as part of my dissertation at the University of Pennsylvania. Thank you to my Ph.D. advisor, Steve Zdancewic, and to my thesis committee, Benjamin C. Pierce, Frank Pfenning, Andre Scedrov, and Stephanie Weirich. Their feedback greatly strengthened the ideas in this paper.

References

[1] M. Abadi. Access control in a core calculus of dependency. In *Proceedings of the 11th ACM SIGPLAN International Conference on Functional Programming, ICFP 2006, Portland, Oregon, USA, September 16-21, 2006*, pp. 263–273. ACM, 2006.

[2] M. Abadi, P. Rogaway. Reconciling two views of cryptography (the computational soundness of formal encryption). In *Journal of Cryptology*, 15(2):103–127, 2002.

[3] A. Askarov, D. Hedin, A. Sabelfeld. Cryptographically-masked flows. In *SAS '06*, LNCS. Seoul, Korea, 2006.

[4] A. Askarov, S. Hunt, A. Sabelfeld, D. Sands. Termination-insensitive noninterference leaks more than just a bit. In *ESORICS '08*, pp. 333–348. 2008.

[5] A. Askarov, A. Sabelfeld. Gradual release: Unifying declassification, encryption and key release policies. In *SP '07: Proceedings of the*

2007 *IEEE Symposium on Security and Privacy*, pp. 207–221. IEEE Computer Society, Washington, DC, USA, 2007.

[6] M. Backes, B. Pfitzmann. Relating symbolic and cryptographic secrecy. In *IEEE Trans. Dependable Secur. Comput.*, 2(2):109–123, 2005.

[7] M. Backes, B. Pfitzmann, M. Waidner. A composable cryptographic library with nested operations. In *CCS '03: Proceedings of the 10th ACM Conference on Computer and Communications security*, pp. 220–230. ACM Press, Washington D.C., USA, 2003.

[8] G. Barthe, B. Grégoire, S. Zanella Béguelin. Formal certification of code-based cryptographic proofs. In *POPL '09: Proceedings of the 36th annual ACM SIGPLAN-SIGACT symposium on Principles of programming languages*, pp. 90–101. ACM, New York, NY, USA, 2009.

[9] L. Bauer, S. Garriss, M. K. Reiter. Distributed proving in access-control systems. In *Proceedings of the 2005 IEEE Symposium on Security & Privacy*, pp. 81–95. 2005.

[10] N. Benton, P. Buchlovsky. Semantics of an effect analysis for exceptions. In *Proceedings of the Third ACM SIGPLAN Workshop on Types in Language Design and Implementation (TLDI '07)*. ACM, Nice, France, 2007.

[11] M. Blume, U. A. Acar, W. Chae. Exception handlers as extensible cases. In *Proceedings of the Sixth ASIAN Symposium on Programming Languages and Systems (APLAS 2008)*. Bangalore, India, 2008. To appear.

[12] H. B. Curry, R. Feys, W. Craig. *Combinatory Logic*, vol. 1. North-Holland, Amsterdam, 1958.

[13] D. Dolev, A. Yao. On the security of public key protocols. In *IEEE Transactions on Information Theory*, 2(29), 1983.

[14] C. Fournet, A. D. Gordon, S. Maffeis. A type discipline for authorization in distributed systems. In *Proc. of the 20th IEEE Computer Security Foundations Symposium*. 2007.

[15] C. Fournet, T. Rezk. Cryptographically sound implementations for typed information-flow security. In *POPL '08*, pp. 323–335. 2008.

[16] C. Gentry. Fully homomorphic encryption using ideal lattices. In *STOC '09*. 2009.

[17] R. Goldblatt. Mathematical modal logic: a view of its evolution. In *J. of Applied Logic*, 1(5-6):309–392, 2003.

[18] N. Heintze, J. G. Riecke. The SLam calculus: programming with secrecy and integrity. In *POPL '98*, pp. 365–377. ACM Press, New York, NY, 1998.

[19] W. A. Howard. The formulae-as-types notion of construction. In J. P. Seldin, J. R. Hindly, eds., *To H. B. Curry: Essays on Combinatory Logic, Lambda-Calculus, and Formalism*, pp. 479–490. Academic Press, New York, 1980.

[20] L. Jia, J. A. Vaughan, K. Mazurak, J. Zhao, L. Zarko, J. Schorr, S. Zdancewic. Aura: A programming language for authorization and audit. In *ICFP '08*, pp. 27–38. 2008. Extended version U. Penn. Tech. Rep. MS-CIS-08-10.

[21] L. Jia, D. Walker. Modal proofs as distributed programs (extended abstract). In *ESOP '04*. 2004. Full version Princeton Tech. Rep. TR-671-03.

[22] L. Jia, S. Zdancewic. Encoding information flow in aura. In *PLAS '09*. 2009.

[23] P. Laud, V. Vene. A type system for computationally secure information flow. In *FCT '05*, pp. 365–377. Lübeck, Germany, 2005.

[24] P. Li, S. Zdancewic. Encoding information flow in haskell. In *CSFW '06*. 2006.

[25] J. Liu, M. D. George, K. Vikram, X. Qi, L. Waye, A. C. Myers. Fabric: a platform for secure distributed computation and storage. In *SOSP '09: Proceedings of the ACM SIGOPS 22nd symposium on Operating systems principles*, pp. 321–334. ACM, New York, NY, USA, 2009.

[26] J. M. Lucassen, D. K. Gifford. Polymorphic effect systems. In *POPL '88*. 1988.

[27] T. Murphy, VII. *Modal Types for Mobile Code*. Ph.D. thesis, CMU, 2008.

[28] T. Murphy, VII, K. Crary, R. Harper, F. Pfenning. A symmetric modal lambda calculus for distributed computing. In *LICS '04*. IEEE Press, 2004.

[29] A. Myers, B. Liskov. Protecting privacy using the decentralized label model. In *ACM Trans. on Software Engineering and Methodology*, 9(4):410–442, 2000.

[30] F. Pfenning, R. Davies. A judgmental reconstruction of modal logic. In *Mathematical. Structures in Comp. Sci.*, 11(4):511–540, 2001.

[31] D. K. Rappe. *Homomorphic Cryptosystems and Their Applications*. Ph.D. thesis, University of Dortmund, Germany, 2004.

[32] A. Sabelfeld, A. C. Myers. Language-based information-flow security. In *IEEE Journal on Selected Areas in Communications*, 21(1):5–19, 2003.

[33] G. Smith, R. Alpízar. Secure information flow with random assignment and encryption. In *FSME'06*, pp. 33–43. Alexandria, Virgina, USA, 2006.

[34] E. Sumii, B. C. Pierce. A bisimulation for dynamic sealing. In *POPL '04*. 2004.

[35] N. Swamy, J. Chen, R. Chugh. Enforcing stateful authorization and information flow policies in Fine. In *ESOP '10*. 2010.

[36] J.-P. Talpin, P. Jouvelot. The type and effect discipline. In *LICS '92*. 1992.

[37] J. A. Vaughan. *Aura: Programming with Authorization and Audit*. Ph.D. thesis, University of Pennsylvania, Philadelphia, PA, USA, 2009.

[38] J. A. Vaughan, L. Jia, K. Mazurak, S. Zdancewic. Evidence-based audit. In *CSF '08*, pp. 177–191. 2008. Extended version U. Penn. Tech. Rep. MS-CIS-08-09.

[39] J. A. Vaughan, S. Zdancewic. A cryptographic decentralized label model. In *IEEE Security and Privacy*, pp. 192–206. Berkeley, California, 2007.

[40] D. Volpano, G. Smith, C. Irvine. A sound type system for secure flow analysis. In *Journal of Computer Security*, 4(3):167–187, 1996.

Information Flow Enforcement in Monadic Libraries

Dominique Devriese
K.U.Leuven, Belgium
dominique.devriese@cs.kuleuven.be

Frank Piessens
K.U.Leuven, Belgium
frank.piessens@cs.kuleuven.be

Abstract

In various scenarios, there is a need to expose a certain API to client programs which are not fully trusted. In cases where the client programs need access to sensitive data, confidentiality can be enforced using an information flow policy. This is a general and powerful type of policy that has been widely studied and implemented.

Previous work has shown how information flow policy enforcement can be implemented in a lightweight fashion in the form of a library. However, these approaches all suffer from a number of limitations. Often, the policy and its enforcement are not cleanly separated from the underlying API, and the user of the API is exposed to a strongly and unnaturally modified interface. Some of the approaches are limited to functional APIs and have difficulty handling imperative features like I/O and mutable state variables. In addition, this previous work uses classic static information flow enforcement techniques, and does not consider more recent dynamic information flow enforcement techniques.

In this paper, we show that information flow policies can be enforced on imperative-style monadic APIs in a modular and reasonably general way with only a minor impact on the interface provided to API users. The main idea of this paper is that we implement the policy enforcement in a monad transformer while the underlying monadic API remains unaware and unmodified. The policy is specified through the lifting of underlying monad operations.

We show the generality of our approach by presenting implementations of three important information flow enforcement techniques, including a purely dynamic, a purely static and a hybrid technique. Two of the techniques require the use of a generalisation of the `Monad` type class, but impact on the API interface stays limited. We show that our technique lends itself to formal reasoning by sketching a proof that our implementation of the static technique is faithful to the original presentation. Finally, we discuss fundamental limitations of our approach and how it fits in general information flow enforcement theory.

Categories and Subject Descriptors D.4.6 [*Security and Protection*]: Information flow controls

General Terms Security, Languages

Keywords information flow enforcement, monads, monad transformer, parameterised monads

TLDI'11, January 25, 2011, Austin, Texas, USA.

1. Introduction

In various scenarios, there is a need to expose a certain API to a program without fully trusting it. Examples are JavaScript applications running in a web browser, plug-ins in user applications or even independent programs in a general-purpose OS. In order to protect against faulty or malicious use of the API, policies are defined establishing what constitutes valid use of the API. Such a policy is then enforced statically (type systems or other compile-time analysis) or dynamically (run-time monitoring).

Information flow policies are an important general class of policies. Given an ordered set of security levels, and a classification of all input and output operations at certain security levels, such a policy mandates that input at a certain security level must not in any way influence output at lower security levels. In the common case with only two security levels, secure information flow mandates that confidential information does not leak to public outputs.

It has been shown [13, 19, 22] that enforcement of information flow policies can be implemented in a lightweight fashion in the form of a library. However, these approaches suffer from a number of limitations. Often, the policy and its enforcement are not cleanly separated from the underlying API, and the user of the API is exposed to a strongly and unnaturally modified interface. Some of the approaches are limited to functional APIs and have difficulty handling imperative features like I/O and mutable state variables. In addition, all of these libraries use a form of static analysis (either at compile-time or at runtime). None of them show how to implement the dynamic information flow enforcement techniques that are increasingly being studied in information flow research [2, 4, 12, 21].

In this paper, we present a general technique for enforcing information flow policies in monadic libraries in Haskell. The enforcement of the policy occurs in a monad transformer, wrapping the monadic API of the underlying library, which remains unaware and unmodified. Policies are specified through the lifting of base monad operations into the transformed monad. We show that our technique is suited for implementing a wide range of enforcement techniques, including dynamic, static and hybrid ones. We show that this is possible while maintaining most of the "look and feel" of the underlying monadic library API.

Contrary to previous work, we do not limit ourselves to information flow enforcement techniques based on static analysis. We present implementations of three important information flow enforcement techniques, including a purely dynamic, a purely static and a hybrid technique. The two latter techniques require some form of static analysis of user code, which we implement using a generalisation of the *Monad* concept, called parameterised monads [9]. This allows us to type the monadic operations *return*, $(\gg)$ (sequence) and $(\ggg)$ (bind) differently, allowing us to perform the static analysis we need without relying on explicit developer-provided casts.

In section 7, we provide a formal result and a proof sketch demonstrating the faithfulness of our account of Volpano et al.'s classic type system-based enforcement [24], which we implement in section 6. We show that we can translate programs in a model language extended with output statements to calculations in our monad transformer, where the typing judgements of a straightforward extension of Volpano et al.'s type system correspond in a precisely defined manner to the types of our transformed monad calculations. We do not expect corresponding results for our other implementations to be significantly harder to formulate and prove.

Finally, we look into the limits of our approach. In the context of dynamic information flow enforcement, we can think of our approach as a type of monitor where the monitorable events are the monadic sequence ($\gg$) and bind ($\gg\!=$) operators. We discuss that for at least one recent dynamic information flow enforcement technique [2], these monitorable events do not suffice, making it impossible to implement the technique as a monad transformer.

In summary, the contributions of this paper are:

- We propose an approach to implementing information flow policy enforcement for monadic libraries. Contrary to existing work, it allows for a clean separation between policy enforcement and the underlying API, and does not impose unnatural modifications of the interface provided to users of the library.
- We provide evidence for the generality of the approach by presenting implementations of three information flow enforcement techniques, including a dynamic, a static and a hybrid technique, where existing libraries only work with static analysis. We are not aware of any previous implementations of dynamic information flow enforcement as a library.
- We give a formal statement of the faithfulness of our account of a static enforcement technique to the original presentation, and provide a proof sketch.
- We discuss the limitations of our approach, in which all compile-time or run-time interception takes place at the level of monadic operations, making it unsuitable for at least one dynamic enforcement technique [2].

2. The basic idea

In order to explain the basic design of our library, we show an example of a monadic API on which we want to enforce an information flow policy.

2.1 An E-mail Client Example

Our example API starts from a simplistic scenario where an e-mail application provides a plug-in infrastructure allowing user- or institution-provided plugins to intercept e-mails while they are being sent. Plug-ins are allowed to modify e-mails (e.g. in order to add quotes or disclaimers at the bottom of the e-mail), send the mail to multiple recipients (e.g. to the original recipient and to an archiving system). In order to do this, they are allowed to retrieve external resources (e.g. a company standard disclaimer or a quotes database), identified by URLs.

In order to prevent malicious plug-ins from leaking users' private information through resource requests, an information flow policy is defined. The result of any *readMail* operation is considered confidential information, and it is only allowed to influence *sendMail* operations, which are considered as output at the confidential security level (note that malicious plug-ins could send e-mails to other recipients than the original, but we assume for simplicity that this is prevented in some other way). Invocations of *downloadResource* and the URLs passed to them are considered public, as they can be observed on the network or by the resource server owners. The result of *downloadResource* calls is public information. With this classification of base monad operations at security levels, an information flow policy is defined, stating that the contents of a user e-mail must not in any way influence requests for external resources. In further sections, we show how to specify and enforce this policy using different enforcement monad transformers.

```
class (Monad m) ⇒ EmailM m where
  readMail :: m String
  sendMail :: String → m ()
  downloadResource :: String → m String
instance EmailM IO where
  sendMail = putStrLn ∘ ("Sending mail: "++)
  readMail = putStr ": " ≫ getLine
  downloadResource = (≫return "prefix; ") ∘
    putStrLn ∘ ("Downloading resource: "++)
instance (EmailM m) ⇒ EmailM (StateT a m) where
  sendMail = lift ∘ sendMail
  readMail = lift readMail
  downloadResource = lift ∘ downloadResource
```

Figure 1. An example API presented to plug-in developers in an e-mail application, along with an example implementation in the IO monad. We also provide classic automatic lifting of the *EmailM* operations through the state monad transformer.

The API presented to plug-in developers is shown in Figure 1. The API is defined in the *EmailM* type class. This type class extends the Monad type class and provides *readMail*, *sendMail* and *downloadResource* operations. The *readMail* operation returns the contents of a mail input by the user, the *sendMail* operation ships off a mail to be sent and the *downloadResource* operation takes the URL of a resource and returns its contents. The figure also shows a model implementation in the IO monad and an automatic lifting of the *EmailM* type class through a *StateT* monad transformer (similar to how this is done with e.g. the standard *MonadReader* type class).

2.2 Information flow enforcement in a Monad transformer

The basic observation behind our implementation approach for information flow enforcement libraries is that in a monadic API, a lot can be learned about the program's information flow from the invocations of *Monad* operations $\gg$ and $\gg\!=$. For example, when two calculations a and b are sequenced ($a \gg b$), we are sure that the result value of a can not influence computation b. On the contrary, when a monadic calculation a is bound to a continuation f ($a \gg\!= f$), we can interpret this as a generalised form of a branching statement, where the result value of a determines the calculations that will be executed next.

The next observation we make is that intercepting monadic operations in a base monad is precisely what Haskell's *Monad* transformers allow us to do. And with this second observation, the basis of our approach is clear: we will implement information flow enforcement techniques as monad transformers and use the information we can obtain from intercepted *Monad* operations to approximate the flow of information in a program.

There is one important problem with this approach however, namely that the calls to *Monad* operations do not always correctly represent the actual information flow in a program. For example, in the program **do** $x \leftarrow$ *getLine*; *return* (), it would be wrong to assume that the result of *getLine* influences the result of the combination. Nevertheless, a Haskell compiler will "desugar" the example to *getLine* $\gg\!= \lambda x \rightarrow$ *return* (), and our monad trans-

```
badflow = do sec ← getSec
             putSecret sec
             pub ← getPub
             putPublic $ pub ++ ", done."

goodflow = do sec ← getSec
              putSecret sec
         ≫ do pub ← getPub
              putPublic $ pub ++ ", done."
```

Figure 2. An example requiring non-standard use of the do-notation to provide proper scoping information for use in the information flow enforcement. In the expression *badflow* it will not be clear to the enforcement transformer that the information coming from *getSec* is not used in the call to *putPublic*. The scoping in the expression *goodflow* makes this clear.

formers will have to assume that the result value of *getLine* is used by the function $\lambda x \rightarrow return\ ()$, leading to an overapproximation of the information flow in the program. The solution we will adopt to this problem is that we impose the requirement on users of the API to accurately reflect the flow of sensitive information in their programs through a proper scoping of variables. For example the example above should instead be written as **do** *getLine*; *return* () or *getLine* ≫ *return* (). In this case, the use of ≫ instead of ≫= allows the enforcement technique to detect that the result of the left-hand side calculation is not used in the other one. Figure 2 shows a more complicated example where two separate do-statements are explicitly sequenced to correctly reflect the example's information flow in the structure of the *Monad* operation calls.

Note that a consequence of this approach is that we do not treat a sequence of two calculations *ma* ≫ *mb* as identical to *ma* ≫= *const mb*, contrary to what Haskell programmers are used to. However, we want to point out that sematically identical constructs are often treated differently by information flow enforcement techniques. Consider how $x := s - s$ would be treated differently from $x := 0$ by most techniques or how **if** *sec* **then** $x :=$ true **else** $x :=$ false would be treated differently from $x := sec$ by Austin and Flanagan's enforcement technique [2]). This imprecision is inherent to enforcement techniques employing the syntactic structure of programs, rather than their actual behaviour. Devriese and Piessens have recently presented a fundamentally different technique which does not suffer from this problem [4].

2.3 Telling the good from the bad

Figures 3 and 4 show examples of plug-ins using the *EmailM* interface. Both employ explicit sequencing of two separate do-statements, as discussed in the previous section. We will use these examples throughout this paper to demonstrate our implementation.

The first example (*plugin1*) shows a plug-in which prefixes the user mail with the contents of an external resource, appends a newline and sends the mail. No information about the mail leaks to the resource server, so this plug-in respects the information flow policy. On the other hand, *plugin2* will only download the external resource if a certain property holds for the user e-mail, thus violating the policy: the owner of the resource server can deduce that the user sent a mail satisfying the *isInteresting* property. Note that in this case, information is only leaked because the request for the external resource is issued in a branch on secret data, which is sometimes called an "implicit" leak in the information flow literature. If we replace the if-then-else block with *downloadResource* $ *res* ++ "?q=" ++ *escape m*, then there is an "explicit" leak of information.

```
res :: String
res = "http://example.com/res.txt"
plugin1 :: (EmailM m, MonadState String m) ⇒ m ()
plugin1 = do m ← readMail
             put $ m ++ "\n"
        ≫ do p ← downloadResource res
             m ← get
             sendMail $ p ++ m
```

Figure 3. Example plug-in *plugin1*, respecting the information flow policy.

```
isInteresting :: String → Bool
isInteresting = elem "Haskell" ∘ words
plugin2 :: (EmailM m, MonadState String m) ⇒ m ()
plugin2 = do m ← readMail
             put $ m ++ "\n"
        ≫ do m ← get
             if isInteresting m
               then downloadResource res
               else return ""
             sendMail m
```

Figure 4. Example plug-in *plugin2*, which does not respect the information flow policy, because it leaks information about the user mail to the external resource server.

With these two examples, we have set the objective for the rest of this text. In the next sections, we implement three different monad transformers, implementing information flow enforcement techniques to be able to detect illegal information flows, such as the one in *plugin2* without interfering with correct plug-ins like *plugin1*.

3. Dynamic information flow enforcement with security level ascriptions

The first information flow enforcement technique we implement is Sabelfeld and Russo's simple flow-insensitive dynamic enforcement [21]. They employ a fixed programmer-provided assignment of security levels to variables. With this information, they can deduce a security level for each expression, and track the security level of all information in the program. In order to prevent implicit leaks, they additionally keep a stack of security levels for the "program counter", representing the maximum security level of all information that determined the currently executing branch to be chosen. This allows them to detect implicit information leaks when public output is produced in a branch whose execution was determined by confidential information. It's a simple technique, so we do not go further into the details, but we think they will quickly become clear in our implementation.

Before we start, we need a type to represent security levels at run-time.

```
data DynSL = L | H deriving (Show, Eq, Ord)
```

In order to implement Sabelfeld and Russo's monitor in a monad, we represent a calculation in the monad as a function of type $DynSL \rightarrow m\ (DynSL, a)$. The calculation takes as input the current security level of the program counter, executes in the base monad and returns not just the value, but also the security level of the calculated result.

$$\textbf{newtype}\ \mathit{DynFlowSabT}\ m\ a = \mathit{DynFlowSabT}\ \{\ \mathit{runDynFlowSabT} :: \mathit{DynSL} \to m\ (\mathit{DynSL}, a)\ \}$$

It is interesting to note the similarity with a StateT transformer monad carrying the program counter security level around as its state. This similarity does not carry through however in the instance of the *Monad* type class.

```
instance (Monad m) ⇒
  Monad (DynFlowSabT m) where
    return v = DynFlowSabT $ λpc → return (pc, v)
    x ≫ y = DynFlowSabT $ λpc →
      runDynFlowSabT x pc ≫
      runDynFlowSabT y pc
    x ≫= f = DynFlowSabT $ λpc →
      do (l, v) ← runDynFlowSabT x pc
         let xo = f v
         runDynFlowSabT xo $ max pc l
```

The essence here is the security levels of the result of combined calculations and the security level of the program counter passed to the components. We make an essential difference between the sequence (≫) and bind (≫=) operators. The first will simply drop the result of a left hand side calculation and not pass it on to the right hand side, so the result of the combined calculation is considered at the same security level as the right hand side result. Both are executed at the same program counter level. The bind operation is more complicated, as the value of the left calculation can determine not just the result of the right calculation, but can even result in a completely different calculation to be combined. Therefore we need to augment the program counter security level passed to the second calculation to at least the security level of the result of the first calculation. This perfectly reflects the rules for branching constructs in Sabelfeld and Russo's monitor. The return operation simply returns the program counter security level it is passed as the security level for its result.

With these ~20 lines of code, our implementation of Sabelfeld's monitor is almost ready. What we still need is a custom lifting operation which will enforce the security policy on a base monad calculation. It is important to note that two security levels need to be specified. First of all, if a base monad operation produces output visible at a certain security level, then we need to make sure it is not executed when the program counter is at a higher security level, because that would constitute an information leak. In addition, if the base monad calculation produces a result value, then we need to assign a correct security level to it, so that it cannot be leaked in the rest of the program. We will call these two security levels respectively the "input" (*li*) and "output" (*lo*) security levels and require them to be specified when a base monad operation is lifted.

```
liftAt :: (Monad m) ⇒ DynSL → DynSL → m a →
    DynFlowSabT m a
liftAt li lo c =
  let levelError pc =
    "Output at level " ++ show li ++ " with " ++
    "program counter at level " ++ show pc ++ "!"
  in DynFlowSabT $ λpc →
    if pc ⩽ li then do v ← c; return (lo, v)
               else fail $ levelError pc
```

The functions *readMail*, *downloadImage*, *sendMail* and *get* and *put*, can now be lifted. The function *downloadResource* produces public effects and a public result, so it is lifted using the function *liftAt L L*. On the contrary, *readMail* produces no publicly visible effects, so it can be executed with a high program counter level, but it produces a confidential result, so we lift with *liftAt H H*. The function *sendMail* is allowed to take confidential input and produces a public (unit value) result, resulting in *liftAt H L*. The String state variable is assigned a confidential value, leading to respectively *H H* and *H L* as input and output security levels for the *get* and *put* functions. Note that because of the workings of the *MonadState* type class, we are limited to a single state variable. We have a version of the code where we remove this restriction and allow the user to allocate extra state variables using a monad transformer version of Launchbury et al.'s *ST* monad [10], but we are not going further into this because of space limitations and because it is unclear to us how and if this can be extended to the technique we will implement in section 5.

```
instance (EmailM m) ⇒
  EmailM (DynFlowSabT m) where
    downloadResource = liftAt L L ∘ downloadResource
    readMail = liftAt H H readMail
    sendMail = liftAt H L ∘ sendMail

instance (MonadState String m) ⇒
  MonadState String (DynFlowSabT m) where
    get = liftAt H H get
    put = liftAt H L ∘ put

runplugin1 = evalStateT
  (runDynFlowSabT plugin1 L) ""
runplugin2 = evalStateT
  (runDynFlowSabT plugin2 L) ""
```

When we now execute the examples in GHCi, we see that our simple monitor works as intended, and succeeds in detecting and preventing the illegal information flow, while not modifying those executions which respect the information flow policy.

```
*Main> runplugin1
: Haskell invented currying?
Downloading resource: http://example.com/res.txt
Sending mail: prefix; Haskell invented currying?

*Main> runplugin2
: Haskell invented currying?
*** Exception: user error (Output at level L
      with program counter at level H!)
*Main> runplugin2
: Some other mail contents...
Sending mail: Some other mail contents...
```

Our first information flow monitor monad transformer is ready. We have defined a basic dynamic information flow monitor as a monad transformer and used a special lifting function to specify security levels for base monad operations. In sections 5 and 6, we show that we can similarly implement two other information flow enforcement techniques. But before we continue, we first need to introduce a technique called parameterised monads, which we require for the implementation of static analysis on the user code.

4. Parameterised Monads

Monads in Haskell are defined through the *Monad* type class, shown in Figure 5. It defines the *return*, *fail*, (≫) and (≫=) operations, and their type signature. For some applications, this type signature is too restrictive. In our case, the problem is that for the two enforcement techniques that we will discuss next, we

```
class Monad m where
  return :: a → m a
  (≫=) :: m a → (a → m b) → m b
  (≫)  :: m a → m b → m b
  fail  :: String → m a
```

Figure 5. Definition of Monad class and its operations from the standard Haskell Prelude.

```
import qualified Control.Monad as Old
class Sequence m m′ m″ | m m′ → m″ where
  (≫) :: m a → m′ b → m″ b
class Bind m m′ m″ | m m′ → m″ where
  (≫=) :: m a → (a → m′ b) → (m″ b)
class Fail m where
  fail :: String → m a
class Return m where
  returnM :: a → m a
```

Figure 6. The *Sequence*, *Bind*, *Fail* and *Return* type classes, as used in this paper instead of the standard *Monad* class.

need to be able to keep some compile-time data about calculations in information flow enforcing monads. We will represent this data in the type of the monadic calculation, but for this, we need to be able to combine values of different types using the monadic combinators. Because this is impossible with the standard *Monad* type class, we turn to a technique that allows us to bypass this restriction: parameterised monads.

Various forms of parameterised monads have been introduced, but for our purposes, we will use a library developed by Edward Kmett [9]. The basic idea in this library is to use the GHC NoImplicitPrelude [6] Haskell extension to redefine the monadic operators in separate type classes, and to use the GHC MultiParamTypeClasses and FunctionalDependencies extensions to allow different monadic types to be combined and derive the result type from the combined types. We go slightly further than Kmett even, by also separating (≫) from (≫=) in separate type classes. Our definitions can be seen in Figure 6.

An important consideration when using these parameterised monads is the impact on type inference. Because monadic calculations of different types can now be combined, the compiler can no longer infer the type of one of the arguments of the (≫) or (≫=) operators from the other. This would be especially problematic for the *return* operator, for which the type is almost always determined by the calculations it is sequenced or bound with, so if it were typed as $a \rightarrow m\ a$, then explicit programmer type ascription would always be required to determine the type m.

Kmett instead proposes to type *return* as $a \rightarrow Identity\ a$ with *Identity* the standard identity monad. In this way, less type inference is required to determine the type of *return* calls, and *return* calculations are now combined with a monad through the the (≫) and (≫=) operators with their extended type signature. An old-style *return* call is still available in the new type class *Return* under the name *returnM* and standard definitions for *Bind Identity m m*, *Bind m Identity m*, *Sequence m Identity m* and *Sequence Identity m m* are defined using it. The resulting definitions can be seen in Figure 7.

It turns out that in practice, this "trick" can make parameterized monads feel quite natural to programmers used to standard monads

```
return :: a → Identity a
return = Old.return
instance Bind Identity m m where
  lm ≫= f = f (runIdentity lm)
instance (Return m, Bind m m m) ⇒
    Bind m Identity m where
  lm ≫= (f :: a → Identity a′) =
    lm ≫= (returnM ∘ runIdentity ∘ f :: a → m a′)
instance Bind Identity Identity Identity where
  m ≫= f = f $ runIdentity m
instance Sequence Identity m m where
  lm ≫ rm = rm
instance Sequence Identity Identity Identity where
  lm ≫ rm = rm
instance (Return m, Sequence m m m) ⇒
    Sequence m Identity m where
  lm ≫ (rm :: Identity a′) =
    lm ≫ (returnM $ runIdentity rm :: m a′)
```

Figure 7. Kmett's definition of the *return* function returning an instance of the *Identity* monad, behaves better w.r.t. type inference. Special instances of the *Bind* and *Sequence* type classes make sure it interacts well with other monads.

in Haskell. Also important in this respect is that GHC supports the do-notation for parameterised monads since version 6.8.3 [5], by simply executing the canonic translation for **do**-blocks in function of whatever versions of *fail*, (≫) and (≫=) are in scope.

5. Dynamic enforcement, without annotations.

The second information flow enforcement technique we implement is a hybrid (dynamic, supported by static analysis) flow-sensitive technique developed by Le Guernic et al.[12] The technique is flow-sensitive, indicating that variables can be assigned different security levels throughout the execution of a program. The security levels of variables are inferred by the enforcement technique and do not have to be provided by the programmer.

To present the technique, it is instructive to first consider a more naive attempt at getting rid of the security level annotations. Naively, it seems possible to just infer an appropriate security level for the information stored in a variable every time a value is assigned to it. An appropriate security level could be calculated as the maximum of the level of the assigned value and that of the program counter. We can implement special lifting functions that do this in our DynFlowSabT monad transformer as follows.

```
instance (MonadState (DynSL, Bool) m) ⇒
  MonadState Bool (DynFlowSabT m) where
    get = DynFlowSabT $ const get
    put v = DynFlowSabT $ λpc →
      do put (pc, v)
         return (L, ())
```

Now, this is not very difficult to implement, but unfortunately, this approach is not sound, as can be seen in the following example.

```
leak = do put True
          m ← readMail
          let p = isInteresting m
          if ¬ p then put False else return ()
     ≫ do p ← get
          if ¬ p
```

```
            then return ""
            else downloadResource res
          return ()
runleak :: (EmailM m) => m (DynSL, ())
runleak = evalStateT (runDynFlowSabT leak L) (L, False)
```

As we can see in GHCi, the *leak* plugin will download the resource identified by URL *res* if a certain property of a user e-mail holds, thus leaking one bit of secret information and bypassing our information flow policy.

```
*Main> runleak
: Some other mail contents...
(H,())
*Main> runleak
: Haskell invented Currying?
Downloading resource: http://example.com/res.txt
(L,())
```

The reason that our monitor fails to detect the illegal information flow in this example lies in what happens in the first if-statement. There, if p is *False*, then the branch *put False* will be chosen, and our lifted *put* function will correctly mark the variable as confidential. However, in the case that p is *True*, no assignment takes place, and the security level for the state variable is not updated, even though its new value does depend on confidential data. Afterwards, our monitor does not consider it a problem when we make a request for a public resource in a branch on this variable, because it is marked as non-confidential. One could say that the information leak occurs through the non-assignment of a variable in a conditional branch that is not executed.

This example may seem relatively harmless at first sight, but by adapting the code, the trick can be exploited to consistently leak any amount of information, not just a single bit. In fact, our example is an adaptation from a classical example that plays an essential role in Russo and Sabelfeld's proof of the non-existence of a sound and precise flow-sensitive purely dynamic monitor [18].

Russo and Sabelfeld's result implies that a sound and precise flow-sensitive monitor must use some form of static analysis of user code. The classic example of this solution is the monitor developed by Le Guernic et al. [12]. They propose to tackle the problem by combining the dynamic tracking of state variables' security level with such a static analysis and an additional rule for conditional statements like **if** and **while**. After executing the chosen branch of such a statement, the monitor will in addition update the security level of all variables which could possibly have been assigned in the other branch of the conditional. This set of variables is precalculated using a compile-time static analysis and for all of these variables, the security level is increased to at least the security level of the program counter and the conditional expression. Le Guernic et al. prove that this idea effectively solves the problem and guarantees secure information flow.

Clearly, what is difficult to implement about this technique in our framework, is the static analysis. First, it is not straightforward to perform such a static analysis outside of the compiler, but secondly, we also have to generalise the rules defined by Le Guernic et al. to our monadic interception facilities. For the second problem, it turns out that Le Guernic's technique adapts nicely to our handling of the monadic binding operator (>>=) as a generalised branching construct. For a binding of a calculation m to a continuation f (m >>= f), we will perform a static analysis of f to determine the complete set of variables that can be assigned by it, and update their security levels to at least the level of the conditional expression and the program counter. This update can be sequenced after the continuation, just like Le Guernic et al. execute the updates after the chosen branch of an **if** expression.

In order to solve the first problem (actually performing the static analysis of the continuation f), we apply a simple form of effect typing to our monadic operations. For any variable used, we define a ghost type, and require that it be an instance of the type class *LGStateEffect*. The function *updateLabel* in this class takes a dummy value of the ghost type and a security level, and returns a calculation that increases the variable's security level to at least the given level. Note how the functional dependency $st \rightarrow m$ couples a token to the monad in which the state variable is kept.

```
class LGStateEffect st m | st -> m where
  updateLabel :: st -> DynSL -> m ()
```

Because a piece of code can clearly update more than a single state variable, we need a type-level representation for lists of tokens. We define a type *Nil* representing the empty list and a type *Cons* parameterised by a first element of a list and a tail list. Using the GHC MultiParamTypeClasses, FunctionalDependencies, OverlappingInstances, UndecidableInstances and TypeFamilies Haskell extensions, we define type families Add and Merge, respectively adding a *token* to a list of tokens and merging two lists, removing duplicate entries along the way. We also use the EmptyDataDecls and TypeOperators extensions for some syntactic sugar.

```
data Nil
data Cons a r
type Singleton a = Cons a Nil

class Add a b c | a b -> c
instance Add Nil a (Cons a Nil)
instance Add (Cons a r) a (Cons a r)
instance (Add a r r') => Add (Cons b r) a (Cons b r')

class Merge a b c | a b -> c
instance Merge Nil l l
instance (Add l a l', Merge r l' l'') =>
  Merge (Cons a r) l l''
```

We can now instantiate the LGStateEffect class for lists of effects (using the ScopedtypeVariables Haskell extension).

```
instance LGStateEffect Nil Identity where
  updateLabel _ _ = return ()
instance (LGStateEffect t m, LGStateEffect t' m',
      Sequence m m' m'') =>
    LGStateEffect (Cons t t') m'' where
      updateLabel tok l =
        updateLabel (⊥ :: t) l >>
        updateLabel (⊥ :: t') l :: m'' ()
```

The *DynFlowLGT* monad transformer is identical to the previous *DynFlowSabT*, except for the annotation with the effect type tag:

```
data DynFlowLGT t m a = DynFlowLGT {
  runDynFlowLGT :: DynSL -> m (DynSL, a)
}
```

With this, we define the function *otherBranchExec*, which returns a calculation updating the security level for all variables for which assignments occur in a block of code to at least a given security level.

```
otherBranchExec :: forall t m mt a ∘
  (LGStateEffect t mt)
  => DynFlowLGT t m a -> DynSL -> mt ()
otherBranchExec _ l = updateLabel (⊥ :: t) l
```

The monadic combinators (>>) and (>>=) now perform several tasks. In their type signature, they propagate and merge the effect type tags. Their implementation performs the same function as for the *DynFlowSabT* transformer, and in addition the combinator (≫=) employs the *otherBranchExec* function to update security levels for all variables that can possibly assigned in its right hand side continuation. Evidently, for the propagation of effect tokens, these definitions depend crucially on the parameterized monads introduced before.

```
instance (Sequence m m' m'', Merge t t' t'') ⇒
  Sequence (DynFlowLGT t m) (DynFlowLGT t' m')
           (DynFlowLGT t'' m'')
  where (DynFlowLGT ex) ≫ (DynFlowLGT ey) =
    DynFlowLGT $ λpc → ex pc ≫ ey pc
instance (Bind m mt'' m'', Merge t t' t'',
  Bind m' mt' mt'',
  Sequence mt' Identity mt',
  LGStateEffect t mt, LGStateEffect t' mt') ⇒
  Bind (DynFlowLGT t m) (DynFlowLGT t' m')
    (DynFlowLGT t'' m'') where
  (DynFlowLGT x) ≫= f =
    DynFlowLGT $ λpc →
      do (ll, lv) ← x pc
         let rm = f lv
         result ← runDynFlowLGT rm $ max pc ll
         otherBranchExec rm $ max pc ll
         return result
instance (Return m) ⇒
    Return (DynFlowLGT t m) where
  returnM v = DynFlowLGT $ λpc → returnM (pc, v)
```

State lifting functions are now identical to the unsafe versions defined above, except that their results are tagged with the state token needed for the static analysis. Non-state operations are lifted as before, and get the empty list *Nil* as effect tag, indicating they do not affect any state.

```
liftGet :: m (DynSL, s) → DynFlowLGT t m s
liftGet g = DynFlowLGT $ const g
liftPut :: (Sequence m Identity m,
  LGStateEffect t m) ⇒
  ((DynSL, s) → m ()) → s
    → DynFlowLGT t m ()
liftPut p v = DynFlowLGT $ λpc →
  do p (pc, v)
     return (L, ())

liftAt :: (Fail m, Bind m Identity m) ⇒
  DynSL → DynSL → m a → DynFlowLGT Nil m a
liftAt li lo c =
  let levelError pc =
    "Output at level " ++ (show li) ++ " with " ++
    "program counter at level " ++ (show pc) ++ "!"
  in DynFlowLGT $ λpc →
    if pc ≤ li
      then do v ← c; return (max pc lo, v)
      else fail $ levelError pc
```

The definitions of the API functions need to be changed because their type becomes more complicated with the effect annotations, and type inference is less powerful in the context of parameterised monads. Indeed, API providers need to more strongly fix the types of lifted base monad operations, to avoid requiring more type ascription from plug-in writers. Here, we reuse the names of the lifted operations, so that we can keep our previous examples unmodified (only a recompilation required). We use the old definitions through a qualified import under the prefix *Old*.

```
type BaseMonad = StateT (DynSL, String) IO
type MonadStack t a = DynFlowLGT t BaseMonad a

readMail :: MonadStack Nil String
readMail = liftAt H H Old.readMail
sendMail :: String → MonadStack Nil ()
sendMail = liftAt H L ∘ Old.sendMail
downloadResource :: String → MonadStack Nil String
downloadResource = liftAt L L ∘ Old.downloadResource
```

For the state operations, we need to define an effect token ghost type, include the effect token in the type of the put operation, and instantiate the LGStateEffect type class. Again, we reuse the previously used *get* and *put* names.

```
data VarAToken

get :: MonadStack Nil String
get = liftGet Old.get
put :: String → MonadStack (Singleton VarAToken) ()
put = liftPut Old.put
instance (MonadState (DynSL, s) m, Bind m m m) ⇒
  LGStateEffect VarAToken m where
  updateLabel _ pc = do
    (l, v) ← Old.get :: m (DynSL, s)
    Old.put (max l pc, v) :: m ()
```

We can now recompile and execute our example plug-ins *plugin1* and *plugin2* again. Note that we need to replace the call to *return* by a call to *returnM* because of the new type for *return* in our parameterised monads, and recompile the programs with the new definitions of the API.

```
plugin1 = do m ← readMail
             put $ m ++ "\n"
         ≫ do p ← downloadResource res
             m ← get
             sendMail $ p ++ m
plugin2 = do m ← readMail
             put $ m ++ "\n"
         ≫ do m ← get
             if isInteresting m
               then downloadResource res
               else returnM ""
             sendMail m
runplugin1 :: IO (DynSL, ())
runplugin1 = evalStateT
  (runDynFlowLGT plugin1 L) (L, "")
runplugin2 :: IO (DynSL, ())
runplugin2 = evalStateT
  (runDynFlowLGT plugin2 L) (L, "")
```

When we execute these examples in GHCi, we get the expected results, this time without having required programmer-provided security level annotations for state variables.

```
*Main> runplugin1
: Haskell invented currying?
Downloading resource: http://example.com/res.txt
Sending mail: prefix; Haskell invented currying?

*Main> runplugin2
: Haskell invented currying?
*** Exception: user error (Output at level L
    with program counter at level H!)
*Main> runplugin2
: Some other mail contents...
Sending mail: Some other mail contents...
```

Similarly, for an omitted adaptation of the *leak* example from the beginning of this section, we see that Le Guernic's solution also detects the illegal information flow in that example:

```
*Main> runleak
: Haskell invented currying?
*** Exception: user error (Output at level L
      with program counter at level H!)
*Main> runleak
: Some other mail contents...
(H,())
```

Unfortunately however, Le Guernic's technique has only been shown to support lexically scoped stack variables, without aliasing. Features like heap data or even references cannot easily be supported, because they make it impossible in general to statically analyse the set of variables that could potentially be assigned by a branch of a conditional statement. In the context of real world API's in real world languages, we think this restriction can prove to be fairly strong and make the technique unusable.

6. Static enforcement

The third and last information flow enforcement technique we implement in this text is the classic compile-time flow-insensitive type-system based enforcement developed by Volpano in 1996 [24]. Like Sabelfeld's dynamic technique (see section 3), this technique requires programmer-provided security level annotations for variables and uses this to type all (pure) expressions at a certain security level (written $e : l$). A subtyping rule states that if $e : l$ and $l < l'$ then $e : l'$. In addition to that, statements' types represent the lowest security level on which their effects are visible. For example, an assignment s to a variable annotated with security level l will be typed $s : l\,\mathrm{cmd}$. Contrary to expression types, these statement types are subject to a contravariant subtyping, i.e. if $s : l\,\mathrm{cmd}$ and $l > l'$ then $s : l'\,\mathrm{cmd}$.

Using this typing information, enforcing secure information flow becomes relatively easy. In assignment or output statements, explicit flows are prevented by requiring the assigned expression to be associated to the variable's security level or higher. In branching statements, implicit flows are prevented by requiring the security level of the conditional expression to be lower or equal to the effect levels of any of its branches. We discuss all of this in more detail in section 7.

In this section, we implement this type system in a monad transformer, in such a way that the transformed monad behaves identically to the original at runtime, but the information flow type system is checked at compile-time. Making the security types part of the transformed monad calculations' types and providing custom types for the monad operations (as parameterized monads), allows us to implement the type checking in a relatively cheap way, making the Haskell compiler do most of the work for us.

Clearly, the first thing we need to do to achieve this, is to represent security levels at the type level. We use the Haskell extensions MultiParamTypeClasses, EmptyDataDecls, TypeFamilies, TypeOperators and UndecidableInstances to provide both powerful, convenient and elegant type-level computation primitives for working with our security level types. The *UndecidableInstances* extension is not generally accepted in the Haskell community, but we cannot avoid it for the static analysis we want to perform. We define the different levels we need as empty data types, and define a type class $\cdot \geqslant \cdot$. We also define type families $\cdot \wedge \cdot$ and $\cdot \vee \cdot$ (commonly known as join and meet operators using terminology from mathematical lattices), representing respectively a least upper bound and greatest lower bound of two security levels.

```
data H
data L

class ll ⩾ lr
instance H ⩾ H
instance H ⩾ L
instance L ⩾ L

type family ll ∧ rl
type instance H ∧ sl = H
type instance sl ∧ H = H
type instance L ∧ L = L

type family ll ∨ rl
type instance H ∨ H = H
type instance sl ∨ L  = L
type instance L ∨ sl = L
```

Before we continue, there is a slight extension that we need to make to Volpano et al.'s type system. Contrary to their model language, our monadic calculations can behave as both an expression and a statement. A base monadic calculation $m\ v$ produces a result of type v, but can also produce side effects in the background. This means that in the type for our transformed monad, we need to track both a covariant *result security level* representing the security level of the result of the calculation, and a contravariant *effect security level* representing the lowest level at which it produces side effects. We write this as $StaticFlowT\ lr\ le\ m\ a$ where m is the base monad, v the result type, lr the result security level and le the effect security level. Note that this elegant extension of Volpano et al.'s type system is not our contribution, but was previously investigated by Crary et al. [3] (see section 8). We look further into the correspondence between the classic types and ours in section 7.

Except for this annotation with security level types, our transformed monads are identical to the underlying base monad:

```
newtype StaticFlowT lr le m v = StaticFlowT {
  runStaticFlowT :: m v
  }
```

We make our *StaticFlowT* monad transformer an instance of the *MonadTrans* class, so that a base monad operation can be lifted using the standard *lift* function.

```
instance MonadTrans (StaticFlowT lr le) where
  lift c = StaticFlowT c
```

Note how the lifting operation is fully polymorphic in the security levels. The idea here is that the caller of the lift function can simply use explicit type ascription to annotate base monad operations with correct security levels. We demonstrate this for the e-mail application plug-in API.

```
type BaseMonad = StateT String IO
type MonadStack lr le a =
  StaticFlowT lr le BaseMonad a

readMail :: MonadStack H L String
readMail = lift Old.readMail
sendMail :: String → MonadStack L H ()
sendMail = lift ∘ Old.sendMail
downloadResource :: String → MonadStack L L String
downloadResource = lift ∘ Old.downloadResource
```

For state variables, we lift *put* and *get* operations similarly.

```
get :: MonadStack H H String
get = lift MS.get
put :: String → MonadStack L H ()
put = lift ∘ MS.put
```

The final task in implementing our static information flow enforcement monad transformer is defining the monadic operations:

$$
\begin{array}{l}
\textbf{instance}\ (\mathit{Bind}\ \mathit{lm}\ \mathit{rm}\ \mathit{fm}, \mathit{rle} \geqslant \mathit{llr}, \\
\quad \mathit{llr} \wedge \mathit{rlr}{\sim}\mathit{flr}, \mathit{lle} \vee \mathit{rle}{\sim}\mathit{fle}) \Rightarrow \\
\quad \mathit{Bind}\ (\mathit{StaticFlowT}\ \mathit{llr}\ \mathit{lle}\ \mathit{lm}) \\
\qquad\qquad (\mathit{StaticFlowT}\ \mathit{rlr}\ \mathit{rle}\ \mathit{rm}) \\
\qquad\qquad (\mathit{StaticFlowT}\ \mathit{flr}\ \mathit{fle}\ \mathit{fm})\ \textbf{where} \\
\quad (\mathit{StaticFlowT}\ \mathit{le}) \gg\!= f = \\
\qquad \mathit{StaticFlowT}\ \$\ \textbf{do}\ x \leftarrow \mathit{le}; \\
\qquad\qquad\qquad\qquad\qquad \mathit{runStaticFlowT}\ \$\ f\ x \\
\textbf{instance}\ (\mathit{Sequence}\ \mathit{lm}\ \mathit{rm}\ \mathit{fm}, \mathit{lle} \vee \mathit{rle}{\sim}\mathit{fle}) \Rightarrow \\
\quad \mathit{Sequence}\ (\mathit{StaticFlowT}\ \mathit{llr}\ \mathit{lle}\ \mathit{lm}) \\
\qquad\qquad\quad (\mathit{StaticFlowT}\ \mathit{rlr}\ \mathit{rle}\ \mathit{rm}) \\
\qquad\qquad\quad (\mathit{StaticFlowT}\ \mathit{rlr}\ \mathit{fle}\ \mathit{fm})\ \textbf{where} \\
\quad (\mathit{StaticFlowT}\ \mathit{le}) \gg (\mathit{StaticFlowT}\ \mathit{re}) = \\
\qquad \mathit{StaticFlowT}\ \$\ \mathit{le} \gg \mathit{re} \\
\textbf{instance}\ (\mathit{Return}\ m) \Rightarrow \\
\qquad \mathit{Return}\ (\mathit{StaticFlowT}\ \mathit{lr}\ \mathit{le}\ m)\ \textbf{where} \\
\quad \mathit{returnM} = \mathit{StaticFlowT} \circ \mathit{returnM}
\end{array}
$$

These are intimidating type signatures, but before looking at them, it is interesting to first look what the code actually does. Interestingly, all that it does is pass on the monadic operations to the underlying monad. This is clearly what we want, since this is a purely compile-time enforcement technique, not performing any work at run-time.

Looking at the type signatures, we see that for the monadic sequencing operation $\gg$, the result security level of the left hand side calculation is thrown away together with the result itself, and the right-hand side result security level is used as the result security level of the calculation. Slightly less evident, the effects of the combined calculation are considered at the meet (minimum) of the effect levels of the calculations being combined. This is natural, since an observer at that security level can observe at least one of the effects.

The monadic binding operation $\gg\!=$ has an even more complicated type. The result security level of the combined calculation here is the join (maximum) of the levels of both calculations' results, since both results can influence the combined result. The effect security level is, as before the meet (minimum) of both effect levels. In addition to this, the $\gg\!=$ type signature also performs a check to see if the bind is actually allowed. This is done using the constraint $\mathit{rle} \geqslant \mathit{llr}$, which makes sure that information at a certain security level can not be used to produce effects at a lower security level.

We don't repeat the *plugin1* and *plugin2* examples, since they look exactly the same as in section 5. We do need to recompile them, because of the new definitions of the API functions, and we need to compile each separately, because one is supposed to give a compilation error and the other one isn't.

$$
\begin{array}{l}
\mathit{runplugin1} :: \mathit{IO}\ () \\
\mathit{runplugin1} = \mathit{evalStateT}\ (\mathit{runStaticFlowT}\ \mathit{plugin1})\ \texttt{""}
\end{array}
$$

Running the *runplugin1* program in GHCi, the program is accepted. The compiler statically determines that the program respects the information flow policy. Its execution is unmodified and does not incur any run-time overhead.

```
*Main> runplugin1
: Safe info flowing through...
Downloading resource: http://example.com/res.txt
Sending mail: prefix; Safe info flowing through...
```

The *runplugin2* example now gives the following compile-time type error:

```
No instance for (GT L H)
  arising from a do statement at (...)
Possible fix: add an instance declaration for
  (GT L H)
In a stmt of a 'do' expression: y <- getA
In the second argument of '(>>)', namely
    'do { y <- getA;
          if y /= 0
          then putInt y else returnM () }'
(...)
```

We can still improve the error message a little, by playing a standard trick on the compiler.

$$
\begin{array}{l}
\textbf{data}\ \mathit{IllegalInformationFlow} \\
\textbf{class}\ \mathit{Failure}\ a \\
\textbf{instance}\ (\mathit{Failure}\ \mathit{IllegalInformationFlow}) \Rightarrow L \geqslant H
\end{array}
$$

The improved error message has the same error location info, but starts like this:

```
No instance for (Failure IllegalInformationFlow)
...
```

With this, our third and last information flow enforcement monad transformer is also ready and working correctly on at least the two examples we started with.

7. Proof

In this text, we do not provide a proof of the correctness of all for the three information flow enforcement techniques we implement. What we do provide, in this section, is a formal result about our implementation of the static enforcement technique in section 6. What we demonstrate is that a model language and type system similar to the one from Volpano et al.'s presentation [24] can be translated into our implementation and that under this translation, types on both ends correspond in a precise manner that we will define below. It is important to note that we do not prove the semantic correctness of our translation, but we consider that given a semantically correct set of base monad state and input/output functions, this correctness is at least credible given the relative simplicity of the translation.

Figure 8 shows the syntax of the simple model imperative programming language we will use. The language is the one we used previously in our paper about an information flow enforcement technique called secure multi-execution [4]. It is not the one used by Volpano et al., but it is similar except for the added basic input and output statements. Values denoted i and o represent identifiers of input and output channels, respectively.

Figure 9 shows an version of the classic type system, adapted to our situation. These typing rules assume a fixed, user-provided assignment of variables to security levels Γ, and fixed classifications σ_{in} and σ_{out} of input and output channels into security levels. We further assume an extension of the user-provided typing for variables to a typing for all expressions. An expression of type $e : l$ denotes an expression containing information at security level l. The covariant subtyping for expression types indicates that information at a certain security level can be used wherever more confidential information can. A statement typing $s\ :\ l\,\text{cmd}$ denotes that the statement can produce effects visible on security level l. The contravariant subtyping for statement types indicates that statements with effects at a given level can be used wherever statements with lower level effects can.

Figure 11 now shows the translation function ϕ, translating a program $P\ :\ l\,\text{cmd}$ in our model language to a calculation of type $\mathit{StaticFlowT}\ \ l\ \ L\ \ \mathit{BaseMonad}\ \ ()$ (see theorem 1 below). For a program P using a set of state variables

$$command ::= x := e \mid c; c \mid \textbf{if } e \textbf{ then } c \textbf{ else } c \mid \textbf{while } e \textbf{ do } c \mid \textbf{skip} \mid \textbf{input } x \textbf{ from } i \mid \textbf{output } e \textbf{ to } o$$

Figure 8. Command syntax of a simple model imperative language. We assume a standard syntax for effect-free expressions e.

$$\frac{\Gamma(x) = l \quad \Gamma \vdash e : l}{\Gamma \vdash x := e : l\,\text{cmd}} \quad (1)$$

$$\frac{\Gamma \vdash c : l\,\text{cmd} \quad \Gamma \vdash c' : l\,\text{cmd}}{\Gamma \vdash c; c' : l\,\text{cmd}} \quad (2)$$

$$\frac{\Gamma \vdash e : l \quad \Gamma \vdash c : l\,\text{cmd} \quad \Gamma \vdash c' : l\,\text{cmd}}{\Gamma \vdash \textbf{if } e \textbf{ then } c \textbf{ else } c' : l\,\text{cmd}} \quad (3)$$

$$\frac{\Gamma \vdash e : l \quad \Gamma \vdash c : l\,\text{cmd}}{\Gamma \vdash \textbf{while } e \textbf{ do } c : l\,\text{cmd}} \quad (4)$$

$$\frac{\Gamma(x) = l \quad \sigma_{\text{in}}(i) = l}{\Gamma \vdash \textbf{input } x \textbf{ from } i : l\,\text{cmd}} \quad (5)$$

$$\frac{\Gamma \vdash e : l \quad \sigma_{\text{out}}(o) = l}{\Gamma \vdash \textbf{output } e \textbf{ to } o : l\,\text{cmd}} \quad (6)$$

$$\Gamma \vdash \textbf{skip} : l \quad (7)$$

$$\frac{\Gamma \vdash e : l \quad l \leqslant l'}{\Gamma \vdash e : l'} \quad (8)$$

$$\frac{\Gamma \vdash c : l\,\text{cmd} \quad l \geqslant l'}{\Gamma \vdash c : l'\,\text{cmd}} \quad (9)$$

Figure 9. Adapted information flow enforcement typing rules, based on those developed by Volpano et al [24]. Typing rules for expressions are assumed, reflecting the maximum security level of any variable used in the expression. Also assumed is a security level typing Γ for variables, based on programmer-provided variable security level ascriptions.

$\{v_1, \ldots, v_n\}$, we assume that the variables are assigned security levels $\{l_{v_1}, \ldots, l_{v_n}\}$. We assume that properly typed Haskell values $getV_i :: StaticFlowT\ H\ l_{v_i}\ BaseMonad\ Int$, $putV_i :: Int \rightarrow StaticFlowT\ l_{v_i}\ L\ BaseMonad\ ()$ are defined. We assume that P uses input and output channels $\{i_1, \ldots, i_{n_i}\}$ and $\{o_1, \ldots, o_{n_o}\}$, classified at security levels $\{l_{i_1}, \ldots, l_{i_n}\}$ and $\{l_{o_1}, \ldots, l_{o_n}\}$ and that properly typed Haskell values $readI_j :: StaticFlowT\ H\ l_{i_j}\ BaseMonad\ Int$ and $writeO_i :: Int \rightarrow StaticFlowT\ l_{o_i}\ L\ BaseMonad\ ()$ are defined. Finally, the translation assumes a function *Vars* returning the set of variables used in a given expression, and a translation function for expressions ϕ_{ex}, translating references to variables into references of correspondingly named Haskell values. With all of these, ϕ will translate the given program P in a straightforward manner. Maybe the only unintuitive feature of this translation is the use of helper function *upcastLeft* from Figure 10, which make sure the **if**-statement type-checks by upcasting the lowest typed of the two branch statements. **while**-statements are translated to a recursive monadic expression.

We now come to the central theorem of this section. In order to understand this correspondence, it is important to remark that our typing scheme assigns a single type to any monadic calculation, whereas Volpano et al. allow subtyping. For example, a calculation $StaticFlowT\ L\ l\ m\ ()$ corresponds to a statement s such that $s : l'\,\text{cmd}$ for all $l' \leqslant l$. This is taken into account in the formulation of the next theorem.

$$\begin{aligned}
&upcastLeft :: StaticFlowT\ l\ L\ bm\ () \rightarrow \\
&\quad StaticFlowT\ l'\ L\ bm\ () \rightarrow \\
&\quad StaticFlowT\ (Min\ l\ l')\ L\ bm\ () \\
&upcastLeft\ a\ b = MkStaticFlowT\ (unMkStaticFlowT\ a)
\end{aligned}$$

Figure 10. Utility function *upcastLeft* for use in the translation function ϕ in Figure 11.

$$\frac{c = \textbf{if } e \textbf{ then } c_{\text{true}} \textbf{ else } c_{\text{false}} \quad Vars(e) = \{v_{i_1}, \ldots, v_{i_n}\} \quad cond = \phi_{ex}(e) \quad m_{\text{true}} = \phi(c_{\text{true}}) \quad m_{\text{false}} = \phi(c_{\text{false}})}{\begin{aligned}\phi(c) = \ & getV_{i_1} \ggg\!= \lambda v_{i_1} \rightarrow \ldots \rightarrow getV_{i_n} \ggg\!= \lambda v_{i_n} \rightarrow \\ & \textbf{if } cond \textbf{ then } upcastLeft\ m_{\text{true}}\ m_{\text{false}} \\ & \textbf{else } upcastLeft\ m_{\text{false}}\ m_{\text{true}}\end{aligned}} \quad (1)$$

$$\frac{m_1 = \phi(c_1) \quad m_2 = \phi(c_2)}{\phi(c_1; c_2) = m_1 \gg m_2} \quad (2)$$

$$\phi(\textbf{skip}) = returnM\ () :: StaticFlowT\ H\ L\ BaseMonad\ () \quad (3)$$

$$\frac{c = \textbf{while } e \textbf{ do } c_{\text{loop}} \quad Vars(e) = \{v_1, \ldots, v_n\} \quad cond = \phi_{ex}(e) \quad m_{loop} = \phi(c_{\text{loop}})}{\begin{aligned}\phi(c) = \ & fix\ \$\ \lambda self \rightarrow \\ & getV_{i_1} \ggg\!= \lambda v_{i_1} \rightarrow \ldots \rightarrow getV_{i_n} \ggg\!= \lambda v_{i_n} \rightarrow \\ & \textbf{if } cond \textbf{ then } m_{loop} \gg self \textbf{ else } returnM\ ()\end{aligned}} \quad (4)$$

$$\frac{val = \phi_{ex}(e) \quad Vars(e) = \{v_1, \ldots, v_n\}}{\begin{aligned}\phi(v_i := e) = \ & getV_{i_1} \ggg\!= \lambda v_{i_1} \rightarrow \ldots \rightarrow \\ & getV_{i_n} \ggg\!= \lambda v_{i_n} \rightarrow putV_i\ val\end{aligned}} \quad (5)$$

$$\frac{val = \phi_{ex}(e) \quad Vars(e) = \{v_1, \ldots, v_n\}}{\begin{aligned}\phi(\textbf{output } e \textbf{ to } o_i) = \ & getV_{i_1} \ggg\!= \lambda v_{i_1} \rightarrow \ldots \rightarrow \\ & getV_{i_n} \ggg\!= \lambda v_{i_n} \rightarrow writeO_i\ val\end{aligned}} \quad (6)$$

$$\frac{c = \textbf{input } vi \textbf{ from } i_j}{\phi(c) = readI_j \ggg\!= putV_i} \quad (7)$$

Figure 11. Translation function ϕ from our model language to calculations in the transformed monad.

Theorem 1. *Suppose a program P as before, using variables $\{v_1, \ldots, v_n\}$. Suppose $\{l_{v_1}, \ldots, l_{v_n}\}$, $getV_i$, $putV_i$, $\{i_1, \ldots, i_{n_i}\}$, $\{o_1, \ldots, o_{n_o}\}$, $\{l_{i_1}, \ldots, l_{i_n}\}$, $\{l_{o_1}, \ldots, l_{o_n}\}$, $readI_j$ and $writeO_i$, all as before.*

Then we have that $\phi(P)::StaticFlowT\ l'\ L\ BaseMonad\ ()$ if and only if $P : l\,\text{cmd}$ for all $l' \geqslant l$.

Proof sketch. "only if": induction on the syntactic structure of P.

- Suppose $P = \textbf{if } e \textbf{ then } c_{\text{true}} \textbf{ else } c_{\text{false}}$, with $e : l$, $c_{\text{true}}, c_{\text{false}} : l\,\text{cmd}$. By the induction hypothesis, we know that $\phi(c_{\text{true}}) = m_{\text{true}} :: StaticFlowT\ l'\ L\ BaseMonad\ ()$, $l' \geqslant l$ and $\phi(c_{\text{false}}) = m_{\text{false}} :: StaticFlowT\ l''\ L\ BaseMonad\ ()$, $l'' \geqslant l$. Case (1) in Figure 11, the typing of the $(\ggg\!=)$ operator, the types of the $getV_i$, and the assumption on the typing of expressions (that it is determined by the security levels of the variables used), together with Haskell typing rules, give us that $\phi(c)$::$StaticFlowT\ l'''\ L\ BaseMonad$ () with $l''' \geqslant l$.

- Suppose $P = c_1; c_2$, with $c_1 : l$ cmd and $c_2 : l$ cmd. We know that $m_1 = \phi(c_1)$::$StaticFlowT\ l'\ L\ BaseMonad$ (), $m_2 = \phi(c_2)$::$StaticFlowT\ l''\ L\ BaseMonad$ (), for some $l' \geqslant l$ and $l'' \geqslant l$. Case (2) in Figure 11, the type of the ($\gg$) operator and the Haskell typing rules tell us that $\phi(P)$::$StaticFlowT\ l'''\ L\ BaseMonad$ () with $l''' \geqslant l$.
- The cases for **skip**, **while**, **output**, **input** are similar or straightforward.

For the "if" direction, we also work by induction on the syntactic structure of P.

- Suppose now that P = **if** e **then** c_{true} **else** c_{false}, that $\phi(P)$::$StaticFlowT\ l\ L\ BaseMonad$ (). Take l' and l'' such that $\phi(c_{\text{true}})$::$StaticFlowT\ l'\ L\ BaseMonad$ () and $\phi(c_{\text{false}})$::$StaticFlowT\ l''\ L\ BaseMonad$ (). By induction, case (1), the type rules for **if**, we know l' is the same type as l'', that $c_{\text{true}}, c_{\text{false}} : l'''$ cmd for all $(Min\ l'\ l'') \geqslant l'''$. Because the security level of e is determined by the variables used in it, because of the types of the $getV_i$ and the ($\gg=$) operator, we get that $P : l''''$ cmd for all $l \geqslant l''''$.
- Suppose $P = c_1; c_2$, with $m_1 = \phi(c_1)$, $m_2 = \phi(c_2)$. Suppose that m_1 :: $StaticFlowT\ l'\ L\ BaseMonad$ () and m_2 :: $StaticFlowT\ l''\ L\ BaseMonad$ (). The type of the ($\gg$) operator and Haskell typing rules then give us that $\phi(P)$::$StaticFlowT\ l\ L\ BaseMonad$ () with $l{\sim}Min\ l'\ l''$. Induction gives us that c_1 :: l''' cmd, c_2 :: l''' cmd for $l' \geqslant l'''$ and $l'' \geqslant l'''$ and the typing rules in our model language then ensure that P :: l''' cmd for all $l \geqslant l'''$
- **skip**, **while**, **output**, **input** are again similar or straightforward.

□

8. Discussion and Related Work

8.1 The techniques we use

Parameterised monads [1, 9] have already been shown to serve many purposes. Kiselyov uses parametrised monads for typing polymorphic delimited continuations [8]. Harrison and Hook also apply monad transformers for information flow security but in a different manner. Also, our use of parameterised monads and monad transformers in the context of policy enforcement on Haskell libraries is not new. Pucella describes an interesting implementation of session types using these two techniques [17].

8.2 The Monad operations as monitorable events in an information flow monitor

In a theoretical work about fundamental limits of run-time policy enforcement mechanisms, Ligatti et al. [14] discuss how the set of events in the executing programs that can be observed by the monitor is one of the factors that determines the power of the enforcement mechanisms. In this respect, our run-time enforcement monad transformer from section 3 can be regarded as a monitor receiving only applications of the monadic bind ($\gg=$) and sequence ($\gg$) operations as monitorable events. We think we have shown in this text that monitoring this set of events provides us with enough information about information flow in a program to be able to enforce relevant forms of secure information flow, and that we have been able to encode three important enforcement techniques from the literature. Nevertheless, we also want to point out that for at least one other enforcement technique, we do not believe such an implementation is possible.

In section 5, we have explained the general problem related to flow-sensitive purely dynamic information flow monitors and Le Guernic's solution to this problem. Austin and Flanagan discuss an alternative [2], purely dynamic solution to the problem based on the "No Sensitive Upgrade" rule. Under this rule, it is not allowed for a variable's security level to be upgraded to a higher level because of an assignment with the program counter at a higher level. Instead, such an assignment will cause the program to be terminated. Our example *leak* on page 5 section 5 would thus be terminated when the assignment *put p* is executed. Austin and Flanagan prove that this new rule fixes the flow-sensitivity problem and ensures secure information flow.

The problem for implementing this technique using our approach can be seen by looking at how the technique handles the following two statements: **if** sec **then** x := true **else skip** and $x := sec$. Assuming that the variable x was previously assigned a low security level, the no sensitive upgrade rule would terminate the first command. The second command on the other hand is legal, and the monitor would just assign a high security level to the variable x. The problem now becomes apparent if we notice that in a monadic encoding of these examples, we get $getSec \gg= \lambda sec \rightarrow$ **if** sec **then** $putX\ True$ **else** $returnM$ () and $getSec \gg= putX$ respectively. Notice that both cases reduce to an application of the monadic bind operator, making it fundamentally impossible for monad transformer policy enforcers to make the required distinction. Accordingly, we believe Austin and Flanagan's enforcement technique cannot be implemented in our model.

8.3 The information flow enforcement techniques we implement

The information flow enforcement techniques we implement are classic from the literature. For an overview of existing static techniques, we refer to Sabelfeld and Myers [20] and for dynamic techniques to Le Guernic's PhD thesis [11].

The techniques we implement in this paper are those described by Sabelfeld and Russo [21] (section 3), Le Guernic et al. [12] (section 5) and Volpano et al. [24] (section 6). These techniques are tied in an important way to their handling of imperative features like mutable state and side effects, which is why they are relevant to our policy enforcement over monadic APIs. A small but nevertheless relevant contribution in this paper is the way we have adapted these techniques to handle monadic operations. For all three of these techniques, the extensions followed straightforwardly from considering the monadic binding operator as a generalised branching construct and generalising the rule for the **if** statement. Our presentation of Volpano et al.'s type system unified the linear type hierarchies for expressions and statements into a type lattice for monadic calculations, like in Crary et al.'s proposal [3].

An interesting direction for future research comes from the observation that monads in functional languages can be used for more purposes than the encoding of mutable state variables and side effects. Other features like exceptions and even delimited continuations can also be encoded in it. It would be interesting to investigate the application of techniques from the information flow literature for handling these features [15, 16, 23] by lifting the relevant base monad operations into information flow enforcement monad transformers.

8.4 Other information flow enforcement libraries

Finally, as an example of a Haskell information flow library, it is fundamental to compare our work to other interesting papers in this domain. Li and Zdancewic [13] were the first to propose an information flow enforcement library as a light-weight alternative to performing the enforcement as part of the implementation of a language compiler or interpreter. Li and Zdancewic require the programmer to explicitise control flow by encoding the program using the do-notation for arrows [7]. This is similar in spirit to how we approximate information flow using the invocations of monad operations in untrusted code. They perform a static analysis of the resulting dependency graph to detect illegal information flow, but they perform this analysis at runtime. This strikes us as a compromise lacking the advantages of both dynamic checking (e.g. determination of security levels during execution, ignoring dead code) and static checking (no run-time performance impact, errors signaled to developer during compilation). A strong point of Li and Zdancewic' approach is that they provide a full formal proof of the soundness of their enforcement. Unfortunately, they do not handle side effects or imperative features like mutable state, but mention it as interesting future work. Their use of the arrows framework requires the API user to work with an unfamiliar abstraction, and yields code that is quite strongly adapted for and as such coupled to their enforcement mechanism.

Tsai, Russo and Hughes [22] improve upon Li and Zdancewic' work by adding support for typing separate components of structured data differently, mutable references and concurrency primitives to the library, extending and modifying Li and Zdancewic' library significantly. These extensions improve the applicability of the library quite a bit, but they still require API users to write their code in the arrow abstraction. Interestingly, their $FlowArrow$ is parameterised by an "underlying arrow" in a similar way as our monad transformers, but afterwards, they remove this generality by instantiating the underlying arrow with the $a \to IO\ b$ arrow when adding support for references. It would have been more elegant to use some sort of arrow transformer based on something like the ST monad [10]. Unlike Li and Zdancewic, Tsai, Russo and Hughes require a type level representation of security levels (like we do in section 6) to keep track of the security type of the contents of references, and convert back to the dynamic representation a type class when needed in the run-time information flow analysis. This idea is interesting, and could perhaps be used to add support for references in our libraries as well.

Russo, Claessen and Hughes present an information flow enforcement library based on the more widespread monad abstraction instead of arrows [19]. Their approach is simple and corresponds quite strongly to the static enforcement technique we present in section 6. They use the $Sec\ s$ type constructor to protect values at the security level represented by s, and use the $SecIO\ s'$ to represent IO calculations producing side effects visible at security level s'. Their $SecIO\ s\ (Sec\ s'\ v)$ corresponds quite strongly to the type $StaticFlowT\ s'\ s\ IO\ v$ in our implementation.

Like Tsai, Russo and Hughes, they miss the opportunity to parametrise the underlying monad, instead mandating the common IO monad. Their $Sec\ s$ and $SecIO\ s$ type constructors are instances of the $Monad$ type class, but Russo, Claessen and Hughes do not use the parameterised monads technique. Because of this, they require API users to use explicit security level casting functions ($plug$, up) in their programs. This is acceptable, but does not allow the strong separation of information flow enforcement from the underlying API and programs using it that parameterised monads allow us to achieve, thus limiting the modularity of their library. In addition, their use of monadic values ($Sec\ s\ a$) as the values of another monad ($SecIO\ s'$) requires API users to work with monads on two levels, which again leads to unnatural code.

In their text, Russo, Claessen and Hughes subsequently demonstrate an impressive declassification framework using *declassification combinators* and the concept of *escape hatches*. Declassification is something which we have not looked at in this paper, but we think their declassification framework can in fact be translated easily to our implementations. In fact, most of their declassification functions can probably be reused as is by simply lifting them correctly into our transformed monads. This would add important value to our implementations, without much effort.

We think our library improves upon this existing work in a number of respects. First, as we have discussed, our implementations are much more modular, and allow for a much stronger separation between information flow enforcement on the one hand and the underlying API and programs using it on the other. Second, this previous work never featured generality in the specific information flow enforcement technique used. This text, on the other hand, presents implementations of three different classical enforcement techniques. Third, our parameterisation in the base monad is more general and elegant than other libraries' use of the IO monad. Finally, we think that our libraries keep the API presented very natural to the API user, which previous approaches did not achieve, either due to their use of the uncommon arrow abstraction or because of the requirement for working in more than a single monad and using explicit casting functions.

References

[1] R. Atkey. Parameterised notions of computation. *Journal of Functional Programming*, 19(3-4):335–376, 2009.

[2] T. Austin and C. Flanagan. Efficient purely-dynamic information flow analysis. In *PLAS Workshop*, pages 113–124. ACM, 2009.

[3] K. Crary, A. Kliger, and F. Pfenning. A monadic analysis of information flow security with mutable state. *Journal of functional programming*, 15(02):249–291, 2005.

[4] D. Devriese and F. Piessens. Non-interference through secure multi-execution. In *IEEE Symposium on Security and Privacy*, 2010.

[5] I. Dupree. Ghc ticket 1537 - do notation translation. `http://hackage.haskell.org/trac/ghc/ticket/1537`, 2007. Fixed in GHC 6.8.3.

[6] GHC Team. GHC manual - rebindable syntax and the implicit Prelude import. `http://haskell.org/ghc/docs/6.12.2/html/users_guide/syntax-extns.html#rebindable-syntax`, 2010.

[7] J. Hughes. Generalising monads to arrows. *Science of computer programming*, 37(1-3):67–111, 2000.

[8] O. Kiselyov. Genuine shift/reset in haskell. Mailing list message, December 2007.

[9] E. Kmett. Parameterized monads in haskell. *The Comonad.Reader*, 2007. URL `http://comonad.com/reader/2007/parameterized-monads-in-haskell/`.

[10] J. Launchbury, P. Jones, and L. Simon. Lazy functional state threads. In *PLDI*, page 35. ACM, 1994.

[11] G. Le Guernic. *Confidentiality Enforcement Using Dynamic Information Flow Analyses*. PhD thesis, Kansas State University, 2007.

[12] G. Le Guernic, A. Banerjee, T. Jensen, and D. Schmidt. Automata-based confidentiality monitoring. In *ASIAN*, pages 75 – 89, 2006.

[13] P. Li and S. Zdancewic. Encoding information flow in haskell. In *19th IEEE Computer Security Foundations Workshop, 2006*, page 12, 2006.

[14] J. Ligatti, L. Bauer, and D. Walker. Edit automata: Enforcement mechanisms for run-time security policies. *International Journal of Information Security*, 4(1):2–16, 2005.

[15] A. Myers. JFlow: Practical mostly-static information flow control. In *POPL*, pages 228–241. ACM, 1999.

[16] F. Pottier and V. Simonet. Information flow inference for ML. *TOPLAS*, 25(1):117–158, 2003.

[17] R. Pucella and J. Tov. Haskell session types with (almost) no class. *ACM SIGPLAN Notices*, 44(2):25–36, 2009.

[18] A. Russo and A. Sabelfeld. Dynamic vs. static flow-sensitive security analysis. In *Computer Security Foundations*, 2010.

[19] A. Russo, K. Claessen, and J. Hughes. A library for light-weight information-flow security in haskell. In *Haskell Symposium*, pages 13–24. ACM, 2008.

[20] A. Sabelfeld and A. Myers. Language-based information-flow security. *IEEE Journal on selected areas in communications*, 21(1):5–19, 2003.

[21] A. Sabelfeld and A. Russo. From dynamic to static and back: Riding the roller coaster of information-flow control research. In *Perspectives of System Informatics*, 2009.

[22] T.-C. Tsai, A. Russo, and J. Hughes. A library for secure multi-threaded information flow in Haskell. In *CSF*, pages 187–202, 2007.

[23] D. Volpano and G. Smith. Eliminating covert flows with minimum typings. In *CSFW*, pages 156–168, 1997.

[24] D. Volpano, C. Irvine, and G. Smith. A sound type system for secure flow analysis. *Journal of computer security*, 4(2/3):167–188, 1996.

The Essence of Monotonic State

Alexandre Pilkiewicz François Pottier
INRIA
{Alexandre.Pilkiewicz,Francois.Pottier}@inria.fr

Abstract

We extend a static type-and-capability system with new mechanisms for expressing the promise that a certain abstract value evolves monotonically with time; for enforcing this promise; and for taking advantage of this promise to establish non-trivial properties of programs. These mechanisms are independent of the treatment of mutable state, but combine with it to offer a flexible account of "monotonic state".

We apply these mechanisms to solve two reasoning challenges that involve mutable state. First, we show how an implementation of thunks in terms of references can be assigned types that reflect time complexity properties, in the style of Danielsson (2008). Second, we show how an implementation of hash-consing can be assigned a specification that conceals the existence of an internal state yet guarantees that two pieces of input data receive the same code if and only if they are equal.

Categories and Subject Descriptors F.3.1 [*Logics and Meanings of Programs*]: Specifying and Verifying and Reasoning about Programs; F.3.3 [*Logics and Meanings of Programs*]: Studies of Program Constructs—Type structure

General Terms Languages, Theory

Keywords types, capabilities, specification, hidden state, monotonic state, amortized complexity, type-based complexity-checking, thunks, hash-consing

1. Introduction

This paper presents novel type-theoretic mechanisms and techniques for exploiting *monotonicity* in establishing properties of programs that manipulate mutable, heap-allocated data.

Two traditional modes of dealing with state How do the type systems in the literature deal with mutable state? Do they allow the type of mutable data to evolve over time? How do they keep track of this type? How do they deal with aliasing? Although there is a large variety of such systems, two modes seem to prevail:

1. *invariable, duplicable types; uncontrolled aliasing;*

   In most mainstream programming languages, including Java, Haskell, and ML, types are *invariable:* the type of a mutable object is fixed at allocation time, and cannot change with time. In return for this lack of expressiveness comes a gain in flexibility: type information can be *duplicated,* and aliasing can remain *uncontrolled,* without risking unsoundness.

2. *variable, linear types; controlled aliasing;*

   There are systems where the type of a mutable object is permitted to *vary,* in an arbitrary way, during the object's lifetime. The price to pay for this expressiveness is that type information must be *linear,* and aliasing must be *controlled.*

The traditional representatives of the latter mode are systems of *linear types.* By requiring that there exist at most one pointer to an object, these systems conflate the control of ownership and the control of aliasing. Their modern descendants [3, 4, 29] offer greater flexibility by using *linear capabilities* to control ownership and *regions* to control aliasing. In these systems, there may exist multiple pointers to an object. Each object, however, must belong to a region, and access to each region is governed by a capability. A capability can be thought of as a unique token that represents the ownership of a region.

It is sound for the two modes to co-exist: the literature presents numerous systems that mix them. They are most often both viewed as primitive. More economically, the second author has argued in earlier work [24] that the former mode (invariable, uncontrolled objects) can be implemented in terms of the latter mode (variable, controlled objects), with the help of a primitive mechanism for *hiding* a capability within a lexical scope.

This mechanism, known as the *anti-frame rule,* makes it possible to organize the implementation of a mutable object in such a way that aliasing and ownership are controlled within the implementation, but need not be controlled outside of it. As far as clients are concerned, objects appear to be ordinary (stateless, duplicable) values. Our implementations of monotonic counters (§2) and thunks (§5) are carried out in this style.

Monotonic state The above two modes of dealing with state can be informally summarized in the semblance of a security policy, that is, by answering the following two questions:

> Who is permitted to *change* the type of an object?
>
> Who is permitted to *know* the type of an object?

Here, to "know" the type of an object means to record this type at some point in time, and to later use the object at the type that was recorded. The answers are, very roughly, as follows:

1. In the first mode, *nobody* is allowed to change the type of an object; *everybody* is allowed to know it.
2. In the second mode, *only the owner* is allowed to change or know the type of an object.

The purpose of this paper is to study a third mode, which strikes a different compromise. It has, at its heart, a notion of *monotonicity.* This mode can be described, again very roughly, as follows:

TLDI'11, January 25, 2011, Austin, Texas, USA.

3. Only the owner of an object is allowed to change its type, and, furthermore, *only in a monotonic manner*, so that types get "better", in a certain sense, with time. In return for this constraint, *everybody* is allowed to record the type of an object, with the understanding that, by the time this information is exploited, the object may well have a "better" type than the one that was recorded.

The choice of the word "better" is meant to suggest some ordering relation. There is no connection between this ordering and the standard subtype ordering: we do not require types to become more precise with time. The choice of an appropriate ordering, on a case-by-case basis, is in the hands of the programmer.

In this third mode, which we dub "monotonic state", changing the type of an object is a restricted operation: control of ownership and aliasing is still required. However, recording and exploiting the type of an object are unrestricted operations: to a certain extent, this control is relaxed.

Contributions The existence of this interesting compromise has been pointed out in the literature (§7), so it does not constitute, in itself, a contribution of this paper. Our contribution is twofold:

> *Contribution 1.* We study monotonic state in a standard type-theoretic setting and explain it in terms of a handful of primitive mechanisms.

The new mechanisms that we propose are simple and elegant (so we claim, that is!), because they are concerned purely with the essence of the interplay between monotonicity and linearity.

In order to define these mechanisms, we need, as our substrate, a type system equipped with capabilities (both linear and non-linear ones) and with logical assertions (which we view as a particular species of non-linear capabilities). In order to present meaningful applications, we need more, namely: higher kinds, regions, mutable state, and hidden state. This list of extra features is perhaps intimidating, but is in principle independent of the topic of this paper.

As is evident from the verbosity of our code (§4), our calculus is intended to serve as a kernel language, into which more palatable surface languages equipped with some form of monotonicity can be encoded.

> *Contribution 2.* As a non-trivial application, we show how Danielsson's system [6] for analyzing the complexity of pure, lazy programs can be programmed up as a library in our imperative, call-by-value setting.

We show how a simple implementation of suspensions, or thunks, can be ascribed a signature that allows a client of the "thunk" abstraction to reason about amortized execution time. This was a challenge because thunks must be ascribed precise types (the type *thunk* carries an integer index, which represents a time bound), yet there must be no control of ownership or aliasing over thunks.

Our result provides a foundational explanation of Danielsson's system: while Danielsson gives a direct proof of the soundness of his system, we encode it into a richer, lower-level system, which allows reasoning about the amortized complexity of imperative ML programs.

Caveat emptor We do not, at this time, have a proof of type soundness for the full type system exploited in this paper. We build on two earlier papers by Charguéraud and Pottier [3] and by Pottier [24]. In as-yet-unpublished work, the second author has established the soundness of the combination of these papers: this took a 20000 line Coq proof. In order to justify the ideas presented in this paper, this proof must be extended with support for embedding logical assertions within capabilities, support for fates and predictions, and support for time credits. A generic treatment of monotonicity is built into the current machine-checked proof, and is exploited in order to justify singleton and group regions. It is hoped that this machinery can also justify fates and predictions.

$\textbf{let}\ mk\ () = ref\ 0$ — *allocates a fresh counter*
$\textbf{let}\ read\ r = !r$ — *reads a counter*
$\textbf{let}\ inc\ r = r := !r + 1;\ r$ — *increments a counter and returns it*

Figure 1. An implementation of monotonic counters

$\textbf{type}\ sc : \text{VAL}$
$\textbf{val}\ mk : unit \rightarrow sc$
$\textbf{val}\ read : sc \rightarrow int\ (0 \leq .)$
$\textbf{val}\ inc : sc \rightarrow sc$

Figure 2. A signature for simple counters

$\textbf{type}\ tc : \text{SNG} \rightarrow \mathbb{Z} \rightarrow \text{CAP}$
$\textbf{val}\ mk : unit \rightarrow \exists\sigma.\ ([\sigma] * tc\ \sigma\ 0)$
$\textbf{val}\ read : \forall i, \sigma.\ [\sigma] * tc\ \sigma\ i \rightarrow int\ i * tc\ \sigma\ i$
$\textbf{val}\ inc : \forall i, \sigma.\ [\sigma] * tc\ \sigma\ i \rightarrow [\sigma] * tc\ \sigma\ (i + 1)$

Figure 3. A signature for tracked counters

$\textbf{type}\ mc : \mathbb{Z} \rightarrow \text{VAL}$
$\textbf{val}\ mk : unit \rightarrow mc\ 0$
$\textbf{val}\ read : \forall i.\ mc\ i \rightarrow int\ (i \leq .)$
$\textbf{val}\ inc : \forall i.\ mc\ i \rightarrow mc\ (i + 1)$

Figure 4. A signature for monotonic counters

Road map The paper begins with a challenge (§2). After presenting a 3-line implementation of *monotonic counters* (Figure 1) as well as a plausible signature for them (Figure 4), we ask: *in which known type systems can it be checked that this code satisfies this signature?* We argue that the answer appears to be: *none*. In order to address this challenge, we suggest introducing new type-theoretic mechanisms, called *fates* and *predictions*. After informally presenting these mechanisms (§3), we explain how, in combination with a number of orthogonal, pre-existing features, they allow monotonic counters to be type-checked (§4). As a more striking application, we show that they allow transporting Danielsson's analysis of thunks [6] from a purely functional, call-by-need language to an imperative, call-by-value setting (§5). We also present an application to hash-consing (§6). We conclude with a discussion of related work (§7). A summary of the core of our system (§A) appears in an appendix.

2. A challenge: monotonic counters

A *monotonic counter* is an integer counter that offers two operations: *read*, which returns the current value of a counter, and *inc*, which increments a counter, and returns its argument. (The reason for this design choice becomes apparent later on.) A constructor function, *mk*, allows creating fresh counters. An untyped implementation of monotonic counters appears in Figure 1. It is trivial: a counter is just an integer reference.

Monotonic counters pose a simple, yet challenging problem. In the following, we present three natural signatures for them, which correspond to the three modes of dealing with state that were reviewed in the introduction (§1). While the implementation of monotonic counters satisfies the first two signatures, it is not clear how to argue that it also satisfies the last one.

Parenthesis: indexed types In order for the three signatures to differ in interesting ways, we need precise types: that is, we need a type to be able to express an assertion about the integer value of a counter. To this end, we allow types to be parameterized with integer indices, in the style of Xi's Dependent ML [32].

Let us briefly review what this means. We write $\mathbb{Z}$ for the kind of integer indices. We use a singleton type, *int* i, whose unique inhabitant is the integer value i. The addition operator has type $\forall ij.\mathit{int}\ i \to \mathit{int}\ j \to \mathit{int}\ (i+j)$. The traditional, unparameterized type *int* can be viewed as sugar for $\exists i.\mathit{int}\ i$.

We also use the type *int* $(i \leq .)$, whose inhabitants are the integer values *greater than or equal to* i. This type can be defined as $\exists j.(\mathit{int}\ j * \langle i \leq j \rangle)$, where we use *existential quantification* over an integer index j and a *conjunction* of a type, *int* j, and a *proposition* about indices, $\langle i \leq j \rangle$. We note that, if $i \leq j$ holds, then *int* $(j \leq .)$ is a *subtype* of *int* $(i \leq .)$. This fact intuitively reflects the set-theoretic inclusion $[j, \infty) \subseteq [i, \infty)$. Here, it can be derived from the definition of *int* $(i \leq .)$.

A signature for simple counters In the first signature (Figure 2), the operations *read* and *inc* have simple types. The type *sc* of *simple counters* is abstract: it is internally defined as *ref* (*int* $(0 \leq .)$), where *ref* is ML's reference type constructor. (We write VAL for the kind of ordinary types, that is, types that classify values. Other kinds appear later on.) This definition encodes the invariant that the value of a counter is a nonnegative integer. This allows *read* to have codomain *int* $(0 \leq .)$ rather than just *int*.

Because *sc* is an abstract type, the reference *r* is accessible only through *read* and *inc*. This guarantees that counters are monotonic, that is, their value can only grow with time. However, this is only an *informal* guarantee. The type-checker is unaware of this property, which it can neither check nor exploit.

This signature is imprecise: it does not reflect the fact that *inc* increments its argument. In the setting of an ML-like type system, despite the availability of indexed types, this seems to be the best signature that one can express *and implement*.

A signature for tracked counters In a type-and-capability system [3, 4, 29], access to a reference is governed by a linear capability, so that type-varying updates (also known as *strong updates*) are sound. In Charguéraud and Pottier's notation [3], for instance, a counter inhabits a *singleton region* σ. The type of the reference r is written $[\sigma]$, read "at σ", and means that r is the single inhabitant of the region σ. Access to r is governed by a capability of the form $\{\sigma : \mathit{ref}\ (\mathit{int}\ i)\}$, where the integer index i represents the current state of the counter. This capability must be presented when the reference is read or written. A *read* operation returns an identical capability. An *inc* operation returns an updated capability, $\{\sigma : \mathit{ref}\,(\mathit{int}\ (i+1))\}$. This is a strong update.

In such a system, a signature for *tracked counters* can be defined and implemented (Figure 3). There, $\mathit{tc}\,\sigma\, i$ is an *abstract capability*, analogous to an *abstract predicate* in separation logic, which hides the fact that the implementation of a counter is an integer reference. It is internally defined as $\{\sigma : \mathit{ref}\ (\mathit{int}\ i)\}$. (We write SNG for the kind of singleton regions and CAP for the kind of capabilities.)

The function *mk* has codomain $\exists\sigma.([\sigma] * \mathit{tc}\,\sigma\, 0)$. This means that *mk* returns: (i) a region σ; (ii) a value, of which nothing is known, except it inhabits σ; and (iii) a capability $\mathit{tc}\,\sigma\, 0$. This capability guarantees that *the inhabitant of* σ *is a counter in state 0.* At the same time, it represents the *ownership* of this counter, that is, the right to pass this counter as an argument to *read* and *inc*.

Accordingly, the functions *read* and *inc* require not only a value of type $[\sigma]$, but also a capability $\mathit{tc}\,\sigma\, i$, which serves as a proof of ownership and indicates that the counter is initially in state i. Out of this, *read* produces a pair of *the integer* i and an unmodified capability, while *inc* produces a pair of an unmodified value and an updated capability $\mathit{tc}\,\sigma\,(i+1)$.

This interface is strong: thanks to capabilities, the state of a counter is *tracked* in a precise manner. Unfortunately, there is a price to pay: this interface imposes restrictions on aliasing and ownership. The fact that $\mathit{tc}\,\sigma\, i$ is a *linear* capability means that every counter must have a unique owner. This effectively restricts the use of tracked counters to linear data structures, that is, data structures without sharing.

A signature for monotonic counters Is it intuitively sound to make an assertion about the value of a counter without imposing any restriction on aliasing or ownership? Yes. Because the value of a counter *increases* with time, it is possible for a client to maintain a sound *under-approximation* of it. This is permitted by the signature in Figure 4, where the type *mc* of *monotonic counters* is now integer-indexed.

What is the intuitive meaning of the type *mc* i? Certainly, the index i cannot reflect the *exact* internal state of the counter, but must represent a *lower bound*. Indeed, if x has type *mc* i, then, after an application of *inc* to x, the variable x still has type *mc* i, even though the internal state of the counter x has just changed. More deeply, if some variable y also has type *mc* i, then, after this application, y still has type *mc* i. Yet, because x and y may be aliases, the state of the counter y could have just changed as well. So, the intuitive interpretation of *mc* i is:

> *mc* i *is a type of monotonic counters whose internal state is at least* i.

It is straightforward, although not quite trivial, to *informally* convince oneself that this signature is sound. Consider a counter x, of type *mc* i, where i represents a lower bound on x's internal state j, that is, $i \leq j$ holds. Invoking *read* returns j, which has type *int* $(i \leq .)$, as advertised. Invoking *inc* updates the internal state to $j+1$, of which $i+1$ is a lower bound, so it is sound for *inc* to advertise a return type of *mc* $(i+1)$. Furthermore, i remains a lower bound of $j+1$, so it is sound to continue using x at type *mc* i.

An unusual feature of this signature is that, even though *inc* returns its argument, it ascribes a *more precise* type to its result than to its argument! (To permit such a type refinement is the reason why we decided that *inc* should return its argument.) This allows keeping track of a lower bound on the internal state of a counter. For example, *read (inc (mk ()))* has type *int* $(1 \leq .)$. This may seem a tiny achievement; yet, such a feature is essential in our encoding of Danielsson's analysis of thunks. There (§5), the function *pay* is analogous to *inc*, in that it also returns its argument at a better type.

The signature of monotonic counters is stronger than the simple signature of Figure 2. (Indeed, the latter can be implemented in terms of the former, by defining *sc* as $\exists i.(\mathit{mc}\, i * \langle 0 \leq i \rangle)$.) On the other hand, it is incomparable with the signature of tracked counters (Figure 3). The latter allows keeping exact track of the state of a counter, while the former only allows keeping track of a lower bound. On the other hand, the latter comes with restrictions on aliasing and ownership, while the former does not.

The challenge ML, extended with indexed types, allows writing down the signature in Figure 4, and allows clients of this signature to be written and type-checked. However, it does not allow checking that the code in Figure 1, augmented with a suitable definition of *mc*, satisfies this signature. Neither do the type-and-capability systems that we are aware of. In the following, we extend such a system with new mechanisms (§3) that address this challenge (§4).

3. Fates and predictions

Perhaps the most obvious approach to addressing the challenge would be to build monotonicity directly into references, by making *monotonic references* a primitive notion. We quickly abandoned this approach, however, for several reasons.

First, monotonicity is sometimes not a property of a single reference cell, but of a composite data structure. For example, in our application to hash-consing (§6), a hash table encodes a mathematical function whose graph grows with time (with respect to set-theoretic inclusion, $\subseteq$). A primitive notion of a monotonic reference would not support these non-trivial applications.

Second, requiring monotonicity to hold between *any two points* in time would be too inflexible. It is desirable to allow monotonicity to be *temporarily* violated, as long as this remains in some sense *unobservable* from the outside. This is again evident in advanced applications (§6): because updates to a complex data structure are not atomic, monotonicity does not make sense while an update is in progress. Again, perhaps one could build this flexibility into a set of *ad hoc* typing rules for monotonic references; here, however, it is obtained via the anti-frame rule.

Fates Instead of monotonic references, we introduce *monotonic ghost variables,* or *fates,* for short. A fate can be thought of as a mutable memory location that does not exist at runtime and whose value can only grow with time. A fate is controlled by a linear capability, just as if it did exist in the runtime heap.

Fates are not tied to references or objects. Furthermore, as we will see, there is no need for fates to temporarily disobey monotonicity. For these reasons, the rules that govern fates are simple and lightweight. In a sense, fates distill the *essence* of monotonicity: they describe the interplay between linearity and monotonicity, and nothing else.

In order to express the fact that the value of a certain fate reflects the state of a certain reference, or of an entire data structure, one sets up an explicit *invariant*. The anti-frame rule [24] offers a mechanism for this purpose. The invariant, a capability, is invisible (and must hold) outside of a certain lexical scope, and is visible (and can be temporarily violated) within that scope. This approach, it turns out, addresses all three previously mentioned issues.

Types and laws Because a fate does not exist at runtime, it does not contain a *programming language* value (e.g., a machine integer, a λ-abstraction, a memory location, etc.), but a *mathematical* value (e.g., an integer, a set of integers, a function of integers to sets of integers, etc.). In other words, the *type* $\mathbf{T}$ of a fate is a type of the ambient logic. Any sound logic that is powerful enough for the intended application can serve as the ambient logic. For instance, in the case of monotonic counters, Presburger arithmetic would be sufficiently expressive and would permit decidable type-checking. For more advanced examples, the ambient logic could be the Calculus of Inductive Constructions, so that our type-checker ships proof obligations to the Coq proof assistant. (In this paper, for the sake of uniformity, we place ourselves in this case.) A soundness proof for our system should in principle be independent of the choice of an ambient logic.

A fate of type $\mathbf{T}$ must be equipped with a *law* $\mathbf{R}$, that is, a preorder over $\mathbf{T}$. The law defines what it means for the value of a fate to *grow*. Each fate can have its own type $\mathbf{T}$ and law $\mathbf{R}$, which are fixed when it is created. A law need not be a total order: some applications of fates involve partial orders (§6).

In our running example, a fate is used to reflect the value of a monotonic counter. Its type is $\mathbb{Z}$, the type of the mathematical integers; its law is the ordering $\leq$ over $\mathbb{Z}$. For simplicity, we fix this special case in the following explanations.

Creating a fate Since fates do not exist at runtime, none of the primitive operations over fates has a runtime effect. These operations can be thought of as type annotations, and are erased before the program is executed. More precisely, we will view them as *subsumption axioms*. For instance, the creation of a fresh fate is permitted by the following axiom:

$$\emptyset <: \exists\varphi.\{\varphi : i\}$$

Such an axiom means that the capability on the left-hand side can be transformed into the capability on the right-hand side. Here, out of nothing, one obtains a fresh *fate* φ, together with a *capability*, written $\{\varphi : i\}$, which represents both the *ownership* of the fate φ and the *knowledge* that the current value of the fate is i. (Here, i, the initial value of the fate, can be any element of $\mathbb{Z}$.) This capability is *linear:* a fate has at most one owner.

This axiom can be compared with the type of the primitive operation for allocating a fresh reference [3]:

$$\mathit{ref} : \tau \to \exists\sigma.([\sigma] * \{\sigma : \mathit{ref}\,\tau\})$$

When provided with an initial value of type τ, this operation allocates a fresh reference cell in the heap, and returns: (i) a singleton region σ; (ii) a memory location, of type $[\sigma]$, the single inhabitant of this region; (iii) a capability $\{\sigma : \mathit{ref}\,\tau\}$, which represents both the ownership of the region and the knowledge of its type. Creating a fate is analogous to allocating a reference, in that it creates a fresh name and produces a capability. It differs in that no runtime values are involved, and the heap is unaffected.

Updating a fate The owner of a fate is free to update it at any time, provided the new value is provably related to the current value. This is expressed as follows:

$$\{\varphi : i\} * \langle i \leq j\rangle <: \{\varphi : j\}$$

That is, the value of the fate can be changed from i to j, provided the proposition $i \leq j$ holds. If $\mathbf{P}$ is a proposition of the ambient logic, then $\langle\mathbf{P}\rangle$ is a *duplicable* capability, a witness for $\mathbf{P}$. This axiom is analogous to the *strong update* of a reference [3], in that a capability is consumed and a potentially different capability is produced. It differs in that no runtime values are involved and updates are required to be monotonic. The capability $\langle i \leq j\rangle$ on the left-hand side can be thought of as a *proof obligation*.

Tying a fate to a piece of runtime state The internal state of a monotonic counter consists of an integer reference, which inhabits a region σ, and of a fate φ. How do we express the fact that the value of the fate is kept synchronized with the content of the reference? The answer is simple: the capabilities that respectively govern the reference and the fate must *share* an integer index. The composite capability:

$$\exists i.(\{\sigma : \mathit{ref}\,\mathit{int}\ i\} * \{\varphi : i\})$$

not only represents the ownership of both the reference and the fate, but also indicates that they share a common value i. By existentially abstracting over i, we make this capability suitable for use as an *invariant* that remains true even as the counter is incremented. In the following (§4), this invariant is *hidden*, so that it is invisible to a client of the monotonic counter abstraction. It is visible only within the implementation of monotonic counters, where it can be temporarily broken, provided it is restored before control is returned to the client. One cannot forever escape one's fate!

Making predictions We are still missing a piece of the puzzle. A capability $\{\varphi : i\}$ represents, *at the same time,* the ownership of a fate and an assertion about its value. In other words, so far, only the owner of a fate can assert a proposition about its value. However, in our planned application to monotonic counters, a client must be allowed to assert that the state of a counter is at least i, for a certain integer i, even though the client does not own the counter. How could we solve this difficulty?

This is where monotonicity comes into play. Because a fate is constrained to evolve in a monotonic manner, its current value serves as a *prediction* of its future values: if the current value is i, it is safe to assert that any future value j satisfies $i \leq j$. *Making* such a prediction requires knowledge of the current value i, which in turn requires ownership of the fate. However, once such a prediction is made, it can never be contradicted by updating the fate, so it remains valid forever. For this reason, a prediction can be considered a *duplicable capability*, separate of the linear capability that governs of the fate. A prediction is created as follows:

$$\{\varphi : i\} <: \{\varphi : i\} * \langle \varphi : i \rangle$$

We write $\langle \varphi : i \rangle$ for the prediction that *the value of φ will always be at least i*. It can also be understood as an *observation* of some state of φ that is sufficient to guarantee that the value of φ will always be at least i. Both points of view are useful, so, in the following, we make use of both of the words "prediction" and "observation". The above axiom states that the owner of a fate can, at any time, produce an observation of the fate's current state or, equivalently, a prediction of its future states.

How does this solve the difficulty with which we were faced? A prediction $\langle \varphi : i \rangle$ is *non-linear*. It does not represent the ownership of the fate φ, yet it does represent an assertion about its state. So, *it is now possible to make an assertion about a piece of state that one does not own.* Our implementation of monotonic counters (§4) retains ownership of the fate, but creates predictions that it passes to its clients.

Exploiting predictions Predictions—at least in our system!—are true and remain so forever. As a result, comparing an old prediction with the present state allows knowledge to be gained: one learns that the present state conforms to what was predicted. This is stated as follows:

$$\langle \varphi : i \rangle * \{\varphi : j\} <: \langle i \leq j \rangle * \{\varphi : j\}$$

If it was once predicted that the state would always be at least i, and if the present state is j, then $i \leq j$ must hold. In other words, exploiting a prediction produces a new logical fact, which can later be used in a proof.

As explained earlier, our implementation of monotonic counters (§4) uses the internal invariant: $\exists i.(\{\sigma : \mathit{ref\ int}\ i\} * \{\varphi : i\})$. Once unpacked, this becomes: $\{\sigma : \mathit{ref\ int}\ j\} * \{\varphi : j\}$, where a fresh integer index j represents the current state of the reference and the fate. Now, imagine that a client presents us with an old prediction, of the form $\langle \varphi : i \rangle$. This prediction must have been created earlier within the implementation of monotonic counters, handed to a client, carried around for a while by the client, and is now being presented back to us. By exploiting it, we learn $i \leq j$, that is, we learn that the current state is as good as or superior to what the client expects. In its absence, nothing would be known about the current state, since j is just an abstract integer index.

Since the reference has type *ref int* j, reading it yields a value of type *int* j, which, thanks to the proposition $i \leq j$, is a subtype of *int* $(i \leq .)$. In other words, the *read* operation produces a value of type *int* $(i \leq .)$, provided the client hands it the prediction $\langle \varphi : i \rangle$.

Weakening predictions A prediction can be weakened to one that permits more numerous potential futures:

$$\langle i \leq j \rangle * \langle \varphi : j \rangle <: \langle \varphi : i \rangle$$

This is used in the implementation of monotonic counters (§4). In the *inc* operation, after the reference and the fate have been updated from j to $j + 1$, the following capability is available:

$$\{\sigma : \mathit{ref\ int}\ (j + 1)\} * \{\varphi : j + 1\}$$

At this point, we wish to create a new prediction, based on the new state, and return it to the client. So, we construct the prediction $\langle \varphi : j + 1 \rangle$. This prediction is valid; however, it cannot be returned to the client, because it mentions j, a variable that was introduced by unpacking our existentially quantified invariant. The client knows nothing about j, the true current state of the counter; it only knows about i, the value that it has observed in the past. Thus, we *weaken* the prediction $\langle \varphi : j + 1 \rangle$ by changing it into $\langle \varphi : i + 1 \rangle$. This is valid, because we know $i \leq j$, which implies $i + 1 \leq j + 1$. The weakened prediction can now be handed back to the client. In summary, *inc* produces the prediction $\langle \varphi : i + 1 \rangle$, provided the client hands it the prediction $\langle \varphi : i \rangle$.

Joining predictions If it has been predicted that the value of φ will remain above i and above j, then its (unknown) current value must be a common upper bound of i and j. Thus, it is safe to produce a new prediction of *some* common upper bound k of i and j. Ownership of the fate is not required.

$$\langle \varphi : i \rangle * \langle \varphi : j \rangle <: \exists k.(\langle i \mathbf{R} k \rangle * \langle j \mathbf{R} k \rangle * \langle \varphi : k \rangle)$$

The need for this axiom arises when $\mathbf{R}$ is not a total order. For instance, it plays a key role in our application to hash-consing (§6). There, it is not even the case that every two elements i and j admit a common upper bound with respect to $\mathbf{R}$. Even in this case, the axiom is sound, and all the more useful.

4. Application: monotonic counters

We now put everything together and explain how to typecheck monotonic counters. The code, which appears in Figure 5, consists of four definitions, for *mc*, *mk*, *read*, and *inc*.

Surface syntax Whereas this paper is concerned only with type checking in a core calculus, our illustrative examples are expressed in a plausible but informal sugared syntax, with some degree of inference of types and capabilities. In particular, the keywords **let fate**, **set fate**, **make**, and **exploit** are used to create (and name) a fate, update a fate, make (and weaken) a prediction, and exploit a prediction, respectively. We use **let cap** to define an abbreviation for a capability. We use **pack cap** and **unpack cap** to introduce and eliminate existentially quantified capabilities. We use **got cap** to assert that a certain capability is held: this is a machine-checkable comment. The construct "**hide** $I = C$ **outside of** t", proposed by the second author in earlier work [24], has the double effect of introducing I as an abbreviation for the capability C within the term t, and of making the capability I invisible outside of the term t. None of these constructs has a runtime effect: they are used by the type-checker only. In addition, we use ordinary **pack** and **unpack** constructs to introduce and eliminate existential types.

Definition What is, *really*, a monotonic counter with index k? According to the definition of *mc* (lines 1–5), it is:

> for *some* abstract notion of an observation of an integer (line 2),
>
> a pair of two functions, or *methods*, where the *read* method (line 3) accepts an observation of *any* integer i and produces an integer value that is no less than i, and the *inc* method (line 4) expects an observation of *any* integer i and produces an observation of $i + 1$,
>
> packaged together with an observation of k (line 5).

The parameter k occurs *only* in the last component. It does not occur in the type of the methods! In other words, over the lifetime of a monotonic counter, observations of the counter in various states are created, but the vector of methods remains unchanged.

Because *obs* is a non-linear capability, *mc k* is a non-linear type, as desired. (We write DCAP for the kind of non-linear, or *duplicable*, capabilities. It is a sub-kind of CAP.) This is a key point.

Construction How does one construct a monotonic counter? Let us now review the definition of *mk* (lines 7–47).

```
1  type mc k =                          – the type of monotonic counters
2    ∃obs : ℤ → DCAP.
3      ((∀i. unit ∗ obs i → int (i ≤ .)) ×
4       (∀i. unit ∗ obs i → unit ∗ obs (i + 1))) ∗
5      obs k
6
7  let mk : unit → mc 0 =
8  λ().
9    let fate φ : FATE ℤ (≤) = 0 in
10   got cap { φ : 0 };                 – we own the fate, in state 0
11   let cap obs i = ⟨ φ : i ⟩ in       – a notation for observations
12   make obs 0;                        – make an initial observation
13   let σ, (r : [σ]) = ref 0 in        – allocate a fresh reference
14   got cap { σ: ref int 0 };          – we own the reference, in state 0
15
16   let methods :                      – build a vector of methods
17     (∀i. unit ∗ obs i → int (i ≤ .)) ×
18     (∀i. unit ∗ obs i → unit ∗ obs (i + 1)) =
19
20     hide I =                         – I is visible only to the methods
21       ∃j. ({σ : ref int j} ∗ {φ : j})
22     outside of
23     pack cap I;                      – this establishes the invariant
24
25     let read : ∀i. unit ∗ obs i ∗ I → int (i ≤ .) ∗ I =
26     λ().
27       let j = unpack cap I in
28       got cap obs i ∗ {σ : ref int j} ∗ {φ : j};
29       exploit obs i;                 – this yields i ≤ j
30       let c : int j = !r in
31       let c : int(i ≤ .) = c in      – a subsumption step
32       pack cap I;
33       c
34     and inc : ∀i. unit ∗ obs i ∗ I → unit ∗ obs (i + 1) ∗ I =
35     λ().
36       let j = unpack cap I in
37       got cap obs i ∗ {σ : ref int j} ∗ {φ : j};
38       exploit obs i;                 – this yields i ≤ j
39       r := !r + 1;
40       set fate φ := j + 1;           – a monotonic update
41       got cap obs i ∗ {σ : ref int (j + 1)} ∗ {φ : j + 1};
42       make obs (i + 1);              – permitted, since i + 1 ≤ j + 1
43       pack cap I                     – the witness is j + 1
44     in
45     (read, inc)                      – this is the vector of methods
46   in got cap obs 0;                  – still got that initial observation
47   pack methods as mc 0
48
49 let read : ∀k. mc k → int (k ≤ .) =
50 λ(c : mc k).
51   let obs, methods = unpack c in
52   let (read, _) = methods in
53   got cap obs k;
54   read ()
55
56 let inc : ∀k. mc k → mc (k + 1) =
57 λ(c : mc k).
58   let obs, methods = unpack c in
59   let (_, inc) = methods in
60   got cap obs k;
61   inc ();
62   got cap obs (k + 1);
63   pack methods as mc (k + 1)
```

Figure 5. Monotonic counters

In the prologue (lines 9–14), a fresh fate φ and reference r are created. The notation *obs* i is introduced for an observation of the fate φ in state i, and an initial observation *obs* 0 is made.

Next, the methods that read and increment the counter are defined (lines 16–45). There are *two views* of these methods: an internal view, where an invariant I occurs in the type of the methods, and an external view, where I no longer appears. The invariant I, defined on line 20, requires φ and r to share a common (but unspecified) value j. It is immediately established (line 23).

The methods *read* and *inc* are first defined *within* the scope of the **hide** construct. As a result, they have access to I, and must preserve it: the capability I appears in their argument and result types (line 25 and line 34). This is the *internal view* of the methods.

Next, a pair of *read* and *inc* is constructed (line 45) and returned outside of the **hide** construct. It is bound, there, to the name *methods* (line 16). The effect of **hide** [24] is to consume the capability I and to remove the four occurrences of I in the types of *read* and *inc*, so that I does not appear in the type of *methods* (line 16). This is the *external view* of the methods.

The body of *read* is polymorphic in the integer index i, which appears in a *client-provided* observation *obs* i (line 25), and in the integer index j, which is obtained by unpacking the existentially quantified invariant I (line 27). In short, i represents some past state of the counter, which was observed by the client, while j represents its current state. As explained earlier, exploiting these facts yields the proposition $i \leq j$. This proposition is used to justify a subsumption step that converts the type of c, the current value of the counter, from *int* j to *int* $(i \leq .)$ (line 31).

Similarly, the body of *inc* is polymorphic in i and j, and exploits a client-provided observation to establish $i \leq j$. The reference r and the fate φ are incremented. Between these updates, r is in state $j + 1$, while φ is still in state j. This is fine: we are free to break the invariant I, provided it is restored before control is returned to the client. This is done on line 43. There, the use of **pack cap** causes us to *forget* that the current state is $j + 1$. *Before* forgetting this precious information, we make an observation of $j + 1$, and immediately weaken it to an observation of $i + 1$ (line 42). This weakening step is valid because $i + 1 \leq j + 1$ provably holds. In the end, the observation *obs* $(i + 1)$ is returned to the client. This is made explicit in the type of *inc* (line 34).

Because *read* and *inc* are polymorphic in i, they adapt to the level of knowledge that the client has acquired, and is able to exhibit. A greater value of i means a stronger observation is provided by the client, and, accordingly, a stronger result is returned by *read* and *inc*. The current state j does not (and cannot) occur in the types of *read* and *inc*, since it is existentially quantified within I.

In the epilogue (lines 46–47), we package up the *methods* vector together with the initial observation *obs* 0 and abstract away the definition of *obs*. In so doing, we not only obtain a value of type *mc* 0, as desired, but also ensure that φ does not escape its scope: recall that *obs* i is just a notation for $\langle \varphi : i \rangle$.

Access This concludes our explanation of *mk*. The rest is boilerplate: there remains to define *read* and *inc* functions that satisfy the desired signature (Figure 4). Let us comment on *inc* (lines 56–63); *read* is analogous. Unpacking a monotonic counter object of type *mc k* (line 58) yields an abstract observation constructor *obs*, a *methods* vector, and an observation *obs* k (line 60). We extract the *inc* method (line 59) and invoke it (line 61). This invocation is legal, because we hold *obs* k, and produces a new observation *obs* $(k + 1)$ (line 62). By packing the methods vector together with this improved observation, we construct a new monotonic counter object, which, this time, has type *mc* $(k + 1)$. Yet, in a type-erasure interpretation, this new object is the unchanged argument!

Our definition of *mc k* as an existential type, as well as our implementations of *read* and *inc*, follow the pattern of Pierce and

Turner's encoding of objects [23]. One difference is that Pierce and Turner's purpose was to avoid hidden mutable state (which, following Reynolds, they call *procedural abstraction*), in favor of purely functional objects and type abstraction: so, they used existential quantification *over the state*. Our purpose, on the contrary, is to explain procedural abstraction in the presence of monotonicity: so, we use existential quantification *over an observation* of the state.

Broadly speaking, we met the challenge that we set for ourselves: the code in Figure 5 satisfies the signature of Figure 4 and has the desired semantics. We did fail in one aspect, though: we modified the original code. In Figure 1, a counter was just an integer reference. In Figure 5, a counter is a pair of methods, which encapsulate an integer reference. At present, we do not know how to type-check the code in the absence of this encapsulation layer.

5. Application: thunks

We now explain why we are interested in thunks and how their study leads to a problem that is solved by our treatment of monotonic state. One of our long-term interests is to develop a type system that allows time complexity assertions to be expressed and checked. We would like it to be as close to a standard type system as possible, and we would like it to be able to encode the classic notions of *credits* and *debits,* which we now recall.

Credits Tarjan [31] introduced the *banker's method* for deriving *amortized* time complexity bounds. The approach relies on the notion of a *credit*. One posits that, in order to perform just one step of computation, the machine requires, and consumes, one credit. At the beginning of its execution, the program is supplied with a number of credits, say n. Credits can serve as function arguments, as function results, and can be stored within data structures. Because there is no way to duplicate a credit or to create a credit out of nothing, the number of steps that the program can take must be bounded by n. Because credits can be stored and only later retrieved for consumption, this method leads to *amortized* complexity bounds.

One of the simplest examples of amortization is the reversal of a singly-linked list. The actual time complexity of reversal is linear in the length of the list. However, one can "pre-pay" for one reversal by artificially increasing the cost of the *cons* operation and storing one excess credit in each cell. Then, reversing an entire list requires just one credit, because the credit found in each cell pays for the next recursive call. In short, reversal has constant amortized time complexity: its cost has been amortized over the calls to *cons*.

A serious limitation of this method is that, because credits must not be duplicated, any data structure that contains credits must itself be "single-threaded", that is, linear. For instance, the above "pre-paid lists" must be linear: if such a list were carelessly shared, one could reverse it several times and incorrectly pretend that each reversal operation has constant amortized cost.

Debits To address this limitation, Okasaki [22] proposed a modified version of the banker's method that allows data structures to be shared. The idea is to replace credits with debits: because it is sound for a debit to be duplicated, a debit-based analysis does not come with linearity restrictions.

Okasaki's approach is based on primitive suspensions, also known as *thunks*. When one wishes to execute a certain computation, instead of providing up front enough credits to run this computation, one creates a suspension, at a constant immediate cost. The cost of the computation must then be paid for, possibly in several increments, before the suspension can be forced.

In this approach, suspensions can be freely shared. This can cause a thunk to be paid for more than once: this is a waste, but leads to a sound approximation. This can also cause a thunk to be forced more than once, which is sound as well, because, thanks

type *thunk*: $\mathbb{N} \rightarrow \text{VAL} \rightarrow \text{VAL}$
val *mk*: $\forall n, \alpha.\ (\mathit{unit} * n\$ \rightarrow \alpha) * 1\$ \rightarrow \mathit{thunk}\ n\ \alpha$
val *pay*: $\forall n, p, \alpha.\ \mathit{thunk}\ n\ \alpha * p\$ * 1\$ \rightarrow \mathit{thunk}\ (n - p)\ \alpha$
val *force*: $\forall \alpha.\ \mathit{thunk}\ 0\ \alpha * 1\$ \rightarrow \alpha$

Figure 6. A signature for thunks

to memoization, the computation is performed just once, and the credits that have been accumulated are spent just once.

Okasaki's approach has been formalized and proved correct by Danielsson [6], in the setting of a purely functional, lazy programming language.

Credits as capabilities We equip an imperative, call-by-value programming language with a type-and-capability system that directly supports Tarjan's approach to complexity analysis, and that, via an encoding of thunks as references, also supports Okasaki and Danielsson's approach.

Credits are static entities, which do not exist at runtime. In other words, credits are capabilities. We introduce a new primitive capability: if n has kind $\mathbb{N}$, then $n\$$ has kind CAP: it is a linear capability and represents n credits. Capabilities can serve as function arguments, as function results, can be stored within data structures, and can form hidden invariants: as a result, so can credits.

We posit the subtyping axiom $(n+p)\$ \equiv n\$ * p\$$, where n and p are in $\mathbb{N}$. (If they were in $\mathbb{Z}$, this axiom would be unsound, as it would allow creating credits out of thin air.) (We write $\equiv$ for subtyping, both ways.)

To ensure that credits represent an actual measure of the computation cost, the type system must be modified in one other way: the typing rule for function applications must be amended so that every call consumes one credit. This is standard: in Hehner's approach [12], every recursive function call steps the clock; in Crary and Weirich's system [5], every function call steps the clock; in Danielsson's system [6], every function definition must be "ticked".

In a functional programming language, without primitive loop forms, function calls are the only non-trivial source of time complexity. Furthermore, time credits cannot be manufactured. As a result, one can prove that, up to a constant factor, the number of reduction steps that can be taken by the program is limited by the number of credits that are initially made available to it. For instance, one can prove the following statement: "if p is a program such that $\vdash p : \forall n, \mathit{int}\ n * n\$ \rightarrow \mathit{unit}$ holds, then p has worst-case linear time complexity: that is, there exists a constant k such that, for every integer n, running the program $p\ n$ takes at most kn steps." This theorem shows that the system derives correct complexity claims about complete programs. There follows that the claims that are derived about program components (open terms) must be correct as well, in some sense. The latter are "amortized" complexity claims in the sense that they eventually lead to a correct worst-case complexity assessment for all complete programs.

A type-and-capability system, equipped with credits-as-capabilities and with the rule that function calls consume one credit, is able to encode amortized time complexity analyses in the style of Tarjan. Such a system, however, has the limitation that data structures that contain credits must be linear. Thunks, in particular, do contain credits: as partial payments are made, more credits are stored; when the thunk is forced, the stored amount drops to zero. Thus, it seems that thunks must be linear. This is a problem: in order to reproduce Okasaki and Danielsson's analyses, it is essential to allow thunks to be freely shared.

This is where our treatment of monotonic state comes in: using the "monotonic counters" coding pattern, a call-by-value version of Danielsson's thunks can be implemented as a library.

```
1  type thunk n α =                         – the type of thunks
2    ∃obs : ℕ → DCAP.
3      ((∀n, p. unit ∗ obs n ∗ p$ → unit ∗ obs (n - p)) ×
4       (unit ∗ obs 0 → α)) ∗
5      obs n
6
7  type state n α =                         – internal state of a thunk:
8    | White ((unit ∗ n$ → α) ∗ 1$)         – not yet evaluated
9    | Gray (unit)                          – being evaluated
10   | Black (α)                            – evaluated
```

Figure 7. Thunks: internal type definitions

A signature for thunks A signature for thunks appears in Figure 6. A thunk is parameterized with its cost n (a "debit") and with its result type α (line 1). The type *thunk* n α has kind VAL: a thunk is an ordinary value, and can be duplicated without restriction. A thunk of cost n is created out of a computation of cost n, that is, a function of *unit* to α that consumes n credits (line 2). At any time, a thunk of cost n can be partially paid for (line 3). This consumes p credits, and produces a thunk of cost $n - p$. (This is subtraction in $\mathbb{N}$.) At runtime, *pay* is a no-op and returns its argument. Finally, a thunk can be forced when it has been paid for, that is, when its cost is zero (line 4).

Each of *mk*, *pay*, and *force* require (and consume) one credit. This effectively means that a call to one of these functions costs two credits, one of which pays for the call, the other of which is passed to the function. This does not have deep significance: the point is that these operations have (amortized) constant time cost.

Implementation The definition of the type *thunk* closely follows the pattern that was introduced for monotonic counters. According to Figure 7, a thunk of cost n is:

> for some abstract notion of an observation of a natural integer (line 2),
>
> a pair of a *pay* method (line 3), which accepts an observation of any integer n, as well as a number of credits p, and returns an observation of $n - p$; and a *force* method (line 4), which expects an observation of 0 and produces a value of type α;
>
> packaged together with an observation of n (line 5).

Under the hood, a thunk is implemented as a hidden reference to a state, which is one of *White*, *Gray*, or *Black* (lines 7–10). We build on an earlier encoding of thunks by the second author [24], which explained how to exploit a hidden reference but did not include a time complexity aspect. Here, we introduce a hidden "piggy bank", where credits are inserted by *pay*, and that is broken by the first call to *force*.

The implementation of thunks appears in Figure 8. In the prologue (lines 3–8), we introduce a fate φ over the natural integers. Its value *decreases* with time and represents the number of credits that remain to be paid. It is initially set to the cost of the suspended computation. We also allocate a reference r, which initially holds the color *White*, the suspended computation *userfun*, and one credit, which we later use to pay for the call to *userfun*.

The invariant I (line 14) is a conjunction of three capabilities, which respectively govern the reference, the piggy bank, and the fate. These capabilities share two integer indices. The index nc, for *necessary credits,* is the number of credits required to force the thunk. Its value is initially n (line 17), and drops to zero when the thunk is first forced. The index ac, for *available credits,* is the number of credits in the piggy bank. The index ac is increased when a payment is made, and diminished by n when the thunk is first forced. It is worth noting that ac does not, by itself, exhibit

```
1  let mk : ∀n, α. (unit ∗ n$ → α) ∗ 1$ → thunk n α =
2  λ(userfun : unit ∗ n$ → α).
3    let fate φ : FATE ℕ (≥) = n in           – a decreasing fate
4    got cap {φ : n};
5    let cap obs i = ⟨φ : i⟩ in
6    make obs n;
7    let σ, (r: [σ]) = ref (White userfun) in
8    got cap {σ: ref (state n α)};            – this uses up our 1$
9
10   let methods :
11     (∀n, p. unit ∗ obs n ∗ p$ → unit ∗ obs (n - p)) ×
12     (unit ∗ obs 0 → α) =
13
14     hide I = ∃nc, ac.
15       {σ : ref ((state nc α) ⊗ I) } ∗ ac$ ∗ {φ : nc - ac}
16     outside of
17     pack cap I;                            – the witnesses are n and 0
18
19     let pay : ∀n, p. unit ∗ obs n ∗ p$ ∗ I
20                → unit ∗ obs (n - p) ∗ I =
21     λ().
22       let nc, ac = unpack cap I in
23       got cap
24         obs n ∗
25         {σ : ref ((state nc α) ⊗ I)} ∗
26         (ac + p)$ ∗                        – our new, combined credit
27         {φ : nc - ac};
28       exploit obs n;                       – this yields n ≥ nc - ac
29       set fate φ := nc - (ac + p);         – a monotonic update
30       make obs (n - p);                    – uses n - p ≥ nc - (ac + p)
31       pack cap I                           – witnesses: nc and ac + p
32
33     and force : unit ∗ obs 0 ∗ I → (α ⊗ I) ∗ I =
34     λ().
35       let nc, ac = unpack cap I in
36       got cap
37         obs 0 ∗
38         {σ : ref ((state nc α) ⊗ I)} ∗
39         ac$ ∗
40         {φ : nc - ac};
41       exploit obs 0;                       – this yields nc - ac = 0
42       match !r with                        – whence ac ≥ nc
43         | White (userfun : unit ∗ nc$ ∗ I → (α ⊗ I) ∗ I) →
44             r := Gray ();
45             got cap
46               {σ : ref ((state 0 α) ⊗ I)} ∗
47               (nc + 1)$ ∗                  – the necessary credit
48               (ac - nc)$ ∗                 – any leftover credit
49               {φ : 0};
50             pack cap I;                    – witnesses: 0 and ac - nc
51             got cap (nc + 1)$ ∗ I;
52             let v : α ⊗ I = userfun () in
53             let _, _ = unpack cap I in
54             r := Black v;
55             pack cap I;                    – witnesses: 0 and 0
56             v
57         | Gray () → fail
58         | Black v → pack cap I; v          – witnesses: nc and ac
59     in (pay, force)
60   in
61   got cap obs n;
62   pack methods as thunk n α
```

Figure 8. Thunks

monotonic behavior. The difference $nc - ac$, which represents the amount that remains to be paid, does: it decreases with time.

For lack of space, the reason why I is recursively defined, as well as the meaning of the tensor $\cdot \otimes I$, are not explained. As far as this paper is concerned, these aspects can be ignored. The reader is referred to the second author's earlier paper on hidden state [24].

The *pay* method (lines 19–31) stores the p credits that it receives as an argument in the piggy bank (line 26), updates the fate so as to reflect a decrease in the amount that remains to be paid (line 29), and publishes a new observation (line 30). This method has absolutely no runtime effect: its type erasure is $\lambda().()$. If the type system supported user-defined *coercions* (a feature that we have not included!), the *pay* method, as well as the external *pay* function (Figure 6, line 3), could be declared as coercions. This would have several benefits: (i) an application of *pay* would be considered a coercion application, as opposed to a function call, so it would cost zero credits, as opposed to two; (ii) an application of *pay* would generate no code whatsoever; (iii) more importantly, this would allow *pay* to be used under a linear, covariant context, a feature that is present in Danielsson's system [6, §11]. Coercions, if included in the system, could also serve to expose the fact that the type *thunk* $n\ \alpha$ is covariant in n and in α.

The *force* method exploits the observation *obs* 0 (line 37) to determine that the available credit *ac* exceeds the necessary credit *nc* (line 41). This allows *nc* credits to be taken out of the piggy bank. Furthermore, in the first branch of the **match** construct, deconstructing *White* makes one extra credit is available. Thus, in total, we have $nc + 1$ credits (line 47). These credits are required to call *userfun* (lines 51–52): one credit is consumed by the call itself, while the other *nc* credits are passed to *userfun*, which consumes them. Note that, prior to invoking *userfun*, the invariant I must be re-established (line 50). This is possible, in spite of the fact that *nc* credits have just been taken out of the piggy bank, because the thunk is now colored gray.

The instruction *r := Black v* (line 54) requires unpacking I before the update (line 53) and re-packing it afterwards (line 55).

The implementation of the external functions *pay* and *force* (whose types appear in Figure 6, lines 3–4) is omitted. As before, they are just wrappers in the style of Pierce and Turner [23]. Because this wrapping involves a function call, the external versions of *pay* and *force* require one credit, whereas the internal methods do not.

6. Application: hash-consing

We now present an application to the specification of hash-consing.

A challenge Let us fix a type *data*. A hash-consing facility usually takes the form of a function of type *data* $\rightarrow$ *data*, with the informal specification that the images of d_1 and d_2 are physically equal if and only if d_1 and d_2 are equal. Here, however, in order to avoid dealing with physical equality, we consider a slightly more basic interface, with equivalent expressive power. We view a *hash-consing function* as a function of type *data* $\rightarrow$ *int*, with the informal specification that the integer hashes associated with d_1 and d_2 are equal if and only if d_1 and d_2 are equal.

Hash-consing is typically implemented using a mutable data structure (say, a hash table) that maps data to integers. When some datum d is presented, one checks whether d already is in the domain of the table: if not, the table is extended with a binding of d to some fresh integer. At this point, a binding of d to some integer i must exist in the table, and i is returned.

The challenge is to check that this implementation is correct with respect to a signature that does not reveal the existence of an internal state, does not impose any linearity restrictions, yet is strong enough to encode the above informal specification.

An ideal signature What is an ideal signature for hash-consing? We wish to claim that *hash* implements an injective mathematical function from data to integers. This is done by the signature in Figure 9, where h is declared to be such a function (lines 1–2), and *hash* is declared to implement h (line 3). There, h is a function in the ambient logic, while *hash* is a programming language function. We write *data* both for the (unparameterized) type of data in the ambient logic and for the (indexed) type of data in the programming language. We stick with the indexed-type approach that we have used throughout this paper, although a notation in the style of Hoare, without indexed types and with pre- and post-conditions, would arguably be more palatable.

1 **logic val** h: *data* $\rightarrow \mathbb{Z}$
2 **logic property**: *injective h*
3 **val** *hash*: $\forall d.$ *data d* $\rightarrow$ *int* $(h\ d)$

Figure 9. An ideal (unattainable?) signature for hash-consing

1 **type** φ: FATE *ifmap* $\subseteq$
2 **val** *hash*: $\forall d.$ *data d* $\rightarrow \exists i.$ *int i* $* \langle \varphi : [d \mapsto i] \rangle$

Figure 10. A novel, pragmatic signature for hash-consing

It is very likely that this ideal signature is sound: as far as clients are concerned, everything is consistent with the illusion that *hash* has no side effect and implements some *fixed* injective mathematical function h.

Unfortunately, it is unclear how to argue that an imperative implementation satisfies this signature. The mutable table is initially empty and is populated only as the program is executed. As a result, it seems impossible to *statically* provide a definition of the mathematical function h. In fact, in two distinct program runs, the mutable table might hold distinct contents!

A solution An informal explanation why hash-consing works is that the hash table holds a map of data to integer codes that remains injective at all times and *can only grow with time*, so that whatever facts the client observes about this map remain true forever. Of course, it is straightforward to model this situation using fates and observations.

We write *ifmap* for the (ambient logic) type of injective finite maps of data to integers. We write $[d \mapsto i]$ for the singleton map that maps d to i. We write $\subseteq$ for map inclusion.

In the implementation of hash-consing that follows, we create a fate, say φ, of kind FATE *ifmap* $(\subseteq)$, and set up a hidden invariant that relates the content of the mutable table with this fate. By doing so, we state (and we must prove) that the table holds an injective map and grows with time.

An additional key idea is that, contrary to our earlier examples (§4, §5), the existence of φ is not hidden. Instead, it is exposed in the signature (Figure 10, line 1). This allows *hash* to be specified as follows: when passed a datum d, *hash* produces an integer i, *together with a prediction* of the singleton map $[d \mapsto i]$ (Figure 10, line 2). This can be understood as a guarantee that the binding of d to i is in the map, now and forever.

This signature does not involve any linear entities, so *hash* can be used as if it were side-effect-free. In particular, it can be invoked by multiple clients without requiring them to cooperate with one another, as would be the case if the use of *hash* was governed by a linear capability.

Before showing how a typical imperative implementation can satisfy this new signature, let us first find out how expressive it is. Does it express the property that the integer hashes associated with d_1 and d_2 are equal if and only if d_1 and d_2 are equal? Yes—here is how. Imagine that a client invokes *hash*, at two arbitrary points in time, with respective arguments d_1 and d_2. She receives, in exchange, two predictions $\langle \varphi : [d_1 \mapsto i_1] \rangle$ and $\langle \varphi : [d_2 \mapsto i_2] \rangle$.

```
1  type htbl: SNG → VAL                 – type of a hash table
2  type cht: SNG → fmap → CAP           – capability over a hash table
3
4  val create:
5    unit → ∃ρ. (htbl ρ ∗ cht ρ ∅)
6  val add: ∀d i ρ m.
7    data d × int i × htbl ρ ∗ cht ρ m →
8    unit ∗ cht ρ (m[d ↦ i])
9  val find: ∀d ρ m.
10   data d × htbl ρ ∗ cht ρ m →
11   ((∃i. int i ∗ ⟨[d ↦ i] ⊆ m⟩) + (unit ∗ ⟨d ∉ dom(m)⟩))
12   ∗ cht ρ m
```

Figure 11. A strong specification of hash tables

```
1  type lock : CAP → VAL                – locks are duplicable
2  val newlock: ∀γ. unit → lock γ       – initially in a locked state
3  val lock: ∀γ. lock γ → unit ∗ γ      – locking yields γ
4  val unlock: ∀γ. lock γ ∗ γ → unit    – unlocking consumes γ
```

Figure 12. A signature for locks

By joining these predictions (§3), she obtains the existence of an *injective* finite map m such that $[d_1 \mapsto i_1] \subseteq m$ and $[d_2 \mapsto i_2] \subseteq m$ both hold. The fact that m is a map allows her to show that $d_1 = d_2$ implies $i_1 = i_2$, while the fact that m is injective allows her to prove that $i_1 = i_2$ implies $d_1 = d_2$. Thus, she has $d_1 = d_2 \iff i_1 = i_2$, as desired.

In summary, whereas the ideal signature of Figure 9 claims that *hash* implements a fixed injective mathematical function, the pragmatic signature of Figure 10 claims that it implements an injective mathematical function whose graph may be constructed at runtime, and may grow with time. The latter signature is more general than the former. It represents a relaxed definition of the concept of a *pure* function. It is, to the best of our knowledge, a contribution of this paper.

Implementation Let us now see how this signature can be implemented in our setting. Before we look at the code, we need a couple of building blocks.

The first building block is an implementation of hash tables. An arbitrary implementation will do, as long as it satisfies the signature in Figure 11. This is a completely standard specification of hash tables: it is in no way specific to our application to hash-consing. It relies on a logic type *fmap* of finite (but not necessarily injective) maps of data to integers. It publishes an abstract type and an abstract capabillity: *htbl* ρ (line 1) is the type of a pointer to a hash table in region ρ, while *cht* $\rho\, m$ is a capability over such a hash table. The capability *cht* $\rho\, m$ plays a dual role: it represents the ownership of the hash table and encodes the assertion that the contents of the table corresponds to the finite map m. This is analogous to an abstract predicate in separation logic [20]. The function *create* creates a fresh region ρ containing an empty hash table (line 5). It returns a pair of a pointer to the table and a capability for the table. A call to *add* (d, i, h) (lines 7–8) updates the table h with a binding of d to i. It requires a capability *cht* $\rho\, m$ and produces an updated capability *cht* $\rho\, (m[d \mapsto i])$, so as to reflect the update at the logical level. A call to *find* (d, h) (lines 10–12) either returns an integer i together with a proof that d is associated with i in the table, or produces a proof that d is not in the domain of the table. In either case, *find* returns the capability over the unchanged hash table (line 12).

The second building block is an implementation of locks. In contrast with our earlier examples, here, we will not use the anti-frame rule directly. The anti-frame rule is too restrictive [26] in that it would require us to restore the hidden invariant before calling

```
1  logic type ifmap = {m : fmap | injective m}
2
3  let mkhash : unit → ∃φ : FATE ifmap ⊆.
4      ∀d. data d → ∃i. int i ∗ ⟨φ : (d ↦ i)⟩ =
5  λ().
6    let fate φ : FATE ifmap ⊆ = ∅ in
7    let ρ, (h : htbl ρ) = create () in
8    let σ, (r : [σ]) = ref 0 in
9    got cap {φ: ∅} ∗ cht ρ ∅ ∗ {σ: ref int 0};
10   let cap I = ∃c : int. ∃m : ifmap.
11     {φ: m} ∗ cht ρ m ∗
12     {σ: ref int c} ∗
13     ⟨∀i, i ∈ codom(m) → i < c⟩ in
14   pack cap I;                        – witnesses: 0 and ∅
15   let l : lock I = newlock () in
16   unlock l;                          – this consumes I
17
18   let hash : ∀d. data d → ∃i. int i ∗ ⟨φ : (d ↦ i)⟩ =
19   λd.
20     let () = lock l in               – this yields I
21     let c, m = unpack cap I in       – open it up
22     match find (d, h) with
23     | Left i →                       – we have ⟨[d ↦ i] ⊆ m⟩
24       make ⟨φ: [d ↦ i]⟩;             – permitted: we have {φ : m}
25       pack cap I;                    – witnesses: c and m
26       unlock l;                      – this consumes I again
27       pack i
28     | Right () →                     – we have ⟨d ∉ dom(m)⟩
29       let c = !r in
30       add (d, c, h);                 – we have cht ρ (m[d ↦ c])
31       r := c + 1;                    – we have {σ: ref int (c + 1)}
32       set fate φ := m[d ↦ c];
33       got cap ⟨∀i, i ∈ codom(m[d ↦ c]) → i < c + 1⟩;
34       make ⟨φ: [d ↦ c]⟩;
35       pack cap I;                    – witnesses: (c+1)
36       unlock l;                      – and m[d ↦ c]
37       pack c
38   in
39   pack hash                          – witness: φ
```

Figure 13. Implementation of hash-consing

the hash table functions *add* and *find*. However, by restoring the invariant, we would lose the capabillity over the hash table, so we would no longer be able to call *add* or *find*! A solution to this problem is to introduce a dynamic check, and the most elegant way of doing so is to rely on an implementation of *locks*. A signature for locks appears in Figure 12. Our locks are analogous to dynamically allocated locks in separation logic [11, 13, 21]. Unlocking consumes a capability γ (line 4), which can later be recovered by locking (line 3). The capability γ is fixed at lock creation time (line 2). The type *lock* γ is duplicable. Yet, the capability is never duplicated, because the *lock* operation can fail (in a sequential setting) or block (in a concurrent setting). In a sequential setting, locks can be implemented in terms of the anti-frame rule: all it takes is a hidden reference to a Boolean flag. In a concurrent setting, locks can be viewed as primitive.

Let us now turn towards the actual implementation of hash-consing (Figure 13).

We first define the type *ifmap* of *injective* finite maps on top of the type *fmap* of finite maps (line 1). We use Coq's subset notation. An injective map is a pair of a map m and a proof that m is injective. In the following, we adopt the informal convention that an *ifmap* object can be used where an *fmap* object is expected, and vice-versa; in the latter case, a proof obligation is generated.

The function *mkhash* (lines 3–39) is in charge of creating a new instance of the hash-consing facility. Its result type corresponds to the signature of Figure 10. Its code starts by creating a new initially empty increasing fate φ over injective finite maps (line 6), an empty hash table h (line 7) and an integer reference r (line 8). The internal invariant is defined immediately thereafter (lines 10–13). The invariant states that the fate and the table are in a common state m, an injective finite map. It further states that the integer value c stored in the reference r is an upper bound for the codomain of h: that is, c is the next available integer code. The invariant initially holds (line 14). (This generates the proof obligation $\forall i,\ i \in \text{codom}(\emptyset) \rightarrow i < 0$.) The invariant is hidden using a fresh lock l. The lock l is captured in the closure of the function *hash*, which is permitted because l has duplicable type *lock I*.

Lines 18–39 show the actual hash-consing function, *hash*. We retrieve the invariant I out of the lock and unpack it (Lines 20–21). Then, we check whether d is already in the domain of h. If so (lines 23–27), we produce the observation $\langle \varphi : [d \mapsto i] \rangle$. This is permitted because we have the logical proposition $\langle [d \mapsto i] \subseteq m \rangle$ as well as the capability $\{\varphi : m\}$. Otherwise (lines 28–37), we update h so that the datum d is now mapped to c, the current value of the reference r. The reference r is then incremented so that its value remains an upper bound for the codomain of h. We then check that we have the capabilities needed to repack I (lines 32–34). The first one (line 32), namely $\{\varphi : m[d \mapsto c]\}$, generates two proof obligations. First, we must prove that $m[d \mapsto c]$ is an injective map: this holds because m is injective and c is not in the codomain of m. Second, we must prove that m is a subset of $m[d \mapsto c]$: this holds because d is not in the domain of m. The second one (line 33) represents a logical proposition that we must prove, namely $\forall i,\ i \in \text{codom}(m[d \mapsto c]) \rightarrow i < c + 1$. This follows from the equality $\text{codom}(m[d \mapsto c]) = \text{codom}(m) \cup \{c\}$ and from the hypothesis $\forall i,\ i \in \text{codom}(m) \rightarrow i < c$. The last capability (line 34) is an observation. This line produces two trivial proof obligations: first, we must check that $[d \mapsto c]$ is injective; second, we must prove $[d \mapsto c] \subseteq m[d \mapsto c]$.

Although the concrete syntax used in in our code snippets is admittedly informal, we believe that we have explained fairly precisely how a type-and-capability system, equipped with fates and predictions, and supplemented with an expressive logic, can be used to give a specification of a hash-consing facility. This specification conceals the existence of an internal state, yet guarantees that two pieces of input data receive the same code if and only if they are equal. This is an original result: to the best of our knowledge, no such specification of hash-consing has been presented before.

7. Related work

Ghost state and history constraints A fate is a ghost variable that comes with a built-in temporal property: the sequence of its values forms an increasing chain with respect to a certain preorder $\mathbf{R}$. In combination with an ordinary invariant ("the values of reference r and fate φ coincide"), this allows expressing a temporal assertion about the state ("the value of reference r must grow with time"). The idea of introducing ghost variables in order to reduce temporal reasoning to present-time reasoning is not new; see, for instance, Schneider [28, chapter 7].

Liskov and Wing [18] associate a *history constraint*—a predicate over pairs of visible states—with a class definition. This idea has been implemented in the Larch/C++ [15] and JML [16] specification languages. Unfortunately, there seems to exist no clear account of how history properties are verified. Our understanding is that the tools check that the pre- and post-state of every method are related by the history constraint. This is a necessary condition but, in the presence of callbacks, not a sufficient one. Furthermore, these systems offer no way of exploiting a history constraint to establish a new logical fact.

Fähndrich and Leino [10] note that, if the state of an object is constrained to evolve in a monotonic manner, then it is sound to make an assertion about this object, even in a system that does not control aliasing or ownership. We take inspiration from this idea: a prediction represents an assertion about an entity (namely, a fate) that one does not own. Fähndrich and Leino require every field update to be monotonic (that is, to preserve every property that might be known of the object). We adopt a simpler and more expressive approach: our fates and predictions are independent of the treatment of mutable state. While the update of a fate is required to be monotonic with respect to a fixed law $\mathbf{R}$, there is a priori no restriction on updates of references.

Leino and Schulte [17] extend the Spec# program verification system with *history invariants* in order to verify a version of the subject-observer pattern. Their approach is sound in the presence of callbacks and re-entrancy. Furthermore, there is a benefit to declaring history invariants. In the basic Spec# methodology, an invariant associated with object o_1 may refer to an object o_2 only if o_1 owns o_2 (o_2 is a "transitive rep object" of o_1). Leino and Schulte relax this restriction and allow this also when o_2 is declared to be a "subject" of o_1 and the invariant associated with o_1 is stable under the history invariant associated with o_2. Again, this expresses the idea that, provided updates to o_2 are monotonic, it is sound for o_1 to make an assertion about o_2, even though o_1 does not own o_2.

Regions Most type-and-capability calculi use *regions* as a mechanism for assigning a name to a single value or to a set thereof [3, 4, 29]. Regions involve a form of monotonicity, which manifests itself in two ways: (i) once a region name is allocated, it exists forever; (ii) the population of a region can only grow with time. Thus, if a value v inhabits a region ρ, then this fact holds forever. For this reason, the type $[\rho]$ of the inhabitants of region ρ can safely be considered duplicable. This is the same reason why predictions are considered duplicable in the present paper.

Whereas regions denote sets of runtime values, fates take values in some type $\mathbf{T}$ of the ambient logic. This design decision plays an important part in the simplicity of the meta-theory of fates, but makes it impossible to define regions in terms of fates.

Concurrency Fates and predictions are sound in both sequential and concurrent settings. The implementations of monotonic counters and thunks presented in this paper exploit the anti-frame rule, which is sound only in a sequential setting [24]. In a concurrent setting, one would instead use dynamically allocated locks, which hold and hide a capability [11, 13].

Deny-guarantee There is a strong connection between our work and deny-guarantee reasoning [7]. (We are grateful to Hongseok Yang for bringing this to our attention.) In fact, it is possible to sketch an informal encoding of fates and predictions in terms of stable deny-guarantee assertions.

First, the information that a fate variable φ has kind FATE $\mathbf{T}\ \mathbf{R}$ corresponds to a deny on any update of φ that does not respect $\mathbf{R}$. That is, no thread is allowed to perform a non-monotonic update. In our system, this information carried in the kind is duplicable, so it should be encoded as a "duplicable deny". This can be expressed in terms of Dodds *et al.*'s "fractional denies" via existential quantification over a fraction: $\exists a > 0.(a)deny$.

Second, a prediction $\langle \varphi : i \rangle$ corresponds to an assertion that the value of φ is at least i, that is, $i\ \mathbf{R}\ \varphi$. Such an assertion carries no permission, hence is duplicable, as required. Furthermore, this assertion, once conjoined with the deny that forbids non-monotonic updates, is stable.

Last, a fate ownership token $\{\varphi : i\}$ corresponds to a conjunction of the assertion $i = \varphi$ and a full permission over all monotonic updates of φ. Again, once conjoined with the deny that forbids non-monotonic updates, this assertion is stable.

One can informally check that this interpretation validates all of the axioms that govern fates and predictions (§3).

In summary, like deny-guarantee, fates and predictions allow reasoning about state changes. They are less ambitious and simpler in several ways: (i) they do not permit interference between threads; (ii) the law that governs a fate is fixed at allocation time, and, for this reason, fractional permissions are not needed; (iii) fates hold logical values, as opposed to runtime values. Fates and predictions could perhaps be viewed as an interesting "design pattern" in a programming language equipped with deny-guarantee reasoning.

Relational models of monotonic state Ahmed, Dreyer, and Rossberg [1] consider a call-by-value λ-calculus with general references, and endow it with a possible worlds model in which the relational interpretation of a type may grow with time. They use this model to prove certain pairs of programs contextually equivalent, but also (often) to establish facts about a single program, such as the fact that a certain dynamic check is redundant. For this purpose, type-based approaches are applicable and, perhaps, offer better potential for integration in a programming language design.

When restricted to a unary setting, Ahmed *et al.*'s system exhibits strong analogies with Charguéraud and Pottier's calculi [3, 24] as well as with the present paper. Roughly speaking, an island corresponds to a piece of state that is hidden via the anti-frame rule; the island's population, a set of values, grows with time, and corresponds to a fate; and the fixed law that relates the population with a store relation corresponds to an invariant that is imposed via the anti-frame rule and ties a fate to a piece of runtime state.

In Ahmed *et al.*'s motivating example [1, Figure 1], type abstraction is used to protect an extensible table implementation. Integer indices into the table are passed to the client at an abstract type t, so the client cannot forge indices. As a result, every index must be in the domain of the table (which grows with time) and no bounds check is necessary. Type generativity guarantees that distinct table instances give rise to distinct instances of the abstract type t.

Our system also allows proving that no bounds check is necessary; is amenable to mechanical checking; and (perhaps surprisingly) is able to disclose the fact that table indices are just integers.

How does this work? The problem is essentially a simplified version of hash-consing, so our approach is similar to that described earlier (§6). With a table instance, we associate a fate φ, ranging over sets of integers, and whose law is set inclusion. As an internal invariant, we assert that φ represents the domain of the table. Then, we define a "valid table index" as a pair of an integer index i and an observation that i is in the domain of the table: that is, we define the type $\mathit{index}\ \varphi$ as $\exists i.(\mathit{int}\ i * \langle\varphi : \{i\}\rangle)$. This type plays the role of t in Ahmed *et al.*'s paper.

When supplied by the client with a value of type $\mathit{index}\ \varphi$, we confront the observation $\langle\varphi : \{i\}\rangle$ with the current state of φ, a capability of the form $\{\varphi : I\}$, where the set of integers I represents the current domain of the table. This yields $i \in I$, which guarantees that the index is within bounds.

In Ahmed *et al.*'s "irreversible state change" example [1, §5.5], the challenge is to prove that $!x$ evaluates to 1, even though the unknown function f might (via a re-entrant call) affect x:

$$\textbf{let}\ x = \mathit{ref}\, 0\ \mathit{in}\ \lambda f.(x := 1; f(); !x)$$

This is proved by introducing a fate to express the fact that the value of x grows with time, and by using the anti-frame rule to hide the existence of the cell x and of its fate, together with the invariant that x is 0 or 1. The update $x := 1$ is provably monotonic, since 1 is the greatest permitted value for x. An observation of the fate in state 1 is created before the call to $f()$ and is exploited, after the call, to establish that x still holds the value 1.

Dreyer *et al.* [9] revisit Ahmed *et al.*'s framework and introduce so-called "state transition systems" to model the way in which properties of local state evolve over time. In their most basic form, state transition systems have "public transitions" only. In that case, they are just pre-orders, and allow reasoning about monotonic hidden state much in the same way as we do, as illustrated by the above examples. In their most general form, state transition systems also have "private transitions", which offer a way of taking advantage of the well-bracketing of function calls and returns. The second author's unpublished generalized anti-frame rule [25] stems from a similar motivation, and also allows exploiting well-bracketing. The basic anti-frame rule requires a fixed invariant, so a piece of hidden state is typically governed by a single fate throughout its lifetime. In contrast, the generalized anti-frame rule accepts a parameterized invariant, and uses universal quantification to express well-bracketing, so a piece of hidden state can be usefully tied to different fates at different points in time. Roughly speaking, dynamically allocating a new fate and tying it to the state corresponds to creating a fresh instance of a state transition system, or, in Dreyer *et al.*'s approach, to taking a private transition. In summary, the two approaches are closely related. Ours differs in that it is expressed as a type system and (we believe) is presented in a more orthogonal fashion. In particular, the rules that govern fates and predictions are independent of those that govern hidden state.

Sumii's environmental bisimulations [30] also involve a form of monotonicity, as the set of values that are accessible to the environment grows with time. We are unfortunately unable to offer a more informed comparison of the two approaches. The examples that Sumii presents are borrowed from Ahmed *et al.* and can be dealt with using our type- and assertion-based approach.

Type-based complexity analysis Although *automated* time complexity analysis is a research field of its own, the development of expressive type systems that can *check* user-provided time complexity assertions has received surprisingly little attention.

The type systems by Dornic *et al.* [8], Reistad and Gifford [27], and Crary and Weirich [5] annotate function types with a worst-case cost. The type-and-capability system that we have sketched (§5) is significantly more expressive. This is evidenced, we hope, by our encoding of Okasaki and Danielsson's analysis of thunks.

The idea that a *space credit* is a linear entity, which can be passed around and stored, is not new: Hofmann [14] uses it quite elegantly to keep track of heap space usage. The idea that a *time credit* is a linear entity, which can similarly be passed around and stored, is explicit in Tarjan's work [31], and is formalized, for instance, by Atkey [2]. Atkey's system is analogous to ours in its motivation and in its treatment of credits. It is less expressive in several ways: because it lacks a treatment of hidden state and of monotonicity, we believe that it does not allow an encoding of Danielsson's thunks.

References

[1] Amal Ahmed, Derek Dreyer, and Andreas Rossberg. State-dependent representation independence. In *ACM Symposium on Principles of Programming Languages (POPL)*, pages 340–353, January 2009.

[2] Robert Atkey. Amortised resource analysis with separation logic. In *European Symposium on Programming (ESOP)*, volume 6012 of *Lecture Notes in Computer Science*, pages 85–103. Springer, 2010.

[3] Arthur Charguéraud and François Pottier. Functional translation of a calculus of capabilities. In *ACM International Conference on Functional Programming (ICFP)*, pages 213–224, September 2008.

[4] Karl Crary, David Walker, and Greg Morrisett. Typed memory management in a calculus of capabilities. In *ACM Symposium on Principles of Programming Languages (POPL)*, pages 262–275, January 1999.

[5] Karl Crary and Stephanie Weirich. Resource bound certification. In *ACM Symposium on Principles of Programming Languages (POPL)*, pages 184–198, January 2000.

[6] Nils Anders Danielsson. Lightweight semiformal time complexity analysis for purely functional data structures. In *ACM Symposium on Principles of Programming Languages (POPL)*, January 2008.

[7] Mike Dodds, Xinyu Feng, Matthew J. Parkinson, and Viktor Vafeiadis. Deny-guarantee reasoning. In *European Symposium on Programming (ESOP)*, volume 5502 of *Lecture Notes in Computer Science*, pages 363–377. Springer, March 2009.

[8] Vincent Dornic, Pierre Jouvelot, and David K. Gifford. Polymorphic time systems for estimating program complexity. *ACM Letters on Programming Languages and Systems*, 1(1):33–45, 1992.

[9] Derek Dreyer, Georg Neis, and Lars Birkedal. The impact of higher-order state and control effects on local relational reasoning. In *ACM International Conference on Functional Programming (ICFP)*, pages 143–156, September 2010.

[10] Manuel Fähndrich and Rustan Leino. Heap monotonic typestates. In *International Workshop on Alias Confinement and Ownership (IWACO)*, July 2003.

[11] Alexey Gotsman, Josh Berdine, Byron Cook, Noam Rinetzky, and Mooly Sagiv. Local reasoning for storable locks and threads. Technical Report MSR-TR-2007-39, Microsoft Research, September 2007.

[12] Eric C. R. Hehner. *Abstractions of Time*, pages 191–210. Prentice Hall, 1994.

[13] Aquinas Hobor, Andrew W. Appel, and Francesco Zappa Nardelli. Oracle semantics for concurrent separation logic. In *European Symposium on Programming (ESOP)*, volume 4960 of *Lecture Notes in Computer Science*, pages 353–367. Springer, April 2008.

[14] Martin Hofmann. A type system for bounded space and functional in-place update. *Nordic Journal of Computing*, 7(4):258–289, 2000.

[15] Gary T. Leavens and Albert L. Baker. Enhancing the pre- and postcondition technique for more expressive specifications. In *Formal Methods (FM)*, volume 1709 of *Lecture Notes in Computer Science*, pages 1087–1106. Springer, January 1999.

[16] Gary T. Leavens, Erik Poll, Curtis Clifton, Yoonsik Cheon, Clyde Ruby, David Cok, Peter Müller, Joseph Kiniry, Patrice Chalin, and Daniel M. Zimmerman. *JML Reference Manual*, May 2008.

[17] K. Rustan M. Leino and Wolfram Schulte. Using history invariants to verify observers. In *European Symposium on Programming (ESOP)*, volume 4421 of *Lecture Notes in Computer Science*, pages 80–94. Springer, 2007.

[18] Barbara Liskov and Jeannette M. Wing. A behavioral notion of subtyping. *ACM Transactions on Programming Languages and Systems*, 16(6):1811–1841, 1994.

[19] Karl Mazurak, Jianzhou Zhao, and Steve Zdancewic. Lightweight linear types in system F°. In *Workshop on Types in Language Design and Implementation (TLDI)*, pages 77–88, January 2010.

[20] Aleksandar Nanevski, Amal Ahmed, Greg Morrisett, and Lars Birkedal. Abstract predicates and mutable ADTs in Hoare type theory. In *European Symposium on Programming (ESOP)*, volume 4421 of *Lecture Notes in Computer Science*, pages 189–204. Springer, March 2007.

[21] Peter W. O'Hearn. Resources, concurrency and local reasoning. *Theoretical Computer Science*, 375(1–3):271–307, May 2007.

[22] Chris Okasaki. *Purely Functional Data Structures*. Cambridge University Press, 1999.

[23] Benjamin C. Pierce and David N. Turner. Simple type-theoretic foundations for object-oriented programming. *Journal of Functional Programming*, 4(2):207–247, April 1994.

[24] François Pottier. Hiding local state in direct style: a higher-order anti-frame rule. In *IEEE Symposium on Logic in Computer Science (LICS)*, pages 331–340, June 2008.

[25] François Pottier. Generalizing the higher-order frame and anti-frame rules. Unpublished, July 2009.

[26] François Pottier. Three comments on the anti-frame rule. Unpublished, July 2009.

[27] Brian Reistad and David K. Gifford. Static dependent costs for estimating execution time. In *ACM Symposium on Lisp and Functional Programming (LFP)*, pages 65–78, 1994.

[28] Fred B. Schneider. *On Concurrent Programming*. Springer, 1997.

[29] Frederick Smith, David Walker, and Greg Morrisett. Alias types. In *European Symposium on Programming (ESOP)*, volume 1782 of *Lecture Notes in Computer Science*, pages 366–381. Springer, March 2000.

[30] Eijiro Sumii. A complete characterization of observational equivalence in polymorphic lambda-calculus with general references. In *Computer Science Logic*, volume 5771 of *Lecture Notes in Computer Science*, pages 455–469. Springer, September 2009.

[31] Robert Endre Tarjan. Amortized computational complexity. *SIAM Journal on Algebraic and Discrete Methods*, 6(2):306–318, 1985.

[32] Hongwei Xi. Dependent ML: an approach to practical programming with dependent types. *Journal of Functional Programming*, 17(2):215–286, 2007.

A. Quick reference

We very briefly summarize how to equip a type-and-capability system in the style of Charguéraud and Pottier [3] with fates and predictions. In order to do this, the system must have existential quantification; a distinction between duplicable and linear capabilities; and logical assertions (viewed as duplicable capabilities). Everything else (products, sums, functions, regions, references, recursive types, hidden state) is orthogonal and described elsewhere [3, 24].

The kinds are listed in Figure 14. There, the judgement $\vdash_{\text{CIC}}$ is the typing judgement of the ambient logic, which we take to be the Calculus of Inductive Constructions. In this and the following figures, uses of $\vdash_{\text{CIC}}$ correspond to proof obligations, which, in an implementation, would be shipped to an external theorem prover. Metavariables in bold face stand for objects of the ambient logic: typically, $\mathbf{T}$ ranges over types, $\mathbf{R}$ over preorders, $\mathbf{t}$ over terms, $\mathbf{P}$ over propositions.

The syntax of types and capabilities appears in Figure 15. They are presented as a single syntactic category of *objects* o. A kind assignment system (Figure 16) allows telling which objects are types and which are capabilities; which objects are linear and which are duplicable; etc. This kind-driven approach to linearity has been independently studied by Mazurak *et al.* [19].

A kinding environment K maps type variables to kinds. We write $\lfloor K \rfloor_{\text{CIC}}$ for the restriction of K to bindings of the form $\alpha :: \mathbf{T}$. Value types (VAL) form a subset of computation types (CMP); similarly, duplicable capabilities (DCAP) form a subset of capabilities (CAP). The conjunction $(*)$ of a type and a capability is duplicable if and only if both conjuncts are duplicable. The ownership of a fate is considered a linear capability, whereas predictions and logical assertions are duplicable capabilities.

The typing judgements and typing rules are exactly as in Charguéraud and Pottier [3]. The delta with this previous work lies in the following subtyping axioms. The axioms that govern fates and predictions appear in Figure 17. They are subject to the implicit side condition that φ has kind FATE $\mathbf{T}$ $\mathbf{R}$. The axioms that govern propositions appear in Figure 18. Last, in order to allow duplicable capabilities to be copied, we add the axiom $D <: D * D$, where D has kind DCAP.

$$
\begin{array}{rcll}
\kappa & := & \mathrm{VAL} & \textit{a (duplicable) value type} \\
 & \mid & \mathrm{CMP} & \textit{a (linear) computation type} \\
 & \mid & \mathrm{DCAP} & \textit{a duplicable capability} \\
 & \mid & \mathrm{CAP} & \textit{a linear capability} \\
 & \mid & \mathbf{T} & \textit{a logical value (an index)} \\
 & \mid & \mathrm{FATE}\ \mathbf{T}\ \mathbf{R} & \textit{a fate}
\end{array}
$$

$$
\frac{\vdash_{\mathrm{CIC}} \mathbf{T} : \mathtt{Type}}{\mathbf{T} \text{ is well-formed}}
\qquad
\frac{\begin{array}{c}\vdash_{\mathrm{CIC}} \mathbf{T} : \mathtt{Type} \\ \vdash_{\mathrm{CIC}} \mathbf{R} : \mathbf{T} \to \mathbf{T} \to \mathtt{Prop} \\ \vdash_{\mathrm{CIC}} \mathbf{R} \text{ is a preorder}\end{array}}{\mathrm{FATE}\ \mathbf{T}\ \mathbf{R} \text{ is well-formed}}
$$

Figure 14. Kinds

$$
\begin{array}{rcll}
o & := & \alpha & \textit{variable} \\
 & \mid & o \to o & \textit{arrow} \\
 & \mid & o * o & \textit{conjunction} \\
 & \mid & \exists \alpha :: \kappa . o & \textit{existential quantification} \\
 & \mid & \emptyset & \textit{null capability} \\
 & \mid & \{o : o\} & \textit{ownership of a fate} \\
 & \mid & \langle o : o \rangle & \textit{prediction (observation)} \\
 & \mid & \langle \mathbf{P} \rangle & \textit{logical proposition} \\
 & \mid & \mathbf{t} & \textit{logical value (index)}
\end{array}
$$

Figure 15. Types and capabilities

$$
\frac{\alpha :: \kappa \in K}{K \vdash \alpha :: \kappa}
\qquad
\frac{\begin{array}{c}K \vdash o_1 :: \mathrm{CMP} \\ K \vdash o_2 :: \mathrm{CMP}\end{array}}{K \vdash o_1 \to o_2 :: \mathrm{VAL}}
\qquad
\frac{\begin{array}{c}K \vdash o_1 :: \kappa \\ K \vdash o_2 :: \mathrm{DCAP} \\ \kappa \in \{\mathrm{VAL}, \mathrm{DCAP}\}\end{array}}{K \vdash o_1 * o_2 :: \kappa}
\qquad
\frac{\begin{array}{c}K \vdash o_1 :: \kappa \\ K \vdash o_2 :: \mathrm{CAP} \\ \kappa \in \{\mathrm{CMP}, \mathrm{CAP}\}\end{array}}{K \vdash o_1 * o_2 :: \kappa}
\qquad
\frac{K, \alpha :: \kappa_1 \vdash o :: \kappa_2}{K \vdash \exists \alpha :: \kappa_1 . o :: \kappa_2}
\qquad
\frac{}{K \vdash \emptyset :: \mathrm{DCAP}}
$$

$$
\frac{\lfloor K \rfloor_{\mathrm{CIC}} \vdash_{\mathrm{CIC}} \mathbf{t} : \mathbf{T}}{K \vdash \mathbf{t} :: \mathbf{T}}
\qquad
\frac{\begin{array}{c}K \vdash o_1 :: \mathrm{FATE}\ \mathbf{T}\ \mathbf{R} \\ K \vdash o_2 :: \mathbf{T}\end{array}}{\begin{array}{c}K \vdash \{o_1 : o_2\} :: \mathrm{CAP} \\ K \vdash \langle o_1 : o_2 \rangle :: \mathrm{DCAP}\end{array}}
\qquad
\frac{\lfloor K \rfloor_{\mathrm{CIC}} \vdash_{\mathrm{CIC}} \mathbf{P} : \mathtt{Prop}}{K \vdash \langle \mathbf{P} \rangle :: \mathrm{DCAP}}
\qquad
\frac{K \vdash o :: \mathrm{VAL}}{K \vdash o :: \mathrm{CMP}}
\qquad
\frac{K \vdash o :: \mathrm{DCAP}}{K \vdash o :: \mathrm{CAP}}
$$

Figure 16. Kind assignment

$$
\begin{array}{ll}
\textsc{fate-create} & \emptyset <: \exists \varphi . \{\varphi : \mathbf{t}\} \\
\textsc{fate-update} & \{\varphi : \mathbf{t}_1\} * \langle \mathbf{t}_1\ \mathbf{R}\ \mathbf{t}_2 \rangle <: \{\varphi : \mathbf{t}_2\} \\
\textsc{obs-create} & \{\varphi : \mathbf{t}\} <: \{\varphi : \mathbf{t}\} * \langle \varphi : \mathbf{t} \rangle \\
\textsc{obs-weaken} & \langle \varphi : \mathbf{t}_2 \rangle * \langle \mathbf{t}_1\ \mathbf{R}\ \mathbf{t}_2 \rangle <: \langle \varphi : \mathbf{t}_1 \rangle \\
\textsc{obs-exploit} & \{\varphi : \mathbf{t}_2\} * \langle \varphi : \mathbf{t}_1 \rangle <: \{\varphi : \mathbf{t}_2\} * \langle \mathbf{t}_1\ \mathbf{R}\ \mathbf{t}_2 \rangle \\
\textsc{obs-join} & \langle \varphi : \mathbf{t}_1 \rangle * \langle \varphi : \mathbf{t}_2 \rangle <: \\
 & \exists \alpha_3 :: \mathbf{T} . (\langle \mathbf{t}_1\ \mathbf{R}\ \alpha_3 \rangle * \langle \mathbf{t}_2\ \mathbf{R}\ \alpha_3 \rangle * \langle \varphi : \alpha_3 \rangle)
\end{array}
$$

Figure 17. Subtyping axioms: fates

$$
\begin{array}{ll}
\emptyset \equiv \langle \mathtt{True} \rangle & \\
\langle \mathbf{P}_1 \rangle * \langle \mathbf{P}_2 \rangle \equiv \langle \mathbf{P}_1 \wedge \mathbf{P}_2 \rangle & \\
\langle \exists \alpha : \mathbf{T} . \mathbf{P} \rangle \equiv \exists \alpha :: \mathbf{T} . \langle \mathbf{P} \rangle & \\
\langle \mathbf{P}_1 \rangle <: \langle \mathbf{P}_2 \rangle & \text{if } \vdash_{\mathrm{CIC}} \mathbf{P}_1 \Rightarrow \mathbf{P}_2
\end{array}
$$

Figure 18. Subtyping axioms: propositions

www.ingramcontent.com/pod-product-compliance
Lightning Source LLC
Chambersburg PA
CBHW081510200326
41518CB00015B/2453